GONE VIKING II

Bill Arnott

GONE VIKING II

BEYOND BOUNDARIES

BILL ARNOTT

RMB

For information on purchasing bulk quantities of this book, or to obtain media excerpts or invite the author to speak at an event, please visit rmbooks.com and select the "Contact" tab.

RMB | Rocky Mountain Books Ltd.
rmbooks.com
@rmbooks
facebook.com/rmbooks

Cataloguing data available from Library and Archives Canada
ISBN 9781771605434 (softcover)
ISBN 9781771605441 (electronic)

Printed and bound in Canada

We would like to also take this opportunity to acknowledge the traditional territories upon which we live and work. In Calgary, Alberta, we acknowledge the Niitsítapi (Blackfoot) and the people of the Treaty 7 region in Southern Alberta, which includes the Siksika, the Piikuni, the Kainai, the Tsuut'ina, and the Stoney Nakoda First Nations, including Chiniki, Bearpaw, and Wesley First Nations. The City of Calgary is also home to Métis Nation of Alberta, Region III. In Victoria, British Columbia, we acknowledge the traditional territories of the Lkwungen (Esquimalt and Songhees), Malahat, Pacheedaht, Scia'new, T'Sou-ke, and W̱SÁNEĆ (Pauquachin, Tsartlip, Tsawout, Tseycum) peoples.

We acknowledge the financial support of the Government of Canada through the Canada Book Fund and the Canada Council for the Arts, and of the province of British Columbia through the British Columbia Arts Council and the Book Publishing Tax Credit.

To our amazing #GoneVikingCommunity

And for my dad

CONTENTS

EPILOGUE TO
GONE VIKING: A TRAVEL SAGA

Back home. Following eight years of travel, exploration and research. Eight years of "viking," or voyaging, the northern hemisphere in the wake of some of the world's most adventurous explorers. I was enjoying a Vancouver view – water, mountains, the bustle of tugs, tankers and helijets, all plying sea and sky.

Hillside homes reflected sun in bursts of fiery gold and beyond the bay, where inlet sprawls into ocean, bulkers glowed in morning light. Moored sailboats pinged a rhythmic and nautical tintinnabulation, a toe-tapping score, as a solitary freighter slid west beneath the big green bridge, bound for who knows where. Maybe Avalon. Over the pole, Icelandic horses were changing colour with the season, akin to amber leaves now littering the city.

And I thought of a sign that resonated on Haida Gwaii, hidden in forest. "Do not look back," it read. "There is much more to see, feel and love." While a bench in a park near our home is embossed with a plaque that states, "If you're going to look back, laugh."

GONE VIKING II:
BEYOND BOUNDARIES
MAP

INTRODUCTION

I was coming up for air following the release of *Gone Viking: A Travel Saga*, delighted and humbled by the connections with new friends and readers around the world. And while that odyssey took me across half the planet, the explorer in me, unsurprisingly, remained unsated.

Much of that journey's appeal was those moments of mystery akin to the original Scandinavian Sagas, when there wasn't always a conclusion. No answer, solution nor even a clearly marked finish line. Those dreamy expanses where horizon and cloud commingle in misty swirls. You convince yourself that where you are is real, and beyond that, perhaps, lies the magic that fuels everything. Meanwhile, tangible, imagined, physical, emotional, geographical and spiritual boundaries remain. At times by our own making, other times, imposed upon us.

While *Gone Viking: A Travel Saga* embraced the adventure, playfulness and discovery inherent in travel, it remained, I believe, within acceptable parameters. Now I've gone viking again, a series of voyages toward the unknown. Only this time I'm setting rule books aside. We'll play fair, make no mistake, just not necessarily within guidelines. And I welcome you. There's always room for another adventurous wanderer, another Viking. But this time our destination lies elsewhere.

This venture was unlike any I've experienced – the result of travel restrictions, yet through it all, the world opening anew – a depth and breadth of connectivity that simply wasn't there before pandemic was our norm. This may also be the most ambitious expedition I've undertaken. As a recently appointed Fellow of the Royal Geographical Society, I felt an obligation to do justice to what every traveller craves, the experiences we pursue – exploration no longer being merely shuttling one's husk between locales accumulating passport stamps, but mental, emotional and tactile transport between places, times and sensory touchstones, occasionally glimpsing just what it is we're doing here.

Gone Viking II takes place over a number of years – before, during and after the voyages of *Gone Viking: A Travel Saga* – what preceded the first epic trek, what else occurred at that time and what followed. All of this reflecting a changing world in which travel restrictions became our new normal.

Invariably these wanderings, recording the world around us, emerge as scribbles in journals, our present-day version of scribes putting quill ink to vellum. Once more I've done the same, with a weatherproof pack and blank notebooks. Again I've gone viking. Only now, it's a journey beyond boundaries.

From what may be my favourite journal, dog-eared
and embossed with a map of the world, frayed pages
held in place by an elasticized band, while taped to the
inside back cover is a photo of me and my dad:

Travel. The allure of escape, exoticism, and, yes, for some, bragging rights. For the rest of us it represents time-warp slivers of childhood – when this world remained a place of mystery, adventure. Where you can live, for a spell, a hero's life – desert sand, high seas and buried treasure. X marks the spot to other worlds, imagination, moments when the universe is nothing more than pure potential.

I was on the sofa in our tiny high-rise apartment, the ambient score a rattle of shopping cart wheels on sidewalk, reminiscent of passenger trains slowing through town, crossing roadways. *Clack-clack, clack-clack...clack-clack, clack-clack.* Identical journeys in their way. Somehow synesthetic. The same familial line of sensory sounds associated with every peregrination – whirr of rubber on bitumen, rumble of engines asea and the wind-fuelled rustle and snap of mainsail and jib.

I remembered losing myself in the incubating *whoosh* of a bow-parting ocean in feathers of froth, a blend of cocooned isolation combined with utter connection. And the comforting, familiar yet foreign hum of coach tires speeding on sand – New Zealand highway where road was literally the coast, low tide sand that stretched for miles to the dunes at Te Paki. Speed limit on the beach: 100 km/h. The light there at that time was the same as where I am now – flat, dampened sunshine, the kind that makes you squint, tear up and question your emotions. Every photo from that long, dreamy trip is over- or underexposed, muted in a way I now realize captures the experience precisely.

Back to the train, or more accurately, trains. We'd been living with COVID for what seemed a very long time – numbers spiking again at an alarming rate. And I was attending a lecture virtually. Propped up in a nest of plump pillows, feeling like a sultan, a steaming cup of coffee to hand. Travel author Monisha Rajesh spoke to us through laptop screens, as she was the presenter for London's Royal Geographical Society lecture series. The subject? Her travels around the world on 80 trains, some of the world's most scenic.

It had been a year since my own travel plans had been cancelled as a result of the pandemic – flights, accommodations, rental cars and commuter trains – refunds received, some forgone, airline points reinstated and turned into cash. From a traveller's perspective, things looked dire, other than a pleasant but fleeting debit balance on the credit card. So, along with a stack of travel-lit, -logues and memoirs, I was doing my best to quell wanderlust as best I could. And for a jonesing dromomaniac, Monisha's globe-spanning lecture was an ideal, albeit temporary, cure.

When we eventually swapped messages, I was pleased to learn one of her favourite experiences on that expansive journey had been her travels in western Canada, specifically through British Columbia and the Canadian Rockies. Interestingly, the same pockets of planet a globetrotting friend from Greenland described as her favourites as well. When I rode a similar route aboard Via Rail, I felt much the same. Even as a local, I was awed, slicing through mountains of sandstone, limestone and shale, a route I'd bisected many times in a car, but somehow from the sliding perspective of a train the same land's renewed. Invigorated. Old stone reborn.

Join me for that rail-bound journey across western Canada, skirting the American border with a northerly lilt, a sharp jog north, then a gentle traverse south, returning to the Pacific. If you've read my memoir *Dromomania*, some of this trek will be familiar. While the beauty of that ongoing journey, individuals met and those windows onto life's meaning remain ajar, I believe this viking voyage, shared space and travel, resonates now more than ever.

THE AMERICAS

1

BY RAIL

From the same weathered journal, buckled from sweat
and from rain, stitching frayed to the point where
pages had been lost, the book's profile a wedge:

Fellow travellers were going through pre-overnight rituals;
sleep aids and noise-cancelling headphones,
while I opted for another large serving
of care-cancelling liquor.

"Ahhhhh-board!" a conductor hollered from the platform, walking the length of our passenger train. As he climbed three metal steps we began to roll, shimmying from Winnipeg Station along the Assiniboine, rattling west.

A woman named Claire (shoulder-length brown hair, tortoiseshell glasses and neckerchief knotted to the left) introduced herself and passed me sparkling wine, the bubbles served with hardening cold cuts, stiff from handling and age – Via Rail's interpretation of canapés. Claire would be my coach porter for the trip, she said, and told me to let her know if I needed anything. There weren't many passengers, she explained, so I'd be seeing her a lot. It was the last time I saw her. How someone manages to vanish in a thin tube with a single corridor remains a mystery.

I was riding in Silver and Blue Class, suspecting, at a glance, that denoted passenger hair colour. Even in middle age I was the youngest passenger by 30 years. I staggered my way through the long, tight passageway, jostled by the shimmy of the train as though in a Metallica concert pit. I'd had the same vibrating experience at a St. Paddy's Day show at the Commodore Ballroom with Spirit of the West, perpetually body-slammed by an aggressively affectionate woman whose name I never did learn.

As I eventually reached the Pullman car, I was nearly starving, ready for a big, sit-down dinner. I'd been given a chit with a three on it.

"What's this mean?" I asked a dining car attendant, having to raise my voice over the rumble of my stomach.

"That means you're in the third seating for dinner; at 9 p.m.," she said.

It was 5 p.m. "So, in *four hours* from now?" I asked, punctuated with another stomach growl.

"Oh, no," she replied. "9 p.m. new time: *five* hours from now."

I sighed heavily and bumped my way to the bar car to fill up on booze and see if I couldn't rustle up more fossilized cold cuts.

Of the 120 passengers on board, 40 were a tour group from England. I was convinced it was a 50-year cast reunion of *Coronation Street*. When I was finally seated for dinner, I sat with Ken and Deirdre Barlow and Norris, I believe, although they used different names. They all looked to be 60, although they were probably in their 70s.

Norris, who went by Louis, said he'd just gotten a call from his son, who'd told him he was going to start an MBA.

"Good for him," I said.

"Yes," Norris/Louis replied. "He told me his books will be free now that he's 65."

Ken, Deirdre and I stared, somewhat dumbfounded.

"I'm sorry," I said. "Did you say your *son* is 65?"

"That's right," he replied.

"Cor!" Deirdre said. "You look *60*!"

"Oh, well, we're just friends now," he said, as though that explained everything.

It turned out he was 85, and the four of us visited and laughed as though we'd been friends for years. We ate pickerel in white sauce, discussing travel, politics and, naturally, fish.

It was nearly midnight when we made our way from the dining

car, but Norris/Louis, Ken and Deirdre stopped in the bar car where most of their tour group were having boisterous fun and playing cards. There was no sign of the party letting up. I was exhausted and headed straight to my sleeper cabin, where I'd fold in sink, toilet, slide out the narrow little bed (disturbingly known as a coffin) and, ironically, sleep like the dead.

Passing through the bar car filled with partying septuagenarians (plus Norris/Lewis), I gave a wave and said good night to all.

"GOOD NIGHT!!!" the car chorused, and I went to bed with a smile.

Tucked in my coffin, I pondered mortality. Through drifting thoughts, I recounted time spent in Canada's midriff, in Winnipeg. Much of it was spent around the Forks, the historically significant confluence of the Red and Assiniboine rivers, where I'd jogged along the water while seagulls cried and fish splashed loudly. A guy rode past on a bike with a fishing rod poking from a backpack, making me envious and vowing to never travel without a collapsible rod and some tackle, a vow I forgot almost immediately. My route took me past the provincial Parliament and outsized sculptures where a statue of parliamentarian/traitor Louis Riel stood (at the time), resembling Burton Cummings when he was with The Guess Who. I passed the Nutty Club and wondered how they chose members, expecting it should be closer to the legislature, then carried on to the Salisbury House restaurant, a local diner featuring small, tasty burgers called Nips. They were the daily special. I ate heartily and got change from a five-dollar bill.

I'd been told not to walk to or from my downtown hotel after dark, so I was in a taxi, being driven a short distance by a lean Ethiopian. It was in the midst of the US financial bailout.

"Seven-hundred billion!" he wailed. "SEVEN-HUNDRED BILLION!!! That's enough to fix everything in my country. EVERYTHING! Do you know how many HOMES that could build?!"

I had no idea what a house went for in Addis Ababa, but his point was made just the same. I was sickened by it too, of course, like watching an accident happen, unable to stop it. And sitting in the back of the cab, in a business suit at the time, I felt part of the establishment, guilty by association. Everything the cabbie said was true. I just nodded, then shook my head. What could I possibly say?

On another occasion, making my way (daytime, on foot) to Winnipeg's train station, I met Mohammed. He asked directions and I did my best in a city I knew somewhat. We visited a short while. He introduced himself as a Somalian, so I asked him if chardonnay went with salmon. He explained Somalia is a country in Africa, and that sauvignon blanc would be better.

We walked together, headed in roughly the same direction. He was going to a town hall meeting where a Member of Parliament would discuss current issues. Mohammed said he felt it was important to hear what the politicians had to say, leaving me somewhat ashamed for my apathy.

Some time later, I was again in a cab, disliking the city, its perpetual filth from floods and long winters – salt, sand and grime coating the streets year-round. People bundled in the cold – angered with crime, addiction, directionless youth, surviving bitter weather ten months of the year, the remaining few weeks given over to insatiable insects. This was what I thought, slumped in the cab, eager to leave.

The driver was a huge smile atop a lean frame. He was keen to talk and told me of how he came to Winnipeg from Africa.

"Friendly Manitoba!" he said. "I learned this. It's the provincial slogan, you know? Friendly Manitoba." He made eye contact in the rearview mirror, his smile widening. "It's written on the licence plates – Friendly Manitoba. I dreamed of coming to this place, to Friendly Manitoba. I left my country and had nothing. I have been here for many years now, and I am happy, very happy. It is cold, yes, but I have a family now – a wife and children, and we are here and we are happy."

We turned a corner.

"I was on my own flying here," he explained. "And when the plane touched down, we were still taxiing, and I got out of my seat and dropped to the floor and I kissed it, I did. I was crying, 'Friendly

Manitoba! I am here, in Friendly Manitoba!' I have never been so happy!"

And here I'd thought this poor bastard lived in the worst place possible, when, in fact, this lucky bastard lived in the best place imaginable. As he delivered me I thanked him, a bit excessively, for more than was apparent.

Back aboard the train, from southern Manitoba we veered north as we continued westward. "Trains do not depart," novelist William Gaddis wrote. "They set out, and move at a pace to enhance the landscape, and aggrandize the land they traverse." Which is exactly what happened as we crossed the South and North Saskatchewan rivers, landscape and water in emerald hues reminiscent of a serpentine carving I bought at Vancouver's English Bay from a Manitoban artisan.

He'd gathered the stone from the eastern shore of Lake Winnipeg – the edge of the Canadian Shield and geographical centre of the country. I enjoyed visiting with him, his lineage Cree, Scottish and French-Canadian, a cross-section of national history, his personal pilgrimage akin to that of explorers and settlers. And he travelled west, with this small chunk of greenstone, its provenance his own – an artistic composite of land and people, captured in time, carved and polished into permanence.

Rattling west from the midst of the country, I thought of Dad, who hailed from Winnipeg. And I remembered writing this out (for the first time) in a binder of three-hole-punched loose-leaf, a memory that made us laugh.

It was nearing Christmas. There was a decorative bowl of assorted nuts on the coffee table with a cracker: oddly shaped Brazil nuts, filberts, walnuts, pecans and almonds, none of which appealed to me as a kid as they all seemed to involve a great deal of effort and mess to consume. I was more interested in the Pot of Gold milk chocolates. There was also a dish of mandarin oranges, the little cardboard box they arrived in a perforated window onto the world.

Dad was in his comfy chair, facing the TV from across the room, and asked me to toss him an orange. I knew it must be the holiday season for me to be granted permission to throw fruit in the living room. I picked a good plump one from the bowl, removed the crinkly green tissue paper and hurled it toward him like we did when playing slow-pitch. At that precise moment, however, something on TV caught his attention (probably Anne Murray on Wayne and Shuster's Christmas special), and he was focused on the set rather than the orange missile sailing toward him. I had time to holler, "Dad!" I believe, or maybe that was just in my head, but all I know was the big juicy orange dropped squarely into his crotch with a fleshy *thud*.

Poor Dad folded neatly in half, inadvertently doing an elevated ab-crunch, his head tucking between his knees as he let out a squeaky yip like the time the neighbour's dog Loogie (yeah, I know, but I didn't name it) caught its tail in the trunk of the car.

"Ouch," my sister said, looking at Dad still folded in half.

"Oh, my," Mom added, with genuine concern.

"Sorry, Dad," was all I could muster.

He took a great deal of time to catch his breath, then wheezed, "Oh, son, you got me right in the..." and he said a word I'd never heard before.

Next day at school, I was discussing it with the boys on the playground.

"You know what my dad calls them?" I asked. The boys shook their heads, leaning in, eager to acquire worldly knowledge. I puffed my chest, delighted to be the one in the know.

"Tentacles!" I said, loud and proud. Everyone seemed impressed. We'd all learned a new term for nuts, not to be confused with the festive ones left untouched in the decorative Christmas bowl.

"Say," a boy named Scott piped up. "Isn't that what octopuses have?"

"Uh, yeah," I said, uncertain, but soldiering on. "All I know is it's another name for balls too. My dad said so."

The rest of the gang nodded slowly, realizing they'd learned something new and valuable. We all knew if it came from someone's dad, it had to be true. It was a very long time before it occurred to me I might have misheard dad. But I'm still not convinced I did.

Later Dad fully recovered, tentacles having dropped for a second time, we were on a viking quest, in a manner, travelling not with the tide but in tidy straight lines within our country, outs and backs, each subsequent departure extending our distance from home.

On our first adventure together we went by plane to see an NHL hockey game, flying from Kelowna to Vancouver. I was 6. Mom had packed for the two of us. Three large suitcases. (We would be away for 40 hours.) The flight was late taking off due to fog and we went directly from YVR to the game, arriving at the end of the first period, Dad humping our three outsized suitcases with us to our seats at the arena. We were in row 45, the top row of the Pacific Coliseum, tucked between rafters and a lone, disoriented sparrow.

Perhaps my favourite memory-lane example of Dad and I actually viking was when we embarked on a cross-country road trip in Dad's little Mazda pickup truck. I was off to university and we were moving me to the pleasant, green, slightly haunted town of London, Ontario, a community of schools, hospitals and golf courses populated by students, professors, retired professors, doctors and alcoholics. There was overlap to be sure.

Past birch and maple forests, grain fields and lakes, we drove through Canadiana landscapes, the look of oils on canvas by the Group of Seven. We swapped bad jokes, ate at truck-stop diners, endured tumultuous thunder and lightning on the prairies and crossed Lake Huron on a ferry.

Dad arranged the music for our 8000-kilometre odyssey. Four Sinatra cassettes. That's it. Some of the content being the same songs recorded under different labels. Despite a limited playlist, it was an extraordinary journey. But to this day, with the opening note of a Sinatra song, I sing it from start to finish. Whether I want to or not. Occasionally, when I'm in a rush, I'd rather not have to do the full version of "Summer Wind," but again it's never really been up to me.

From a claret journal with gold leaf and heavy cover that snapped
shut with a magnet; a gift I felt obliged to use, a bit clunky, a
bit frilly and I'm pretty sure it demagnetized my bank card:

*Waking in my little sleeper, the feeling somewhat luxurious
and somewhat grungy, like camping. New deodorant
on old, recycled clothes, and my day's begun.*

Following a jostling night in my Via Rail coffin, my three new dining car companions ordered "The Canadian Breakfast: Pancakes with
Real Maple Syrup!" (The capitalization and exclamation point assur-
ing authenticity.) I had fried Mennonite sausage, with eggs cooked to
someone else's liking.

A petite old Brit, part of the "Corrie" cast reunion, led conversation
at our table; holding court, really. A funny, animated racist. Oddly fair,
mind you, as she managed to disparage every European nation equally.

"On a booze cruise, we were," she explained. "To Calais. And the
woman there, at the duty free shop, she were so rude to me. Like I was
nothing. So I says to her, I says, '*Sprechen sie Deutsch?*' And she says,
all snooty like, '*Mais, non.*' To which I say, 'You're welcome!' Well, the
look on her face, I tell you!"

I admit I rather enjoyed being cast in a real-life episode of *Fawlty
Towers*. Meanwhile, the handful of scrawny trees that had been keeping us company, whizzing past like adolescent phone poles, vanished
completely as we raced through Alberta foothills, then climbed past
bighorn sheep defying gravity on sheer cliffs.

We entered Jasper, rolling to a stop, and the Corrie cast disembarked. They'd be carrying on to British Columbia by coach through
the Rockies and the southern part of the province to Victoria, Canada's
coastal enclave reminiscent of their motherland. Meanwhile, I sat in
my sleeper unit, wrapped in blankets against a frost that somehow

managed to penetrate windows, a sense of lounging in cold storage. I peered through a stubbornly steamy window as the Brits – my new friends – shuffled about, a few snowflakes drifting in the wind. Ice-capped Rockies loomed, brooding, while the little group, all in tweed, stamped feet against the chill. And as the train began to roll I couldn't help but feel we'd deposited them on an ice floe, giving it a little shove as we headed into the mountains.

That night, following a muted dinner and quietened bar car, I lay rocking in my little coffin and watched constellations emerge against darkening sky. As the train rolled through Kamloops, stars hung directly outside vibrating windows, as though the long stretch of hoo-doos fronting the Thompson River were adorned in tiny white twinkle lights.

The last morning aboard the train I woke early and climbed a tight, circular stairwell into one of the glass-domed viewing cars. I sat in front and watched rails race toward me, narrowing in the distance. Mount Baker peered through leaden cloud to the south and the Fraser River moved fast and dirty, paralleling the tracks. Passing through familiar suburban neighbourhoods felt like discovery, the perspective from the rail line, once more, entirely new.

A train rolling past is a lovely thing, like watching a ship or a plane, from the outside. But inside, a passenger vehicle struck me, more often than not, as a kind of zoo – a moving game reserve. No matter how spacious, it's still contained – the restricting confines of a safari, co-incidentally the Swahili word for journey. And so we travel, blessed and challenged with one-way seats on life's Grand Tour.

As the train rumbled along I thought of the expression "Arrivals are departures." Or it may have been "Departures are arrivals." Either works. I first heard it on a travel show, or possibly a beer ad, where it struck me as gag-inducing treacle. Madison Avenue at its worst. But when I read the "arrivals-departures" thing in a Mark Twain journal, it struck me as profound. Maybe I was being a snob. But maybe I just needed context. The right mindset. The simplest journey can, of course, be life-changing. Eventually, a voice came over the PA: "Folks, we're coming into Vancouver." And I was home. Whether departing, arriving or both, the journey continued.

From a slim, unruled notebook with an abstract painting of a tall ship navigating a forest, a book from a turnstile display at a sleepy museum on a dock, off-season, the clerk and I equally surprised by each other's presence:

Iron Maiden's "Rime of the Ancient Mariner" was in my head. Again. Which got me thinking about my high school English literature teacher. While Steve Harris's Powerslave *rendition is better, obviously, it was that kind and influential teacher who turned me on to the original by Sam Coleridge. That class broadened my world through Shelley, Keats and Chaucer, but it was the literary classic* Beowulf *that sparked my wanderer's fuse, slow burning its way across Arctic maps to a cache of once-buried longships that would change my life.*

I'd taken an hour-long bus ride into Vancouver (we lived in the burbs at the time) to see the latest film adaptation of *Beowulf.* Not the roto-scoped one with the A-list Hollywood cast in 3D, mind you. But one filmed in Iceland with government grants and an all-Danish cast. I was on my own as no one I knew – no one – wanted to see the film. I know, right? It boggles the mind.

The bus was a pleasant, temporary escape, granting me the freedom to be a tourist in my own city. Someone else worried about traffic while I relaxed and gave thoughts some off-leash time. I could enjoy a drink or two without worry of driving, plus public transit smelled better than my vehicle. We plunged through a tunnel under a river, crossed two bridges and gradually made our way into town, where I had time before the show to settle into a trendy resto-pub. The thud of dance music vibrating through my solar plexus and scrotum I could've done without, but I quite liked the dark beer they had on tap.

With said beer consumed, still vibrating slightly in my belly with residual bass (think ripples in a puddle as a T-Rex approaches), I made my way to the theatre, scanned the available seats and settled in. There were a total of three of us waiting to see a subtitled *Beowulf*, two losers and me, each of us assuredly thinking the same thing.

Some time later I was once more bound for a train, this time an Amtrak headed south from Vancouver, hugging coastline, deltas and swaths of farmland, bound for Seattle. Deb (my wife) was travelling for work (no plus-ones) and I felt a few days of viking would be a good diversion. I also planned to see the newest version of *Beowulf*. This one being the big-budget, Hollywood production with A-listers in 3D animation, cutting edge tech at the time.

I crossed Vancouver in sharp drizzle, en route to the train, my hood cinched tight, keeping me marginally less wet while tunnelling my vision, the city a rain-blurred squall. Walking through historic Chinatown, I passed construction sites, fencing topped in razor wire, the feel of a prison yard. I quickened my pace in the rain, which somehow matched my speed, falling with increased aggression. Eager to escape the cold and wet, I made for the glowing neon of a welcoming Asian supermarket.

The store was a steamy crush of wet shoppers. I squelched through aisles, killing time and finding snacks for my trip – labels I could neither read nor understand, touted by anime spokespeople. The fish counter was a Food Channel extravaganza – things new and exotic to me: lemon sole resembling Marty Feldman, lobsters handcuffed in rubber bands, a dozen types of oysters and prawns, pink tilapia, striped bass and a tank jammed with a rugby scrum of Dungeness crabs. Another tank was plungered with fat abalone that looked like adhesive toilet-bowl cleaners.

The end cap to the row of burbling displays was a large single tank filled with a solitary king crab I suspect may have lived there forever. It seemed to be daring anyone to buy it. For some reason it reminded me of Snowflake, the albino gorilla from Barcelona Zoo, only bigger. We'd seen Snowflake when we were there, exploring the Costa Brava, and like all zoo experiences it was mildly interesting but mostly sad.

Leaving the giant, quite rightly disgruntled crab behind, I arrived at Pacific Central Station just before early boarding and customs clearance. I bought a postcard – a black and white photo taken when the station was built in 1917 – then made the mistake of using the public bathroom, regretting my decision immediately as my shoes slid about the floor as though it were an oil slick. Every surface, it seemed, had served as targets or backboards for creative ricochets. I turned and shuffle-skated out, not wanting my urine to touch anything.

The customs officer seemed unsure as to why I'd go to Seattle for four days on my own.

"You meeting friends there?" he asked.

"No," I said.

"Not meeting *anyone*?"

"No."

"You don't have *any* friends there?"

I hung my head and muttered a pathetic, "No." Which seemed to satisfy him, having successfully crushed my spirit, and he waved me through.

I took a quick look around the exterior of the train – a boxy locomotive popping, clicking and hissing with two long, tall passenger cars. The car slowly filled. Passengers fussed with heavy coats, tickets, passports and immigration forms, while the hum of fans and the idling engine morphed the interior into a pleasant, purring cocoon. It was surprisingly comfortable in the cozy space and I relaxed. Then I sniffed. Looked around. Sniffed some more. And realized there was a foul, lingering odour permeating the cabin. There was no telling its source and no ignoring it. The most accurate description of the prevailing stink, I decided, was an unfortunate, piquant combination reminiscent of sour cabbage and anus. I realized I'd been in well-used porta-potties at chili cook-offs that smelled much, much better.

Beyond the platform, a row of idling Greyhounds burbled steely exhaust into a wet, wintery evening. I broke the spine on a new copy of Paul Theroux's *The Great Railway Bazaar*, settled in for the ride and felt all was right in the world. Exceedingly well-travelled Theroux wrote in no uncertain terms that Amtrak consistently ran the worst trains in the world. I laughed, gagged on the cabin smell and choked it back to a chortle.

The train rolled from Vancouver through New Westminster and across a swing bridge over the Fraser River. The sky darkened as we passed under Pattullo Bridge and then Alex Fraser Bridge. Orange and white lights reflected long and wavy in the inky black of the water. We continued in a meandering southerly route along tree-lined shore toward Crescent Beach, approaching the American border at the 49th parallel. I pressed my cheek against the window to see the engine and car ahead on a curve as the train whistle blew like an elongated hoot of an owl.

One time I trekked this narrow band of seashore on foot, following the tracks. Because of the rail and sea there's little development, and the swath of prime shoreline's inhabited by bald eagles. I saw no less than two dozen juvies (under 5 years of age), their head plumage still brown and gold. There was no trail to speak of, just a slender finger of steeply sloped gravel and sand buttressing the rail line. And I experienced the sensation Stephen King describes so well in his novella *The Body*, later adapted as the movie *Stand By Me*, as the steel atop the ties began to sing – actually sing – despite seeing nothing, a kind of cautionary, vibrational comprehension, realizing that a speeding locomotive's bearing down on you. I didn't feel in any real danger. There was sufficient space, I felt, between rail line and sea for me to scramble down the short, steep embankment to allow the train to pass. Which it did, thundering by at full throttle, a slightly terrifying, unstoppable blast of countless tons of steel. What I didn't consider, however, was the slipstream effect of the mile-long beast racing past, whipping up gravel like buckshot and peppering me in a nasty volley of cutting rocks. Pinged and winged, I was soon squealing and bloodied by the horrid thing I'd only moments before thought of rather romantically as a sort of travel partner.

Now, however, comfortably ensconced (and unbloodied) aboard one of the world's worst-smelling trains, I was across the aisle from a middle-aged couple going home to Seattle. They called their kids, speaking formally to voicemail – nervous and business-like – the use of tech somehow robbing them of humanity.

A hairy, barrel-chested man in black tee, jeans and white Pumas checked his watch constantly, slowing time. He spoke in a brusque, clipped manner that convinced me he was a homophobe.

Two British businessmen sat behind me. They'd spent the day working in Vancouver and were returning to Seattle. I decided they talked too much and said "cheers" too frequently. Much to my relief, they fell asleep.

Gliding through the dark, the ride became extrasensory. The clack of steel wheels that triggered this recollective thread, a vibrating shudder as we'd cross a road, the occasional moan of our engine's power-chord and the soft hiss of diagonal rain on fast-moving windows. After some time the train began to slow, then rolled to a stop.

A conductor came on the PA: "We'll be stopping briefly in Bellingham and will open one lower door. Please take note of your valuables."

Passengers looked around nervously, gripping handbags. I imagined Bellingham residents must be gangs of filthy thugs with blackened teeth, wearing rags and mobbing the train as one door opens, to spill aboard like pirates, snatching unsuspecting passengers until the train once more began to roll, the homophobe and I left to beat them away from the door, where they'd scuttle and gimp their way back to subterranean lairs to paw their new prizes and fight over swollen tins of expired Chef Boyardee. (Since then I've become friends with a lovely

couple from Bellingham. They have perfectly good teeth and I've yet to
see them rob a train or eat beefaroni. Which doesn't mean they don't.
I just haven't witnessed it.)

Following my mental lapse, one of the British businessmen's phones
kept ringing off and on, continuously waking them. I recognized it as
Gilbert and Sullivan, but the phone was being answered too quickly
for me to identify the song. They must've dozed off again because the
next call rang for a while and to my relief I recognized it as the "Modern
Major-General's Song" from *The Pirates of Penzance*. It seemed a shame
not to mentally sing along, but it was just the music, so I was forced
to fill in the words as best I could. I strongly encourage you to get the
tune going in your head to make the most of it:

I have my wallet and my watch; I have my pair of spectacles
I put my hand into my drawers to check I have my testicles
Defendable and bendable and always most dependable
They are the very model of the modern male genitals

I don't know much astronomy; I can't quote Deuteronomy
But one thing that I know quite well's my masculine anatomy
They hang off half the animals and swing there like root vegetables
They are the very model of the modern male genitals

My twig and berries; meat and two – it's Big Jim and the two twins too
Like two-thirds of the Stooges there's a Larry and there's Curlys too
They're feasible and squeezable and always very pleasable
They are the very model of the modern male genitals

We rumbled into Seattle through industrial suburbs, passing heavy
freight trains, empty and still in the night. We crossed a black body
of water I couldn't identify, dotted with dark outlines of moored tug-
boats. A red neon ampersand spun slowly on a building and then we
dipped suddenly into pitch black before emerging into historic downtown Seattle, where a Florentine-looking fountain, underlit, welcomed
us from the tunnel into King Station.

It was nearly midnight on the bleak November night and I walked from the station in icy rain that fell like a relentless volley of arrows, biting exposed skin and stinging my face and neck. I leaned into the wind, fighting the backwards pull of my pack, and trudged toward my hotel, skirting soaked and curled-up homeless lumps.

It was a gritty part of town – empty stores, broken glass, a dimly lit pawnshop and a narrow stairwell leading to the Showgirls Lounge ("Always Open, Never Clothed"). I walked through flickering neon, then dark. Predatory eyes followed me. I tried to walk with a look of confidence I didn't feel and, after a remarkably long mile, to my relief, saw the glow of the hotel – a lighthouse guiding me through rough water. A guy stood out front, smoking under a dripping canopy. He nodded and I did the same as I went through a wide glass door. In the reflection I saw him throw his lit cigarette into the street and follow me in, exhaling smoke.

I stood at an empty reception counter.

"Hey," the guy from the street said over my shoulder.

"Uh, hey," I replied.

"You alone?" he asked.

"Uh, yeah?" I said, hesitant.

"Cool," he said, and stepped past me behind the counter.

"So, one key?" he asked, and I realized he worked there and was checking me in.

"Yeah, please," I said, relief in my voice.

"You want company?" he asked.

"Uhh..." relief vanishing from my voice.

"You're alone, right? So you want some company for in your room?"

"Um, I'm good. Thanks," I said, feeling I'd made a poor hotel choice. Taking the key, I stepped into the elevator, then turned and asked, "Do many guests take you up on that?"

"Oh, yeah," he nodded with a grin. "They almost all do." Then, as the elevator doors slid shut, I heard him say, "I'm gonna send someone up with Linda for you anyway."

I made a move toward the button, but the door had closed, and with a sickening hum the elevator whisked me up. My mind raced. *Okay, I'll dump my pack in the room, bolt to the theatre to see* Beowulf *as planned, and won't be back until 3 a.m. By that time, Linda should've buggered off and if there's a pimp around, hopefully I won't be too badly shaken down.*

I ducked into the room, which was well appointed – rich, vertically striped wallpaper, Chippendale-style chair and a flat-screen TV. It would be a shame to see it trashed by a vindictive pimp. I tossed my pack and turned to leave when there was a knock at the door. *Shit*! I redistributed things in my pockets – hiding cash and a second credit card. Trying to act much calmer than I felt, I opened the door a crack.

There was a thickset, swarthy guy with a shaved head. He was rather short, and I thought in a pinch, with terror and adrenaline on my side, it might be a fair fight. Funnily, I noticed he had a name tag that read, "John." He shouldered past me into the room.

I glanced up and down the hallway – no sign of anyone else. I turned back into the room. "I think there's been a misunderstanding," I said, my voice unusually high.

"I was told you're alone, so they sent me up with Linda," he said from the middle of the room, and as he turned I realized he was holding a small round fishbowl that had somehow eluded me while I'd been trying to remember how to make a fist.

"This is Linda!" he said with a wide smile. I walked over and swimming in the bowl was a bug-eyed goldfish with a black-tipped dorsal fin, like a tiny shark. She was a homely little thing but did have lovely pouting lips that made her look surprised, a perpetual, "Oh!"

"I'll set her down here," John said. "Housekeeping will feed her and change her depending on the length of your stay. Just don't tap the glass."

Well, how about that, I thought. *This was becoming more like a visit to Amsterdam after all.* I thanked John, relieved not to be robbed, beaten up or, heaven forbid, embarrassed, and tipped him about as much as if we'd had sex anyways.

"Thanks!" he said, and added, "You can keep her. Or even eat her if you like."

I laughed and then remembered room service had stopped for the night. I waited until John was out of sight down the hall and slowly looked back at the bowl with a wolfish grin.

Linda looked back, eyes wide. "Oh!"

A severe weather front was hammering the city, something ugly swirling off the coast. I jogged toward the theatre bent into the wind like *M*A*S*H* medics approaching a chopper. My layers of technical clothing were soaked almost instantly. The streets, running with water, were quiet. Having located the theatre, I couldn't find any way to get in. It was part of a large mall and every entrance was locked. A couple ran to their car and I asked for help.

"Yeah," they laughed. "It's not easy. Go down the alley, into the underground parkade. Look for the elevator. That'll get you into the mall. Then go to the third floor to get to the theatre."

Waving thanks, I found my way into the building from the garage but was soon hopelessly lost in the silent, cavernous space of locked, darkened stores. I wandered around like a UFO-abductee dumped in a cornfield before being rescued by three other moviegoers – a female/male couple and their single male friend Jack, a poster boy for camp. Everything he said came out like a show tune and, remarkably, a spotlight followed him everywhere. The four of us became immediate friends.

We made our way to the ticket office and, despite it being past showtime, we still had to wait for someone to unlock the little glass hut and sell us tickets. It was my first experience with self-serve butter for the popcorn. And as I dumped popcorn to make room for more butter, I could've sworn I heard angels – morbidly obese angels – sing, "U-S-A! U-S-A!"

We settled into seats and an old-fashioned curtain rose, forcing

Jack to cut short a medley from *Oklahoma*. Looking around the theatre, I realized the four of us were the only ones who planned to see
the latest film adaptation of *Beowulf*, quite possibly in all of America.

The following day, I took part in an underground city tour – a
unique look at Seattle's history. A large group of us met in a 19th-cen-
tury tavern, the look of a western saloon. After posing for photos at
the long, dusty bar, we crossed the street to a plain, unmarked door
secured with a padlock. Our tour guide fumbled with keys, popped
the lock and, with a creak of old hinges, we passed through the door
and descended.

Founded on the silty inlet of Elliott Bay, the city was originally built
on thousands of timber pilings driven into the ocean floor – a smaller
version of Venice. For the next 90 minutes we explored the city within
the city, poking around foundations and old, weeping brick, peering
up through purple glass tiles that let daylight pass through from street
level. Specific areas were pointed out to us, showing where much of
the construction had eroded.

"Stupid," I heard a guy in the group say. "Should've used German
engineers. And prostitutes should be legal."

I was unsure if I'd heard things out of context, or if he simply had
strong opinions on sex workers and Teutonic builders. As one does.

What happened next exemplifies the difference between Canadians
and Americans. An obnoxious guy on the tour was talking non-stop
on his cellphone, having to raise his voice (as you can imagine) to be
heard over our guide. People tried shushing cellphone-talker, to no
avail. Now. *This* is the difference between the US and Canada:

In my sternest, no-nonsense voice, I gave cellphone-talker a hard
gaze and said, "Excuse me! Could you *please* stop talking? We're trying to hear the commentary!" Which, naturally, had no effect. But
was immediately followed by an American offering *his* suggestion to
the talker.

"Hey! Asshole! Shut the fuck up!"

Which still didn't work but *did* make the rest of us feel better.

I started the next day at Pike Place Market. The weather was stubbornly foul and I thought of the jokey reference to grey being Seattle's official colour. Wind and rain blew in off the bay as I wound my way through the market. The whole thing felt like a bazaar – weirdos juggling things, flipping sticks, kicking hacky sacks and generally giving the west coast a bad name. The vibe was surly – people ill-tempered and aggressive. I was surprised at the unpleasantness of it all.

I smiled and nodded at a busker, which was a mistake. Then, at a seafood stall, a guy offered me smoked salmon, which I took with a thanks. It tasted awful. And as I stood there, wondering where I could discreetly spit, he gave the rest of the samples to a dog. Another vendor seemed pissed off that I bought something from him, which confused me, so I made my way out, glad to be leaving. Plus, I had a boat to catch.

I was joining a tour to Blake Island Marine State Park for a Suquamish barbecue and cultural show. This patch of land in Puget Sound was a traditional camp used by the tribal Nation and is reported to be the birthplace of Chief Sealth, Seattle's namesake. British explorer Captain George Vancouver arrived in 1792, former first mate of Captain James Cook and namesake of the home I'd temporarily left, a short distance north.

Waiting for the boat, our group huddled in the miserable weather like emperor penguins. There was a restaurant on the pier and its manager took pity on us, opening early and waving us in from the storm. I sat with a foursome from California: Carol and Bob, and Dick and Liz. They'd met and become couples, they explained, when they worked together at NASA. Which made me feel we had a great deal in common as I'd seen the movie *Apollo 11* and was filling my journal using a Fisher Space Pen ("Writes in zero gravity, works upside down, under water, over grease and in extreme temperatures!").

Carol and Liz ordered hot chocolate, while I ordered an enormous beer. Bob and Dick looked at their watches, then ordered giant beers as well. Moments later we were sculling our cocoa and beer and bolting to our ferry.

The ride to Blake Island felt like my midnight sprint to the theatre – cold, windy and wet. We chugged through layers of mist over choppy water and I visited with an Iroquois couple from New York, learning facets of coast-to-coast culture. On deck we watched bald eagles circle the island, reminiscent of those playing an integral role in our first *Gone Viking* adventure.

The Blake Island show was entertaining as well as educational – blanket and mask dances with traditional song, followed by a feast of salmon cooked over alder and cedar, fragrant wild rice, purple potatoes and molasses bread.

On the boat back to the mainland I visited with Preston, a young man retired from the US Navy. We leaned over the railing and watched water roll by. I was bundled up – three thick layers, shivering in the cold. Preston wore an open-necked pullover and looked comfortable. He had short, dark hair, wire-framed glasses and a thoughtful, intelligent look.

"I was a torpedo man," he said softly. "On one of our nuclear subs. It was my job to talk the others down."

"I don't understand," I said.

"Our longest underwater run was 78 days straight," he said. "No light, no booze, no women…extreme." After a while he went on. "I've been all over the world and have no idea where I've been," he smiled, sadly. "I don't know. I don't agree with what the commander's doing over there. They come in to recruit. Tough places where you don't have many choices. They promise you work, an education. I was one of those. You do your first tour and then…what choice you got?" It was quiet again for some time and then he continued. "But I got out after two. People would say, 'But you gotta understand,' and I'd be like, yeah, I *get* it."

Water washed against the hull, the only sound for a long time. Preston's eyes seemed focused on something two oceans away. Eventually, he added, "I don't think he's making good choices." He shook his head. "I don't know."

But I was certain he did.

From the unruled notebook with a tall
ship sailing through evergreens:

*The hotel felt much better by day and it filled with college football
fans, in town to watch UCLA play the Washington Huskies.*

People wore alma mater scarves, hats and jerseys. The atmosphere was
one of good-natured, passionate rivalry. It reminded me of a trip to
Toronto when a pal and I went to a soccer match to see New England
play Toronto FC. We'd jumped aboard a trolley car packed with fans
going to the field overlooking Lake Ontario. The locals were avid sup-
porters – nearly everyone wore a red-and-white striped jersey, toque
or scarf, making the thick cluster of people look like they were off to
a quidditch match or the pages of *Where's Waldo?*

In the Seattle hotel, an evening wine tasting was being held in
the lobby and I settled into a high-backed leather chair to visit with
two women – Lindsay and Alicia – an attractive couple from central Canada. I pushed aside inappropriate sexual thoughts. For later.
Alicia spent most of the time talking animatedly about how shy and
introverted she was.

A fortune teller breezed through the room, part of the evening
event, and made her way to us. Her name was Astrid, or something
equally ethereal. She preferred the term card reader and seemed good
at what she did. She laid out a huge deck of cards and had me choose
four. I drew a hawk, a dog, a turtle and the moon card. She looked surprised, saying there was only a 1 per cent chance of drawing the moon.
She then explained the significance of each; that I would enjoy success, but I needed to be protective of relationships and that I should
sever my ties with false friends.

When our card reading was done, my new friends wanted to take me dancing, but I passed on the offer. As a straight white guy, my dance moves are decidedly lacking. Besides, I was looking forward to a Bear Grylls TV marathon, room service mac-and-cheese and deciding which friends to ditch.

From another journal printed with a ship, this one under full sail, bent into wind, with a nautical compass in the corner:

The day was promising, a robin's egg sky with puffs of creamy cumulus.

The train ride home was uneventful, a morning departure, the coach less smelly. When I disembarked at Pacific Central, a sea of orange-jerseyed fans streamed toward BC Place for the Canadian Football League's Western Final. With no agenda to keep, I chose to go with the flow (literally), making my way with the crowd to the stadium, where I found a single ticket and let the day play itself out.

Back for a time in Vancouver suburbs, I ran along a seawall on a cool, summer morning. Scaups bobbed in the shallows, herons stood motionless on the tide line and pigeons took flight with a sound like shuffling cards. A freight train rumbled past on the old Burlington Northern line, the same tracks as the north–south Amtrak.

There was a granite statue – salt and pepper stone – dedicated to a man who died at the age I was at the time. The carving was of a kayaker, leaning forward in his boat, catching a cresting wave. A small plaque read, "Paddle on to new adventures. Love, your family and friends."

At that moment, rising sun pierced a hole carved through the statue, symbolizing a spirit within the stone. Heat crept up the back of my neck and felt like much more than just sun.

A short distance away another statue sat on a grassy bank, facing the water, a carving called *Metamorphosis*. It was a nude, emerging from the stone, rough and erotic, the figure stretched, reaching toward the shoreline, as though longing for the sea.

Near the statues was an ancient, compact man, his posture a question mark. He was often at the beach, shuffling, hunched over a rolling walker, moving at the speed of the statues. This day, he was seated on the walker, his lap filled with birdseed. Pigeons swarmed, cooing and flapping on his arms, shoulders and knees. The tiny old man, like the carvings, seemed to undergo his own metamorphosis, catching a wave, breaking free, taking flight with his feathery friends.

I stopped to drink at a fountain where another elderly man stood, savouring the vista of Semiahmoo Bay. We smiled and nodded.

"A lot has changed since I was here last," he said.

"When was that?" I asked.

"1967," he said, which happened to be the year I was born. "But," he carried on, "The ocean, the islands, the mountains...that part doesn't change."

Together we enjoyed the view – sea, sky and the snow-capped ridgeline of the Vancouver Island Ranges – layers of watery blue, green and pearly white. Connecting with this man, like nature, felt remarkably comfortable.

"It's beautiful, isn't it?" I said, and added, "My name's Bill."

"*Nature's* beautiful," he replied. "And my name's Bill too." He looked at me, smiled, and a twinkle in his eye made me feel I was looking into the future.

From a simple brown Moleskine, pocket-sized, with a fabric strip that served as a bookmark:

A harbour seal bobbed alongside a slick black cormorant with a mishmash of gulls in white, grey and speckled brown.

Robert Louis Stevenson wrote, "I travel not to go anywhere, but to go." The journey itself the goal. I felt camaraderie, the nomadic gene so many of us share driving a desire to move, our inherent viking DNA.

It was another pleasant Vancouver day, and the Stevenson line tumbled in my head as though in a dryer on permanent press. I was having another run, this one in late summer haze, downtown, False Creek an unpolished mirror, coloured like murky blue sky.

Ground cover running along the seawall had become a produce display: blackberries, red currants and plump rose hips, while heavy orange clusters of mountain ash berries hung overhead. A murder of crows – click-purring like *Predator* aliens – rustled through the branches, methodically stripping the tree of its fruit. Previous runners, walkers, stroller-pushing parents, grandparents and nannies had trampled an assortment of fallen berries, giving a swath of walkway a colourful, tie-dyed look. A few more crows combed the waterline, stepping through seaweed to pick mussels and drop them on concrete bricks, shucking the shiny black shells with loud *cracks*. I trotted under sumac, maple and elm, past a restaurant, a pub and a pottery gallery, where a plate glass window offered a view of two women in half-lotus position, spinning lumps of shapeless brown clay.

An eclectic array of sailboats, luxury cruisers, small open tenders, lilting houseboats and a Chinese junk sat in the inlet, rocking gently while a team of grunting paddlers powered a dragon boat through the middle of it all, the look of Bill Reid's *Loo Taas*, the canoe that led me to Haida Gwaii, a blend of viking and grieving. Across the water, a neat row of residential high-rises lined the shore, tight, bright and pearly white – an outsized, infectious smile. Other than Sydney and pockets of Auckland, I believe no other city so beautifully melds a downtown core with priceless harbour views.

I continued on to the south side of English Bay, around a ship's anchor on Elsie Point, past a centennial totem pole (since removed), Vancouver's Maritime Museum and the *Munin*, a locally constructed longship moored at a floating pier. Although large, *Munin* was a half-size replica of the original housed at Oslo's Viking Ship Museum, high-prowed with a wolf head, teeth bared. We'd visited both on our initial *Gone Viking* travels, the Vancouver-based ship now retired.

When I ran this route at the time, *Munin* was under full sail in the bay, the vertically striped red and white square straight off the pages of Fran Bengtsson's *The Long Ships*, the visual inspiring. But a twinge of panic too was triggered, seeing the ship nearing shore, perhaps distant memories of plaited-hair oarsmen with round shields and axes spilling onto the beach, uninterested in trade. My intuition at the time, oddly enough, was to run home, set our place alight and salt the fields. But our high-rise apartment was concrete and the only produce we had was a tomato plant loaded with ripe fruit. Salting my little crop would only make it tastier. So instead I admired the boat from a distance but left before it got close. A longship full of camera-toting tourists in orange life jackets would simply spoil the visual.

1

PACIFIC

From Paul Theroux's *On the Plain of Snakes*:

"And I thought: I am content. I have achieved that
elusive objective in travel – a destination. I have arrived.
I am happy, one of the hardest moods to describe."

These next viking excursions navigate more of the North American
Pacific – Washington, Oregon and California – a combination of
driving, hiking, commuter trains, ferries, an ocean liner and a solitary horse as we methodically explore the left edge of the continent.

Veering west from the Canada–US border, we traversed the San
Juan Islands in Puget Sound (the Salish Sea). Our vehicle perched precariously in the back corner of a chunky ferry, providing an angled and
undulating view of Gulf Islands. A worker that resembled my nana
jammed a heavy wood chock behind one of our tires, wedging us into
place on the steeply sloped ramp. Then she heaved a water-filled hose
around for who knows what, possibly deck swabbing or a fire drill.
She was small and friendly, doing the work of a team of firefighters.
I danced around the hose, which became a lively barrier, flexing between cars, and made my way to the passenger lounge where a volunteer named Bill was giving an authoritative talk on whales.

Bill's audience was growing. Chairs were wide, squishy, moveable,
and passengers hauled them into auditorium-like seating, bringing
fresh popcorn from food services and getting comfy in a growing *U*.
Eventually, there were about a hundred of us waiting to hear Bill's talk.
His voice was strong and clear. If he didn't know what he was talking
about, it wasn't obvious and didn't really matter.

The one-hour sailing would take a little longer, we were told, as the

Coast Guard was conducting safety drills during our voyage. Mid-crossing we stopped in glass calm, the ship stock-still in dead water. The captain came on the PA intermittently, each announcement beginning with, "Sorry, Bill…" The crowd laughed and listened while Bill nodded, gesturing courteously at ceiling speakers, before resuming his presentation.

These were whale waters, home to grey, humpback, minke and orca. Three types of orcas came here: offshore, transient and resident. Offshore orcas are rare, tending to ply open water west of Vancouver Island, the Olympic Peninsula and the Baja, where they feed on sharks. They attack by flipping sharks onto their backs, making them easy prey. Bill pointed out this handy reminder: in the event of a shark attack, simply flip the shark onto its back. The crowd chuckled. One person wrote it down.

Resident pods, he explained, ate nothing but chinook salmon. Transients, or Bigg's, ate other marine mammals – sea lions, seals, dolphins, porpoises, other whale calves and otters. In order to catch and eat more intelligent prey, transients developed greater intellect and are considerably smarter than their fish-eating cousins. You may want to remember this when choosing food for your next family reunion.

The Sound is most frequented by resident orcas. But salmon stocks were low, the residents nowhere to be seen. On San Juan Island we visited an interpretive centre at Lime Kiln Point State Park, slated as the only place to consistently view orcas from shore. Summer sightings were recorded on a whiteboard calendar where volunteers were working. It was a sad collection of zeroes. Not the volunteers, they were just weird, but the numbers on the calendar – day after day of zero sightings when whales should be seen daily. Whether the change was permanent or not, no one knew.

We hiked around San Juan Island, climbing Mount Young through arbutus, fir, spruce and Garry oak, past fantails, chickadees and a red-headed woodpecker to explore the historical English and American camps, Roche Harbour and the lighthouse at Lime Kiln Point.

As we prepared to leave, sun rose over thick fog and we made a long, easy climb up Mount Finlayson under a partial moon with a face-like profile. A foghorn blew from somewhere, chilly and nautical. The mist-shrouded hill blended with seashore in a blur of scrub, gorse, bull kelp and green water. The ferry ride back to the mainland felt like sliding through cloud. A sailboat drifted past, ghostly in the mist, and our ship's horn blasted into a salty white wall of fog.

From a small journal with lined paper, a journal that stayed in a pocket and went through the laundry, pages clumped into bulging wads like forgotten receipts pulled too late from the wash:

The Oregon coast reminded me of Prince Edward Island, where we stayed in a black and white lighthouse. The Atlantic cliffs were red, but the endless stretch of sea was the same – a touch melancholy, and longingly beautiful.

Oregon became a favourite destination, our first visit being to Cannon Beach with a view of Haystack Rock – a rounded plinth of basalt that's a bird sanctuary, towering from the tide line like a massive head-stone. We were there in the midst of a hot, dry summer. Crossing the Canada–US border at the chunky white Peace Arch, we drove south on Chuckanut Drive with arbutus and evergreen views of Bellingham. ("Please take note of your valuables.")

In the footsteps of George Vancouver we passed the plummeting chute of Deception Pass. A bald eagle soared beneath the bridge as water rushed through the narrows in eddies of deep jade green. We continued south over Whidbey Island's undulating farmland. Scenery breezed by: grassy fields, berry farms and forest, frequent churches, in-frequent homes, more eagles, a falcon at rest and a solitary deer. The temperature rose under sunny sky and we caught a ferry from Clinton to Mukilteo on dazzling water, the snowy blue pyramid of Mount Baker watching as we crossed.

We stopped in Redmond, Washington – a historical town rebuilt by Microsoft, a tidy planned city of trees, water and wide, curving streets. I explored the downtown on a meandering trail through pristine apartments and around a heron rookery – an oasis nestled amongst colourful new builds.

Early next morning, I ran along the Sammamish River, slow-moving, greenish-brown water you'd expect Tom and Huck to pole along on a raft. Swallows skimmed the surface. A salmon jumped through lily pads with a splash. A rabbit darted from undergrowth, nearly through my legs. Sun warmed the blacktop. Blackberry bushes in bloom bordered the trail and tall poplars made a private green corridor. Mallards flew by in a lopsided V, a hummingbird whizzed past and sparrows hopped through dewy grass. I saw the occasional cyclist and walker. Everyone smiled, nodded or said, "Good morning." And I felt as though I'd woken in Stepford. But despite the sterility of a manufactured community, people were warm and genuine.

We explored much of this inviting, rugged state – Crater Lake, Hood River, Mount Hood and Central Oregon, along the coast and up the Willamette River into Portland, a unique, left-coast town, independent and eccentric, the mindset of Seattle but less refined, a green city with edge. In addition to a well-established coffee scene, the state boasts more craft brews and brewpubs than anywhere else in America. As well as beer, Portland has more bookstores than any other American city, creating a delicious slice of hoppy, literary Nirvana. Powell's Books, the world's largest independent new and used bookstore, sits in the heart of the city, a trophy centring a mantel. On our first visit we'd wandered through downtown in search of it, crossing the tracks and finding ourselves in a distinctly transitional neighbourhood. The store itself was a large urban block, a small town in a single building. Store maps were available when you entered, imperative to avoid getting lost.

Wandering through the store, I did my best to tap into the extra-sensory, relaxing and trusting intuition. I tuned out from the tangible and drifted amongst the rows of high shelves, some of which reached four metres or more. As I wandered in a fugue between aware and un-aware, a book fell from above, just to my right. I snatched and caught it, pleased with my reflexes, then turned it over to look at the cover – *The Celestine Prophecy* – essentially about that very thing, heightened awareness and utilizing alternative capabilities. It had literally leapt from the shelf. I smiled, clutching my gift, muttered something resem-bling thanks, and made my way to the till.

I spent four sunny mornings running through Portland, past densely packed food trucks and loosely scattered homeless – weirdly distinct yet blended communities. A local poet's work is carved in red granite by the river: "Mighty Willamette, beautiful friend." And I trot-ted along a paved walkway, feeling that friendship.

It was the first of July (Canada Day) and a flock of Canada geese had taken over the river, paddling in a broad, border-like line, some-how symbolic. Skidmore Fountain splashed nearby, the city's oldest commissioned art. The towering Wells Fargo building commanded the downtown skyline, Orwellian in stature, an imposing white land-mark. Gulls wheeled, pigeons fluttered overhead and I merged into a sweaty, jagged line of joggers, cyclists and pedestrians hugging the edge of the river, washed in morning sun. The *Portland* sat tethered in the water, a retired steam-powered, paddlewheel tugboat, now the Oregon Maritime Museum. Hawthorne, Morrison and Burnside bridges served as measuring landmarks, marking progress for joggers and the city alike. I crossed the river on the Steel Bridge, sharing the span with a whistle-blowing locomotive rattling and vibrating its way over the water.

We spent a hot afternoon under cloudless sky following trails through Washington Park before resting in shade by the Rose Garden Amphitheatre. Robins, crows, squirrels and fantails busied themselves around cedar, birch, hemlock and fern, while a harp echoed across the grounds, plucked notes angelic and dreamy. By early evening it was oddly quiet. Sun slid behind tall buildings. Food trucks closed for the night and we found ourselves on a gritty downtown street. A man shaved at a drinking fountain with an overused razor and tiny round mirror – something from a dental instrument – that he held between thumb and forefinger. He was meticulous, his weathered face shiny smooth, the softest scraping sound as we passed.

Written in rollerball ink on a pocket-sized pad
of plain paper bought at a Dollar Store:

From a block of food trucks I bought Spam musubi – sweet, barbecued Spam with sticky rice in nigiri, a fist-sized Hawaiian snack.

I took a self-guided walking tour of Portland's water features, a dozen fountains around downtown and Portland State University, wending my way through Pioneer Courthouse Square, Lovejoy, Dreamer, the grand Ira Keller Fountain and more. The river draws the ocean into the city, but fountains in concrete, brick and bronze bring the splash of water to every hidden corner.

We explored Portland's Pearl District, around Nob Hill and the high-end retail of Northwest 23rd Avenue, known locally as Trendy-Third. We passed Slabtown, home to Scandinavian and Chinese immigrants 150 years ago. Slabtown referred to slabs – mill cuttings, log edges unusable for building. Slabs were split and sold cheaply for fuel. Wealthy families had fuel storage buildings, while lower-income households piled slabs outside their homes, giving the neighbourhood its moniker. Indigenous Chinook were regular traders in town, travelling along the Willamette. *Chinook Jargon* – a Chinook/English dictionary – was a regional bestseller, as common in Portland homes in the late 19th century as *The Best of Bridge* would be a century later.

From the Dollar Store pad of plain paper:

Between homes, public footbridges crossed the water,
making an engaging run route and providing
intimate glimpses into the community.

In Bend, Oregon, new and old houses, extravagant and modest, clung
to the banks of the Deschutes River. We made the town our home
for a week. Half-hour drives north, south, east and west took us to
scenic hikes: snow-capped volcanic mountains, waterfalls and towering cliffs of purples, reds, oranges and gold, the space shared by hikers, rock climbers and horseback riders. Our hikes ranged from mod-
erate to intense as we climbed Pilot Butte, Tumalo Mountain, around
Tumalo Falls and over Smith Rock State Park's Misery Ridge with expansive vistas of rivers, lakes, colossal stone and the pristine peaks of
the Cascade Range.

The town of Bend is a historical hub surrounded by a gentle sprawl
of squat rural homes. It's a pleasing blend of small (about 100,000) with
the amenities of a larger city, servicing a huge area in the state's centre
with a constant flow of sightseers and year-round adventure seekers.

I strolled through town on the first Friday of the month, and re-
tailers had turned the streets into an open-air evening market and social gathering. Free food and booze flowed, live acoustic music filled
every space and locals and tourists browsed and visited, one of the
most inviting parties I'd ever attended. Farmers' markets were scattered throughout town, nearly one a day during the growing season.
Local fruit abounded, along with dairy and the usual array of baked
goods, herbs, soaps, flowers and crafts.

I noticed in the hotel amenities book loaner guitars were available
to guests. I called the concierge and he asked what I'd like to play. I
said whatever was convenient, preferably a steel string acoustic. He

described a cutaway but suggested I try their Breedlove and within minutes there was a knock on the door and a richly polished, ochre Breedlove acoustic was placed in my hands. The concierge beamed, excited to share something he loved with someone who cared.

"I hope you enjoy this. I play it every weekend," he said. "You need picks?"

"No, thanks," I replied. "I just use fingers."

"Cool," he said, nodding.

Before long, the guitar and I came up with this gentle ballad called "Breedlove":

I remember when I was a boy
Spending my time playing with toys for hours
The years in between when I was a teen
In my room I'd listen to tunes for hours (and hours)
The hours add up into days as they do
Days become years and leave us behind too soon

Boy becomes teen until he's a man
Growing older I understand first-hand
Man on the outside, a child within
Snowy whiskers surrounding a childish grin
Hours add up into days as they do
Days become years and leave us behind too soon

Hours rush by on the clock, and the hands
Sweep away the hourglass sand
Day after day
Every day is a scene that we play
Scenes that are played, they're memories made
Day after day (day after day)

Now I know when I finally grew
That's the day when I met you, my love
The hours, the days and the years that we shared

Memories made and nothing compares, my love
The hours, the days and the years that we shared
Memories made; now nothing compares, my love

Back on the coast we stayed at a cottage in Manzanita. I rode a chest-
nut mare on the beach near Gearhart, splashing along in zigzags as the
horse tiptoed around frothy surf. Had my hair been longer, thicker,
and my pecs better defined, I believe it could've made a fine cover for
a romance novel (he said, huskily).

That evening we grilled salmon on a wood fire and made crab melts
with herbed Boursin on a garlic baguette – one of the finest things
we'd eaten. As our trip wound down, we decided we simply hadn't had
enough and went to a downtown Portland hotel built atop a Macy's
store. Tired of recycled clothes and in-sink laundry, we went downstairs to the department store, bought new socks, tees and underwear,
and stayed for two more days.

Written on a pad of branded hotel stationery, cardboard
backed, a makeshift journal in an uninspiring room:
*From the drudgery of a city hotel on a wide, ugly highway,
the sea felt like liberty – palpable and freeing.*

A hazy bright morning melded surf and smog, an indistinguishable
chalky smear. From the California shoreline a surging tide roared
like a stadium crowd. The salt air was cool – fresh and bracing. Gulls
soared, cormorants dove and pelicans flew in sine–cosine curves just
offshore. In the words of Kerouac, "Behind lay the whole of America
and everything I had known about life, and life on the road."

I lugged an awkward sea kayak over a beach of packed, wet sand to
the water, mounted my orange plastic steed and paddled hard toward
the breakers, bursting through roiling foam. The water calmed and I

made my way south beside crumbling sandstone. Seabirds nested on steep, brittle banks, calling and staining gold cliffs with streaky white guano.

Paddling along the base of the towering rock, I found an opening – a deep, narrow cleft. The swell surged in and out, washing over hidden rocks. I paddled until the cliff curved to my left into a small bay and I steered the boat that way. Vibrant orange garibaldi fish darted through waving kelp. The wall of stone kept curling left and I saw another break in the rock – the back side of the cleft facing the sea. It was a cave – an eroded pass-through. I spun the kayak around and with the next surge of water paddled at the dark opening. I drew my paddle in to slip through the crack in the rock. A receding wave finished the job, pulling me into the cave – a black, yawning void.

Inside was a kind of cathedral – a high, arching nave – dark, dripping stone that echoed with the waves. Eerily calm, the space felt like a shrine to some kraken. The stone was wet and ebony, the water emerald green. Looking down, I saw nothing, the depth indeterminate. As I bobbed, a shaft of daylight pierced the space. With each surge of surf, the kayak was lifted and dropped, methodical and lulling. The boat rose and fell as the lap of waves echoed, acoustically perfect. I could have stayed there a very long time. Maybe I did. But a prickling at the nape of my neck told me to leave, and I paddled to the light, letting an ebbing wave draw me through the gap to open water.

The sudden brightness was overwhelming. I squinted and paddled back the way I'd come, but a small island – a sandy-coloured, spherical mound – had materialized in my path. As I drew near, a cow-sized head broke the surface, exhaling a barking belch. It was a sea lion, which I gave a wide berth but slowed to watch it fish. It drifted with the current like a big buoyant hippo, peering into the depths.

I made my way back a good distance offshore until I was roughly in line with my launch point, then turned the boat landward to approach the back of the breakers where they swelled and curled into froth. I drifted for a while, enjoying the sounds, seabirds and smell of briny air. Then I was aware of something gliding beneath me – long, dark shapes. And realized it was dozens and dozens of sharks, flat-backed, muscled torpedoes the length of my boat, swimming in twos, threes and fours. How had I not seen them before? I recognized them as leopard sharks, supposedly uninterested in the taste of kayaker, but still...

I steeled my nerve and paddled toward land, timing it with the break. Water rose behind me, curling up and rolling under my boat. I paddled furiously and caught the wave, riding it toward shore like a proficient Polynesian. A smug smile spread across my face as I steered in, high on the cresting breaker. And then with a sickening feeling the boat began to turn – the irreversible pivot of a wide, awkward raft, and I knew I'd lost it. I struggled, to no avail. The big wave broke, flipping my boat and sending me flying. All I saw were the big dark shapes of the sharks as I tumbled into them. Somehow I grabbed my hat and sunglasses while the kayak bounced off my head with the *bwoong* sound of a musical saw. Having lost all composure, I leapt from the surf and miraculously rocketed to shore without actually touching the water, speed-walking along the surface. I can only imagine what anyone watching may have thought. Perhaps it renewed a few people's faith.

From a small blue notebook, the size and feel of a passport:

Van Morrison's "Into the Mystic" played in my mind,
the resonating call of foghorns and coming home.

San Francisco lay before us – a living postcard – the towering Transamerica Pyramid, Alcatraz squatting in the harbour and the distant red shimmer of Golden Gate Bridge. As we set sail, fog rolled into the bay, obscuring the bridge span. I stood on deck as we glided toward a thickening wall of white. Sun was setting somewhere beyond the fog and light was all I saw – a glowing drape spanning the harbour. The bridge reappeared, taking shape as a negative – black sweeping lines against white, focusing as we slid beneath. A fiery glow seeped into girders, developing like a Polaroid.

We slipped through the foggy curtain, entering some secret space – a fortune teller's sanctum. An egg yolk sun eased into the water, gilding the ocean in a shimmering band. The ship's horn sounded a vibrating baritone as we passed a signal buoy rocking with the swell, its bell a lonely *clang-clang...clang-clang...clang-clang...*as we sailed home.

Once more at home on the sofa, watching Michael Palin on BBC – travel stuff – one of those inspired examples of repurposing: reducing, reusing, recycling. What I call Al Gore programming. Or Greta Thunberg programming. I give you a choice, so that: a) you can choose based on your age; and b) because one of the two is bound to be out of favour at some point. Regardless, using old stuff is good. Good for the planet, which I love (says the guy shopping for airfares). Plus it's great for production costs, utilizing old footage to make a fresh series with very little outlay. Something else I enjoyed was the timbre of Palin's familiar, almost familial voice – a mentor and *in-absentia* travel companion. Which prompted me to lower my own microscope, re-examining journeys and documentation of those experiences.

In the BBC program I was watching, Ed Byrne stated something about Palin's travels, which can be said for *every* travel and adventure program. "It's like watching James Bond. You *know* he's going to be all right, but you still think, 'How's he going to get out of *this* one?'"

This made me smile, as an attendee at a virtual presentation I'd given had been marvelling at my first *Gone Viking* excursion, in fact many excursions over a number of years. It was remarkable, she said, my derring-do, the risk and inherent danger. When I interrupted to explain, yes, there were a few perilous moments – a couple of times at sea and once or twice on a remote trail or seaside cliff when I may have been somewhat endangered – but the fact remained that, like *all* travellers, the amount of risk is always manageable and assuredly mitigated to some extent. I'm not talking about idiots *pursuing* trouble, eager to roll the dice for a crack at a Pulitzer. That handful of morons aside, the rest of us are, more or less, like Ed Byrne's example of James Bond. As much a tourist, at times, as a traveller.

Let me share one of those examples, a proper adventure with physical demands, discomfort and predatory threat, but the risks involved were, I'm certain, no greater than those endured by any season's cast members of *Survivor*. Still on North America's Pacific coast, I'd be island hopping this time around by ferry, powerboat, a long narrow sea kayak and a winged contraption resembling a plane.

From a weatherproof journal in plasticized yellow, its pages like rain ware, the feel of writing on tent tarps and rubber:

So much fucking rain – it's no longer about being even remotely dry but rather what degree of wetness – should've packed more booze. And shared less.

Seated on a high stool, I tucked into a breakfast fry-up: eggs, hash browns, buttery toast and four rashers of blubber posing as bacon. The World Cup final played on a flat screen above the bar and I happily filled up on TV and fatty food, as I was about to leave for a week of kayaking, whale watching and bare bones living in the rainforest of West Cracroft Island, off the northeast coast of Vancouver Island.

I'd gotten my head nearly shaved for the excursion and was getting used to feeling like a billiard ball. I'd asked the barber if he could make me look like Jason Statham.

"No problem," he'd replied. "First, we take the clippers to your head on setting #1. Then we need to get you to the gym for the next three years straight."

"I see," I'd said. "Maybe just give me the Kojak look."

He'd nodded. "Now *that* we can accomplish without much effort at all."

For a number of years I'd had my hair cut by a barber named Carlito, a warm and friendly Filipino who learned his trade on the American naval base outside Manila. I imagined him buzz cutting his way through GIs like Edward Scissorhands working a hedgerow.

There was a hairstyle menu board on Carlito's wall, offering three options: "Regular," "Military" or "High-and-Tight."

"Hmm," I'd said on my first visit. "What's 'High-and-Tight'?"

"Same as 'Military,'" Carlito replied.

"I see. Well, then, I'll go for the 'Regular.'"

"Good choice," he said, and our relationship began.

I got my first straight razor shave from Carlito. I'd made some money and getting a shave felt like an indulgence. In my mind, I was a gritty Clint Eastwood after a long, hard ride across dusty Italian plains, set to an Ennio Morricone score. I'd uncork a bottle of whiskey with my teeth to slake my thirst before pushing through batwing doors into a saloon, looking for a card game. A player piano would tinkle from a corner. I'd tip my hat to the ladies (and German engineers) leaning over the upstairs railing, and if I had enough money after cards, treat myself to that straight razor shave, the ultimate exercise in trust.

Carlito invited Deb and me to his home to celebrate his birthday, part of a small family group. His tradition was that he did all the food preparation for his party. He stayed up 48 hours straight, sipping scotch and making food, and explained he did this every year. The only sign of fatigue was his speech slowed marginally, but other than that he was the same happy, generous Carlito. We had to shuffle around the perimeter of his apartment as tables of food took up all the space. There was a mountain of crab steamed in curry sauce with fried fish, rice and vegetables, exceptional flavours, with a frosted slab cake to finish.

It reminded me of another culinary experience new to me at the time. I had a meeting with a Fijian–Canadian at his home, and sat down to kava and fried fish. Crisp fillets were slid from hot oil directly onto a Formica table with a soft, sizzling splat. We broke off chunks with our fingers and it was ambrosia. But I hesitated over the narcotic drink, afraid it would send me plummeting down a rabbit hole of spinning images from which there would be no return – an absinthe-like delirium. My mind raced to a dark future where I'd wake in an askew kimono, face down on soiled satin pillows in some opium den in Goa, lolling amidst other sweaty hedonists cutting Moroccan hash. The place would be dimly lit in flickering red and smell of the comings and goings of Gomorrah, without so much of the goings. However, I didn't want to seem rude and slurped up my little bowlful like miso. The kava looked like the brown standing water in the squeegee tub at a gas station and tasted (I suspect) much the same. Fortunately, it didn't leave me slave to the black poppy like Conan Doyle's Holmes but *did* give a pleasant buzz, not unlike well-made rum punch.

En route to my kayak and camping adventure, rather than fried fish I'd be looking for whales, and instead of kava I'd packed a jiggly bag of red wine in my pack, having pulled the plastic bladder from its corrugated box. I crossed the tarmac of the peripheral airport to a tiny Shorts twin prop, which looked like an early Wright brothers plane – one of the unsuccessful ones. It appeared to be a composite of canvas, aluminum foil and duct tape. Doubling over to fit through the door, I squeezed into my small seat, 1A, filling the entire row. From there I watched a young guy load a couple pieces of luggage into the hold and do a walk around the plane, looking at who knows what. Seated where I was, the guy's face was eye level through my window, which appeared remarkably transparent; the "glass" wasn't foggy or scratched like on the big planes.

As I stared at him, he looked in and said in a perfectly clear voice, "How's it going?" and closed my window from the outside.

I jumped, slamming my head into the low ceiling. *Well that would explain the transparent glass*, I thought, rubbing my head.

He had to slam the window a couple of times before it closed, then twisted a small clasp a quarter turn – the kind of lock you'd use to cage a hamster or secure a porta-potty door or, I suppose, seal up a canister of doomed air travellers.

A child entered the plane and offered me a juice box, which felt like a gendarme offering me a cigarette before being blindfolded. I said thanks but no to the girl, as I didn't want to take something I assumed was from her lunchbox. She smiled, put on a headset, climbed into the pilot's seat and taxied us down the runway. The roar of the twin props drowned out my wheezing intake of breath and the grumbling purr of my bowels releasing. I assumed the airline was family run, indifferent to minimum-age labour laws, and it was likely her young brother who loaded the bags and sealed me in to my fate.

It reminded me of a family-run sushi place near our home. The owners' 8-year-old daughter would bring bits of food to the table – much of it being items we'd ordered, along with the occasional single napkin, which she'd set down with pride like a pet bringing you a dead bird.

The flight, although bumpy, was actually enjoyable. We travelled low over small islands – verdant lumps peeking through a navy blue sea. Scallops of sargasso cut the water like doilies, with whitecaps frothed in pearly crescents. We flew through banks of fog and over a bald eagle in flight, looking down at it surreal. Reminding me of an inscription we saw in our previous *Gone Viking* travels: "When you see an eagle, you *know* this is a special place."

The pilot's sister (I presumed) appeared from the co-pilot seat mid-route and reoffered me the juice box with a Dad's chocolate chip cookie, which I accepted, as it's very close to what I'd request for my last meal. I straw-speared the little box and felt the same age as the children flying the plane.

It took me back to my first international flight, as a 10-year-old, going to Honolulu with Mom and Dad on Western Airlines. Eating a meal with small cutlery and tiny salt and pepper made me feel like

a four-foot-ten giant, the coach seat roomy for my fawn-like frame.
The whole thing felt wonderfully posh and stoked my burgeoning
wanderlust.

As we landed in Campbell River, two husky falcons were standing at the edge of the airstrip, looking like security. I picked up my
pack from a pile on the ground and strolled into a lonely little building that closed the moment I passed through. While I waited for a
shuttle into town, an angry man named Reed with a grey buzz cut,
or possibly a "High-and-Tight," snapped at me. He was ex-army and
worked in health care now, he explained, which seemed to infuriate
him for reasons unknown.

"Run it like military," he declared. Everything came out of his
mouth in clipped, loud barks – a cadence – and I fought the urge
to march on the spot. He complained about everything for a while.
"Trouble with men now," he paused, squinting, "*like you*" hanging un-
said, "they expect to be taken care of."

"You make that sound like a *bad* thing," I said, instantly wishing I
hadn't. Surviving the flight had given me a foolhardy sense of invinci-
bility. I hadn't stopped to think before speaking and now realized I
was a rodeo clown tormenting an angry bull, with no barrel to hide in.
Reed's dark eyes widened, he straightened up and was clearly going to
hit me, to start. The only hesitation seemed to be his deciding how best
to immobilize me. I was aware of my camera in my hand – too small to
be used to defend myself, so I improvised and flashed a photo of him.

It threw him off, and he stood, blinking like a bear trying to remember why it was about to charge. Then, with remarkable timing,
the airport shuttle screeched up with a skid, releasing air brakes with
the same *phhewwww* sound I felt at that moment.

I was spending the night in a hotel, as the kayak excursion would
start early the next morning. I checked in and threw my pack on a bed
that sagged alarmingly, thought better of it, and dropped the pack on
the floor, which also sagged alarmingly. I bolted before anything col-
lapsed and got a dinner recommendation from reception.

I walked about a mile along the water, past a marina packed with working boats and the occasional pleasure craft. A sleek, blubbery harbour seal watched me pass and dipped, barely disturbing the water's surface. Sunset and clouds in the east glowed soft pink, hanging like cotton candy over Quadra Island. The restaurant was ideal and close to what I'd envisioned – 20-year-old thinly upholstered chairs, 30-year-old pastel walls, a stern and efficient 50-year-old server and 70-year-old patrons who assuredly wouldn't tip enough.

I ate steak, prawns and Caesar salad, washed it down with beer and wine (house, if you please) and then slightly weaved to a Dairy Queen where I ate something large and sweet I wouldn't remember. Early the next day, I was waiting at a central parking lot – our prescribed meeting place.

According to the excursion brochure I was to be "picked up by Coach" and I admit I was rather excited for the opportunity to meet Craig T. Nelson as I'd always enjoyed his work. (Not ALL my pop culture references will be 20 to 30 years old, just many of them.) But, no, instead of the actor it was a filthy old van that careened into the lot. I'm sure a hubcap would've rolled away in the turn, if it *had* any hubcaps. It lurched to a stop beside me. There was a small Kiwi behind the wheel. Not a fuzzy fruit or flightless bird but a young woman named Robyn who smiled and said hello. Her lovely New Zealand twang made me feel I'd travelled much farther. Sweet and likeable, she would be guide, cook, fixer and friend for the excursion. Although she too was a child, she still had a couple of years on the flight crew that got me here.

There would be three of us together for the week: Robyn, me, and Herta, a woman from Germany. Herta crawled from the back of the van and appeared to have just woken. She resembled a masculine Arnold Schwarzenegger.

I rode shotgun while Robyn drove and Herta fell asleep again on a bench seat in the back. Robyn did her best to make the experience all encompassing and played a CD of gurgling whale songs. Whether it

was the previous night's binge, winding road and lack of shocks or the
recording that sounded like churning stomachs, I turned the greenish hue that tends to precede a hearty throw-up. Robyn took it to be a
critique of the music, which it may have been in part, and asked if we
should listen to something else.

"God, yes!" I managed to say through clenched teeth.

She laughed and jammed in the only other CD in the vehicle, Jack
Johnson's *In Between Dreams*. Then we swapped stories of favourite
kayaking experiences. Robyn loved her adventures on the BC coast,
while I had great memories of drifting in a tandem boat with Deb
over sea turtles in south Maui. Following this, I'd find myself paddling with stingrays in New Zealand's Awaroa River, then up the
Waitangi to horseshoe-shaped Haruru Falls, white water spinning my
boat around, shooting me downriver at a dizzying speed into a tributary of mangroves, where I lay back in the boat to ease through a low,
dense canopy of green-brown branches that reached and clutched like
greedy, sinewy arms.

I recounted kayaking with my friend Doug around Nanaimo's
Hudson Rocks, which of course we called "Rock Hudsons," picking
our way through seals like an obstacle course before leaping into the
shallows and snatching up red rock crabs by hand before they had a
chance to sever our fingers.

As we bounced into Telegraph Cove, Herta woke as her head
double-knocked against the inside of the panel door with a rhythmic
thud-thud. Robyn parked and we hauled our gear from the van to a
water taxi – a small aluminum Boston Whaler skippered by Relic
from *The Beachcombers*. (Okay, the occasional 40-year-old reference,
but that's it!)

When the compact boat was loaded with gear, Relic chugged us
away from the pier into Johnstone Strait. Dall's porpoises rolled and
white-sided dolphins leapt in the distance as we bumped southeast
through the narrows. It turned out Relic was calling himself Denny,
and became a bit of a naturalist en route.

"See that bull kelp there?" he pointed with his chin at lengths of snake-like weeds undulating on the water's rough surface.

"Mmm," I said, my teeth clacking as the boat pounded over the chop.

"Each bulb end has enough CO_2 to kill a cat," he said, punctuating it with a nod.

I liked the fact that the amount of toxin required to kill a cat was a unit of measure the way football fields are for Americans.

After a long ride we burbled into a shallow cove, rising and falling in rough water. Denny said because of rocks and the tide this was as close to shore as we could get. I suspect he'd already been paid and simply couldn't be bothered to beach his boat. So the three of us leapt into cold, waist-deep sea water and carried gear to shore over our heads, army-style, while Denny/Relic sped away, leaving us hoping he'd remember to return in a week.

Thick bull kelp heaved on the surf like a welcome mat of green-brown serpents. Gulls called and there were flashes of silver as salmon jumped. The shore rose into steep wooded mountains, thick with Douglas fir, hemlock, spruce and cedar. Towering basalt cliffs broke through the trees. One angled cliff hung over the water in blocks like the underside of stairs. Massive timbers had been tossed on the beach, stacked like pick-up sticks, leaving us feeling Lilliputian. There was a bald eagle on shore, struggling with a fat salmon while from a tall pine its mate chirped encouragement, or possibly nagged. Unable to lift the big fish, the beachside eagle eventually gave up, leaving it for some other, larger predator.

We dripped our way into the woods where a makeshift camp was set up: lopsided little tents on slatted platforms, a communal tent with a small, coughing, propane heater and a listing tarp, sagging with rainwater. Deep, fresh mountain lion prints cut through the middle of it all.

"Yee-ah," Robyn said, holding her hand above her waist to indicate the animal's size. "But it hasn't been here for a couple of days," she said, as though that made everything better.

I suspected that was simply enough time for it to regain its appetite. I suddenly felt my Leatherman multitool (with the extra-small knife option) was sadly insufficient. I wished I were back in the store, where I'd cut myself so badly while browsing I needed a fist-sized lump of Kleenex from the clerk to staunch the flow. Then the knife seemed plenty lethal enough. Now I wasn't so sure. I took out the sad little blade, which now struck me as a suitable size to serve as a post-meal carnivore toothpick, possibly to aid a cougar in removing nagging threads of sleeping bag from the bicuspid fangs.

We unloaded gear and Herta spoke for what seemed like the first time, her accent pure Schwarzenegger. I longed to hear her say things like "I'll be back" or "*Hasta la vista*, baby," but instead she said, "The cow-girs scare me."

My mind had drifted. "You're afraid of the Dallas cheerleaders?" I asked, confused.

"Oh, no. Da lyintz," she said.

"Ah," I nodded. "The *Lions* cheerleaders scare you. That I understand."

The "Who's on First?" conversation continued for a while. It turned out she hadn't been talking about football at all, as she thought it was soccer, and was referring to the cougar prowling nearby. I rather hoped the big cat would return and consume either one of us (I genuinely didn't care which) just to end our confusing dialogue.

Having dropped our gear, we dragged kayaks over shoreline shingle into the water for an exploratory paddle. I was looking back at shore, the boat knocking awkwardly against my leg when a canon-like boom exploded behind me. I spun to see the residual splash of a breaching orca 50 metres away. Loud *pffooo-pffooos* followed and three big male transients porpoised through our little inlet, two-metre-high dorsal fins spiking from the water. We stood silent and amazed while they curled north, moving slowly up the strait.

That night, between the dark cloud and dense trees, the blackness felt almost solid. It was perversely wet. Rain fell. And fell. The sound of living things scurrying under my tent rustled through the night, leaving me to wonder what they might be. I wrote in a wavering circle from a penlight clenched in my teeth. I had to retrace handwriting, as pencil lead no longer adhered to the wet, my notebook bloated with water.

My sleeping bag slowly changed from grey to charcoal – the colour of saturation – and the underlying sleeping pad became a loaded sponge, squishing with each twist of my body. I lay on my stomach to raise my head above standing water on the floor of the tent. It was pitched on a wooden platform like an elevated raft, leaving me to wonder when the whole thing would simply rise and float me off the island, down the strait and into the Pacific, like a much less courageous Thor Heyerdahl. Once more I found myself in the footsteps of modern-day Vikings.

Water dumped onto the roof of my nylon home with loud *slooshes* like someone rinsing a car with a bucket as branches gave way, incapable of supporting any more water. I rationed a few jalapeno spiced peanuts, Slim Jims and a couple of mouthfuls of red wine, which I drank from the plastic bag – temporary escape. I allowed myself one song a night from an MP3 player, watching the battery slowly die. Invariably, I'd listen to Colin Hay's "Waiting for My Real Life to Begin" and chuckle at the irony. And despite all the reasons why I shouldn't have, I enjoyed myself. I'd signed up for it, sort of. I was experiencing some remarkable things and would get a story out of it, which isn't bad at all. I tucked in earbuds, swirled the last of the wine in my mouth and let Colin's husky whisper lull me to sleep.

From the weatherproof journal, written in an ever-shortening nub of grease pencil:

We pushed through soggy ferns and climbed over rotting stumps and gnarled roots like arthritic giants' knuckles.

For a change of pace, we spent a day off the water and hiked steep trails through dense evergreens – towering, ancient rainforest. After a couple of hours, we broke through to an open ledge, where a rustic little hut clung to a mossy precipice, hundreds of feet above the strait. It was an orca watch post seemingly in the middle of nowhere, and we hoped to find someone new to talk to. A wooden door opened with a creak and four smiling, alarmingly good-looking women greeted us. I'd unwittingly stumbled into a beer ad and my mind leapt uncontrolled to blurred images and the pornographic sound of a slap bass.

They invited us in, offering us fat-free hot chocolate and Vegemite on crackers, which seemed to be the extent of their food supply. They were post-grad university students, spending their summer tracking resident pods of orcas. Every hour or so they would creep to the edge of the cliff, look up and down the strait and enter something into a journal. This, they explained, would enable them to complete their studies. *And*, I thought, *guarantee them a unique but physically uncomfortable summer, a greater admiration for Dr. David Suzuki and a near certainty of unemployment in their chosen field.*

In between journal entries, they removed pieces of clothing to show me tattoos and explain their significance in Haida culture. I nodded and pretended to listen, fighting to keep my expression neutral and remember it all as vividly as possible.

When it was time for another observation of the strait, we eased out to the slippery precipice, using bums and hands, resembling worm-ridden dogs scratching their asses. At the edge, we leaned out and looked north. Nothing. Then we looked south. Nothing. We slid back from the cliff and the workers completed their journal entries: "2 p.m. North. Nothing. South. Nothing." These notes were meticulously written into a tattered book that was then stacked into one of several piles of identical journals, where I was certain they'd remain unread forever.

Back at camp it was my turn to get the poking stick and prod the underside of the rain-filled tarp strung between trees. Water bucketed off, adding to the mud pit that was our camp. The tarp was intended to serve as a canopy but simply redistributed water into a dozen icy shower spouts.

Herta was taking off wet clothes in the heated communal tent, the one intended for drying things. I knew this because from across camp I heard the *creak-stretch-thwap* of someone removing soaked and fitted spandex. The tent, however, never actually dried anything. A rusty little propane heater simply warmed the dank interior. The cloyingly humid space became a wet sauna, like a shaman's sweat tent. But instead of providing a portal to an alternate, heavenly dimension, our tent seemed to open a plummeting shaft to the lower planes of Hades – the *really* brimstoney ones.

I hadn't yet given up on trying to partially dry or at least warm up a couple of pieces of clothing. Herta had changed and left the communal tent, so I went over to do the same. The addition of her foul (I cannot emphasize the magnitude of this), *foul* clothing and undergarments changed the otherwise unpleasantness of the tent into a clammy steam room of such hellish olfactory offence as to render it certifiably toxic – I mean, skull and crossbones, government agents in white haz-mat suits squawking through mic'd gas masks – apocalyptic stink.

Something, I realized, had changed in Herta over the course of our week in the wilderness. Whether it was the stimulation of fresh mountain and ocean air, a waxing moon or she was simply randy, I couldn't say. Perhaps, if I was more of an outdoorsman, in tune with animal instincts, I could've identified it in the overwhelming scent of her clothing. All I knew was that I was the only bipedal male organism around and it had me feeling particularly vulnerable. I took to sleeping with my pocket knife close to hand, fearing not only the *possible* aggression of the local mountain lion but the near *certain* aggression of the Bavarian cougar currently in camp. "No" didn't seem to mean "no" in German. Although peeing around my tent may've succeeded at keeping the resident mountain lion away, I suspect it had quite the opposite effect on the foreign cougar. One night I swore I faintly heard deep nasal inhalation, followed by a mutter that sounded something like, "*Jah, das ees goot mannenspritzen!*"

The moon was near full, the tide extreme. Each night we had to tie our kayaks progressively higher on shore, eventually lashing them amongst trees. The beach was made up of sharp rocks the size of five-pin bowling balls covered in wet, treacherously slick kelp. We fell frequently, and in thin rubber water boots every step hurt. Lugging my boat out one day, limping, I disturbed about a hundred hermit crabs. They skittered away in a tight cluster and I wanted to point out the irony of a bustling community of hermit crabs, but the pain in my feet had me breathless and I only managed a halting exhalation of breath that sounded somewhat like "Fu-uuuuck."

Late one day we were preparing food, huddled around our little propane stove. Dinner was slightly mouldy, foraged berries, bloated grey pasta and cedar bough tea. We were set back from the water, deep amidst hemlock and cedar.

Herta stopped what she was doing, straightened up and, in a voice that can only be described as Schwarzenegger doing his best rendition of the little girl from *Poltergeist*, stated flatly, "They're here." ("Dey hee-ah.")

We trotted through the trees down to the rocky shoreline and, sure enough, there they were – resident orcas rolling through the strait, exhaling plumes of watery breath against a backdrop of tree-blanketed mountainside. I shuddered at her uncanny ability – a cetacean-fixated Radar O'Reilly. (Which maximizes permissible references to *M*A*S*H*.)

Carrying plates of food to the shore, we ate off our laps. Although the same massive log was our bench three nights in a row, each day, high tide tossed it around the wide beach like a twig. Rain eased and a smudge of brightness oozed down the distant sky – sun setting behind banks of dark cloud. Rainwater dripped from leafy ferns and towering evergreens. We were sitting in a living Emily Carr canvas, craning to see it all around us – Hogwarts ghosts in an evergreen frame. Day waned and we listened to orcas in the distance, their *pffooo-pf- fooos* fading with the light until all was black; just the wash of waves, the sighing of forest and diminishing breath of the whales.

It was well into our week-long excursion and Robyn had aged. The emergency radio-phone battery died on day three. There was no cellular service. A slight tension hung in the air, along with determined optimism. Our little group's bond strengthened. The next night, watching another murky sunset, I asked my new friends what they felt was the meaning of life.

Herta lit a slim, menthol cigarette, which thinned the evening mosquitoes. "It is hard for me in English," she said. "But I try." She took a long drag and exhaled. "I know I will be 80 one day and maybe not have met all of my goals," she said. "But I make many goals and work towards them. I do not want to be like those people who are rich – two cars and a house, but just work, work, work. But I also do not want to wind up living with people under a bridge and having to share one set of teeth."

She smiled, making me acutely aware of her teeth. Then she frowned for a moment and added, "If you write of me in your book, say my name is Barbara. I like that name."

I smiled, which she took as consent.

There was a long silence before Robyn spoke up. "I hope I'd make a difference," she said, thinking about it. "Maybe something for the environment. To learn. To always learn, and then to teach and share that." She paused and I wondered if she was done. But then she said, "I believe in reincarnation," and seemed to age again, before adding, "But you always want to do good and make a difference for people... hard task, I reckon." ("Had tisk, I rickun.")

On our last day at camp, assuming Denny/Relic could be bothered to retrieve us, we lugged in extra water and loaded the camp's little shower bucket. It was a raised plastic tub with a hand pump, small hose and nozzle that released intermittent, dripping squirts. It felt like being spat upon, with cold spit, and surprisingly was one of the most luxurious experiences I could recall.

When I started the excursion, my pack weighed 20 kilos. A third of that was liquid – water and wine, which got consumed. At the end of the week, my pack still weighed 20 kilos. I double-checked. I could hardly believe it. My gear was so utterly saturated with water it was 50 per cent heavier. I, however, was a bit lighter and resembled a pale, wrinkly prune. I was forced to throw away my boots. They were beyond salvage, literally falling apart from constant use while remaining soaked, not to mention smelling like unpasteurized Camembert. Back on Vancouver Island I linked up with Deb and she drove me to an outdoor supply store, where I walked in, barefoot, to buy socks and boots. ("No, thanks, I won't need the box.")

From the small notebook in blue that resembled a passport:

It was years before I had a suitable lyrical reference. Which finally came from Foo Fighters and Dave Grohl's "Times Like These," following a submerged and endless, oxygen-starved minute, when I felt I'd learned to live again.

Let's take a leap across water and time: a strait, a lake, an ocean and a shallow bay, most of these places, in fact, the same body of water. And *all* of it the same viking journey. From watery childhood memories – growing up on a lake – I spanned a vast distance, in every sense of the word, on that Western Airlines trip to Hawaii. Despite the shift from fresh water to salt, bobbing in shallows and surf was soon as much a part of my experience as Lego and *Looney Tunes*. One time, however, felt as though I'd been shot from a cannon – boyhood to something more – imparted with a skewer of wisdom I hadn't imagined, nor asked for, and for which I was quite unprepared.

I'd been aware of the big wave approaching, just had no idea *how* big it was in relation to the others – a freak with a vicious rip that towered over my head where I bobbed not far from shore. The forward surge and simultaneous backwash pulled me under, in opposite directions, stretching my little body like an Inquisition rack. Unprepared, my lungs were empty. Dragged down, I wanted to gasp, to gulp, but there was nothing but watery blue – swirling sand below and daylight above, filtered through several feet of frothy wash I couldn't rise above. I fought, only to be pulled harder, held beneath the surface to suffocate in the warm crush of the Pacific.

And as I began to drown I remember thinking, *Well this is gonna wreck the vacation. And I'm just a kid; I haven't even kissed a girl I'm not related to!* Then a sensation of calm washed over me, powerful and indistinguishable from the waves. I resigned myself to my fate and relaxed. Oddly enough, it felt good. Reassuring. Like home. I sank and watched the smothering wave crash over, roiling, pushing and pulling. A second monstrous surge rolled through, moving the sky and changing the light. And, a lifetime later, the waves receded and the water slackened.

I'd watched it all from the sandy ocean floor, content, the pressure in my lungs having eased. When the big waves had gone, it dawned on me my family wouldn't have to be upset after all and I swam to the surface, breathing air with a mix of relief and surprising twinge of disappointment. The whole encounter lasted less than a minute, but I believe in that span I lived the better part of a life. Possibly more.

Years later, typed from memory with a thumb
into Notes on an outdated iPhone:

*Five hundred tourists, mostly heavy, mostly tipsy,
sat at long wooden benches and tables.*

Five hundred tired, hungry, sunburned people in the fading light of a Hawaiian sunset, on a field of trampled grass around a raised, lit stage. Sounds at each table were much the same; the *mmms* and savouring of smoky sweet, imu-roasted pork, the slurping of glassine rice noodles and the predictable "yuck" noises associated with untouched mauve poi. Drums thumped from speakers in leafy palms and dancers took the stage – muscular men grunting and twirling fire and lithe women with coconut breasts in grass skirts, swaying hips, telling stories with a gentle flow of arms, hands and fingers.

A young girl came to the stage, the smallest of the luau's entertainers, cute and precocious. The lights played out to the crowd, searching and agonizing. And a 10-year-old boy was spotted, an easy mark in a loud floral shirt, puka shells and a red-faced blend of too much sun and dawning mortification. Hoots and laughter from the crowd, applause from those who'd finished eating, and the girl came out to the boy and plucked him from the safety of the table and mock horror of the poi onto the stage, to the *actual* horror of performing live, unrehearsed hula to a deafening crowd of strangers hidden through a blind of spot lights.

The boy was me. The memory mine. The horror real. We danced the hukilau, naturally. Over time the memory morphed into something manageable, even pleasant, one of those nasty life experiences we grow from (theoretically). The taste of the pork remained a sweet memory, the poi, not so much. The dancing girl grew up with me in my mind, aging beautifully. And I can still dance the hukilau, more or less, with sufficient encouragement. Or rum punch and kava.

Jotted on an aerial photo of Ho'okipa Beach
in the pages of *Maui Revealed*:

*It was dark when I rolled out of bed, grabbed a swimsuit,
cap and towel, and shuffled out to the car.*

This being years later. I drove for a while on asphalt, then bumped along on dirt, sand and crushed lava. Bits of sun-bleached coral were mixed with the gravel, giving the narrow road a salt-and-pepper look. Tall, slender coconut palms gradually gave way to the occasional koa and ironwood and then all vegetation stopped. I was on the southeast tip of Maui, making my way to La Perouse Bay, named after the explorer who first mapped the area under the French flag. Old brown lava curved down the side of a dormant volcano like a wide, dead river into the ʻĀhihi-Kīnaʻu reserve, haunting but peaceful in predawn light – a tropical moonscape.

Leaving the car at the side of the road, I marched a few hundred metres to the water, crunching over chunky lava and coral. A little group was assembling, yawning, rubbing on sunscreen and hauling big Scupper sea kayaks into the water. Our guide was a *Survivorman* Les Stroud look-alike. His wife, prepping gear on shore, resembled someone from the cover of a Joe Weider magazine. He fussed with PFDs while she did the heavy lifting. I chose a boat, tossed in flip-flops and jumped in.

We were starting later than scheduled and Les kept looking at his watch while studying the water, his brow furrowed. He made some noises I couldn't decipher, then shook his head and told us to go, go, go! An early wind was picking up, along with the swells, and we had to paddle like mad between breakers to clear the wide, black reef. A soft mauve moon hung in the sky, the island peaceful, but on the water, as we cleared the headland, swells grew two metres, breaking frothy and threatening. Strong offshore wind strafed the whitecaps, spraying sea foam in stinging diagonals. Paddling with the current, we muscled our boats up the swells, providing fleeting, sweeping views, before surf-planing into blue-green troughs like a living, watery rollercoaster.

Fighting our way around a black lava point, we entered the Fishbowl – a secluded, sheltered cove. Nearly impossible to find from land in the vast expanse of sharp, undulating lava, the little bay offers spectacular snorkelling, as though you've slid into a well-stocked, exotic fish tank.

Leaving kayaks on shore, we swam with sea turtles and I identified tangs, a boxfish and humuhumunukunukuapua'a, or is it humuhu-munukunukuapua'as? Either way, I saw some – the Hawaiian state fish. They seem to swim with a relaxed, island vibe, despite looking like they've just eaten a bag of sour candies, faces pinched and tight lips puckered.

After a long swim through the bay, I scrambled to shore on steep, loose sand, surprisingly tough to climb. From there I hiked to the headland, munched a granola bar and watched the Pacific heave past. A humpback rolled and dove directly offshore, offering a stunning view of its massive flukes, so close it startled me and left me laughing, shaking my head in wonder.

From a tiny pad printed with seashell designs:

You don't need to know the Bing Crosby song to realize around here "Mele Kalikimaka" is indeed the thing to say.

Let me share a few more Hawaiian vignettes (since we're here), the first of which is meeting the remarkable Tutu. I had a Soprano tucked under my arm. Not a member of Tony's mafia family but a mahogany ukulele. I'd made my way to an open-air square at Kings' Shops on the Big Island, which also served as an informal community centre. Two dozen folding chairs were set in a semi-circle under the shade of coconut palms. I settled in and soon every seat was full, with a few more people standing around the perimeter, all of us holding ukuleles.

Tutu, or Auntie, arrived like a colourful wave – flowing muumuu, long grey hair and fragrant floral lei, with an eight-string tenor made of koa, with rich grain inlays the colour of Kona coffee. Red, yellow and short-stemmed pink flowers were tucked between her tuners, where Keith or Ronnie would wedge a smouldering ciggie.

The group fell silent and smiled. Auntie had an aura. She took us in, holding gazes and casting a peaceful, happy spell without a word. She showed us some chords and together we played Hawaiian classics: "Aloha Oe," "Pearly Shells," "Tiny Bubbles" and others – a happy, unrefined ukulele orchestra. A surprising number were professional players, keen to jam with Tutu and bask in her energy. The rest of us fumbled along and had a great deal of fun. Her voice was angelic and soon we all just sat and listened as she channelled her gift, her music and heritage. Auntie's digits danced across the fret board and, closing my eyes, I could barely believe she had only two hands and ten fingers.

She lightened things up with a traditional tune the locals knew and sang along for the chorus: "Daddy work da' taro field / Mama make da' poi / Sister date a haole boy / ?????" I couldn't make out the last line, but it was delivered with rolling eyes and clucking tongues, followed by peals of laughter; enough to get the gist. When things wound up, Auntie hugged us all in turn, taking extra time with a woman with Down syndrome, rocking her in a nourishing embrace. Then, without being asked, Auntie rummaged through her bag and passed me a piece of sheet music – a Hawaiian Christmas song – a souvenir I treasure. Maybe there was questioning in my face, curiosity, or maybe she simply decided to share, because she began to tell me a bit of her story.

"I had a good job and worked there many years, until I was in my 60s, and then I retired," Auntie said. "Now I just enjoy my music, sharing and playing with my friends, old and new." She punctuated it with her infectious, otherworldly smile.

"And how long ago did you retire?" I asked.

"Oh! That was over 20 years ago now," she said, giggling like a child, then drifted away, as though she were part of a dream.

The next recollections in this thread blend viking explorations by car, then on foot, and conclude with a swim in fresh water next to the sea.

Our rental car idled, adding a mechanical hum to the sound of crashing surf. The creek flowing into the ocean wasn't deep but wide, running fast over ragged rock. We were still a ways from our destination and walking the extra distance seemed unnecessary or uncourageous. I eased the vehicle into the water, voiding insurance and probably common sense. The tires gripped slippery rocks through burbling water and we inched safely to the other side, an excruciatingly long, 15-second crossing. And like a dog that hasn't bothered to shake after a swim, we carried on, the vehicle trailing water from the creek like a tributary.

A little farther on, we parked where the smooth, red mud road widened marginally. Open ocean crashed onto monstrous lava rocks, sending up plumes of frothy white foam. We climbed a short way around the headland and heard it, distinct from the pounding surf – the tumbling wash of a waterfall. Scrambling over rough rocks we saw it, dropping down a lava cliff to fill a deep, dark pool. The only other people were another couple, just leaving. Exchanging hellos they smiled warmly, knowing we were about to experience something special. We kicked off shoes and slid over wet rocks into the natural pool – cold and indescribably fresh. Cascading water created tranquil white noise, splashing down like a musical white curtain. Beyond our sanctuary the Pacific thundered, crashing spray into the sky, leaving us to paddle around the base of the falls in our peaceful little oasis.

Our next island installation jars us awake at 2:55 a.m. A moment of disorientation followed by nausea and then the realization *We've done this to ourselves; we set the alarm.* Questioning choices, I slumped on the edge of the bed, bleary-eyed. A few deep breaths and I got up, splashed water on my face, gathered a pile of warm clothing, pulled a quilt from the closet and staggered to the car to drive from the ocean up Maui's 3000-metre volcanic mountain of Haleakalā.

The roadway climbs steep, hairpin switchbacks. A brilliant full moon lit pre-twilight sky as though the island was prepped for a late-night movie shoot. There were a billion stars above us and we saw none of it, the moon the only thing visible in the sky. We parked in a small lot near the top of the volcano, the temperature near freezing. Pulling on all the clothes we had, we then wrapped the quilt around us and joined a handful of others, all wrapped in blankets, shuffling to a wide viewing platform to shiver and face east in the moonlight.

In Michael Palin's *Sahara*, well into his desert trek, he promised himself he wouldn't describe yet another sunrise but couldn't help himself upon seeing a particularly spectacular one over the Niger. I found myself thinking of this and smiling, knowing I'd be hard-pressed to not write about what we witnessed high atop Haleakalā. The air was thin; I found myself breathing with extra effort and my head swam slightly. A solid band of cloud obscured the eastern sky, creating a billowing, off-white curtain hanging down to cerulean ocean. A thin strip of light bisected the sky, a band arcing ever so slightly, and a brilliant pinprick sliced through like a laser. As we squinted, sun bloomed like a yawning gem come to life, growing before our eyes, announcing a new day.

To conclude our time here, let's take a literal island hop, back to Hawaii's Big Island, where the topaz water of Anaeho'omalu Bay (A-Bay) was warm and calm. With mask, snorkel and flippers, I swam away from shore. To my right, brackish water flowed into the bay from anchialine pools – a series of underwater lava tubes filtering fresh water into the sea. Sea turtles splashed and ate where fresh water met salt; whether it was good feeding, an agreeable current or just fun, I've no idea.

There was a gentle underwater rip, and the oddly moving current created pockets of blurry water beneath the surface, intermittently obscuring my vision and adding a sense of mystery to the dive. An eagle ray glided past, its underwater flight mesmerizing. White polka dots on its back and wings seemed to glow in underwater light.

I swam with a turtle for a while, watching it nibble brain coral, and a boxfish swam by like a brick with lips and a tail. I dodged through a shoal of fingerlings, the experience exhilarating, like something from an IMAX screen. I had the most fun swimming with the school and found myself going back for more, seeking them out and darting with the pack, banking left and right as they streamed at me, past me, and all around, filling my field of vision. It was the only time I recalled carefree fun in a school.

We circumnavigated the island by car, a full day of waterfalls, black sand beaches, banyan trees and parks. A mongoose ran across a stretch of winding road. Wild donkeys grazed improbably in moonscape lava fields, where white coral sat on black lava, the pieces laid out to spell words of happiness and love. We visited Kamehameha's high stone fortress and Pu'uhonua O Hōnaunau National Historical Park, pockets of white sand, neck-craning palms and an abundance of sea turtles in lapis water.

Another day of exploration took us upcountry, into the Big Island interior – *paniolo* (cowboy) country – where land changes at 600 metres, from humid to arid, prickly pear and green-brown fields melding high desert with tropics. We passed paddocks of livestock where egrets sat on horses' backs as though transported from Serengeti rhinos. The stiff-looking, slender birds on horseback reminded me of beaky royals in white breeches, practising dressage.

And with that we bid *aloha* (goodbye) to the Pacific, for now. An unremarkable flight ensued, back to the mainland, a bit of time passed and I was ready to go viking again. Together let's explore the right-hand side of the continent, specifically the Atlantic, the source of red sand memories recollected previously. Staying true to our viking exploration, we'll keep to the coast, our original Scandinavian starting point somewhere out there, a few hundred thousand oar strokes to the east.

ATLANTIC

From a coiled book of lined A4, an unbleached, hardcover journal that flipped back on itself, creating its own compact desk, ideal for writing on pillows or a knee:

The jet slid through greasy grey sky, saturated cloud covering the city. Took an airport taxi into town and the cabbie – smug – said they'd arranged Vancouver weather for my arrival. Prick.

Following an imagined modern-day mariner's rime, we find ourselves in Canada's Maritimes, our soundtrack performed by a duo on stage called McGinty. The bartender poured me another Alexander Keith's IPA and I got comfy as the two played "Heart of Gold." I was visiting with a striking woman named Rachel. I worked Deb into a story. She did the same about her husband and kids, and we were able to enjoy each other's company without any bullshit.

We were at the bar of the Lower Deck Pub on the Halifax waterfront. Patrons were eclectically diverse: guys off the boats in yellow oilskins, banker types in tailored suits, a fleece crowd in Peruvian knit hats and college students, all at wooden picnic tables in the middle of the room. It was a small pub serving a big community – everybody's local.

The bartenders stood behind the bar like offensive linemen – four brutes planted in a broad line, pulling nonstop pints of Budweiser, Labatt, Molson and Keith's. One look at the taps told you the type of place it was. The smell of hot oil and fried food oozed from the kitchen. I picked up snippets of conversations. Shockingly young people swapped stories of their shockingly old children. It was Friday night and everyone seemed to have sitters. The vibe was good, the laughter genuine and the music kept getting better as the bartenders slid pints to us at an alarming rate. Once more I was asked to carry on with a new friend, to find a restaurant and join others, but felt I could no longer keep up with new pints that materialized before me. So instead I bid Rachel goodnight and left with what I hoped was a minimal stagger.

An Atlantic wind hit me with an icy slap, a sobering gust. I pulled my wool beanie down, hunched shoulders and zigzagged away from Halifax Harbour down Barrington Street, where I found an inviting piano bar, changed my mind about turning in and settled in to resume the destruction of brain cells.

A Richard Branson look-alike sat behind a black baby grand, lights in the small room sparkling off his mane of grey-blond hair and remarkable teeth. He played everything in the Domino's style, with extra cheese. And I felt a bit guilty enjoying it so much and still being under the age of 90. It was the kind of place you want to enjoy with everyone you know, or no one you know. Then I realized he was playing an instrumental version of something I knew, but it was tough to identify through the flowery, Liberace ad lib. And then I had it – Ozzy Osbourne's "Crazy Train." Fantastic!

After a while, I figured I'd better get back to my hotel while I still remembered its name. I passed Dalhousie University and weaved along beneath the Citadel, the streets somehow growing steeper and increasingly difficult to navigate. The city had shut down, but I passed a small, lonely eatery that appeared to be my last option for a pre-vomit snack. It was called The King of Donairs. A pair of guys were sitting there, sharing nasty-looking ribbons of meat from an open pita. Neither, I might add, resembled royalty.

The hour had gone from late to early, and the hip of meat rotating under the flickering heat lamp looked more like a femur. I ordered something and the young man working there repeated it back to me with additional phlegm, giving it an authentic Mediterranean feel. He used one of those sheep-shearing tools to shave a puddle of meat onto a soft pita, then glooped jizzimy sauce on it, wrapped it in foil, bagged it and handed it to me, the outside of the bag slick with grease. I smiled, paid and took the wet lump, knowing it would get nowhere near my mouth.

Back in my room, I licked the last of the atrocious donair from my fingers, the bedspread smeared with a great deal of fallout. I yanked the bedcover back, desperate to hide the evidence like spatter at a crime scene, and realized it was only one of many similar stains, the likes of which I could only hope were from previous guests' donairs. Once more I questioned my choice of accommodation.

Next day. The rental vehicle swayed alarmingly in the wind. I was driving to Peggy's Cove and Lunenburg. Wind off the water whipped the small SUV back and forth and I fought the wheel, glad the road was quiet. It was early and my head was still clearing from the previous night's poor choices. I exited the highway to a small community in search of sustenance and a working toilet and found a simple clapboard eatery with stacks of faded wooden lobster traps piled haphazardly outside. The muddy parking lot was filled with cars, which I took as a good sign. I parked and went in.

A man-sized plastic lobster stared me down as I entered, its beady black eyes somehow knowing I'd consumed a relative two nights prior. (A relative of *his*, that is.) Coats were stacked on a coat rack at the door and stiff-brimmed ball caps advertising trucks and tractors seemed mandatory. Conversation was surprisingly lively in the early hour, focused on the coaching of the local bantam hockey team.

I sat at a booth, my server resembling Polly Holliday, who played Flo in *Alice*. And in *Flo*. Flo served me scalding coffee and a platter of rejuvenating breakfast swimming in butter and smelling of haddock – delicious and medicinal. I finished and paid my bill, but a seismic-like rumble emanating from the depths of my intestines warned me I'd better use the facilities, immediately. A short time later, as I sped from the parking lot, tires spitting gravel, in the rear-view mirror I saw Flo nailing up a permanent "Closed" sign and shaking her fist.

Peter Gabriel's "Solsbury Hill" drummed me into Lunenburg. Gold and red maple leaves swirled across the road and gulls hung like kites on strong wind. I strolled through the shipyards to the *Bluenose II*, where a man wound thick rope into fat coils, a greying dog at his feet.

I carried on through residential streets, past a home with laundry hanging from a line, stiff in the wind – plaid mackinaws and a Hudson's Bay blanket. Climbing the hill into town, I was drawn to Saint John's Anglican Church, a 250-year-old structure topped by an iron weather vane adorned with a fish. The church interior was warm and still. Dark old timbers arched overhead and narrow windows of simple stained glass moved the dim interior light, reminiscent of the sea. It was the type of church where Father Mapple would give a sermon from a crow's nest pulpit before the sailing of the *Pequod*.

A welcoming attendant greeted me and encouraged me to sign the guest book, placed indiscreetly beside the donation box. He held his hand, palm up, over the book and box and cleared his throat. Having been shaken down, I sat and warmed up for what I felt was the value of my donation before moving on. I went for lunch and happened across friends who pulled an extra chair to the end of their table. We ate creamy cod chowder made with yellow-fleshed potatoes. They insisted on paying, making me wish I'd ordered more.

Back in the vehicle, I detoured to the memorial site of Swissair Flight 111, which crashed just off the coast in 1998. Coast Guard and local volunteers sped to the scene, a few kilometres offshore, a ragtag flotilla of fishing boats and would-be rescuers in a classic case of maritime co-operation. There were no survivors. No rescue. Only recovery. I stared at a familiar seascape – relentless surf, an indifferent stretch of water, but the view was tainted, a bleak expanse of loss and grief.

I carried on to Peggy's Cove. Wind buffeted bare, rocky headland and crashed plumes of water into the sky. Colourful little homes clung to the rock like determined lichen. The whole place made me shiver; a desolation bright paint couldn't hide.

Back in Halifax, a man named Bob called my room, saying he was waiting for me downstairs. His taxi was immaculate and he explained he was retired but helping a friend. On the half-hour drive to the airport, he pointed out things we passed, proud of his city.

"Lived here 63 years. All my life," he said. We crossed the bridge into Dartmouth and he pointed out to the water. "Lost my brother last week," he said. "He was 67. He was my favourite brother. Talked two, three times a week."

I told him I was sorry.

"Yeah," he said, pointing again. "That's where we scattered his ashes, the wife and me. Then we had a drink of rum and poured one for him." He was quiet then added, "But, you know, you open the paper and it's right there – one corner's obituaries, the other's births – all part of life."

We passed rows of tenements. "See those there?" Bob said. "That's government housing. Subsidized. I'm proud of that. You wouldn't want to go there at night, you understand, but the fact that we *have* them, you know?"

As we pulled up to the terminal Bob apologized that he had to go pick up another fare, and shook my hand for a while. "I would've liked to have shown you more of the city," he said.

I would've liked that as well.

We parted ways and then a funny thing ensued. In addition to having been here for travel research and viking, I was promoting a book and attending a convention. The final few days had been intensely full of conference activities – workshops, breakouts, meet-and-greets – and I was in full-on conventioneer mode, every sentence starting with, "Hi, I'm Bill, from Vancouver..."

As I went into the airport and onto an elevator, the other occupant was a woman in a suit wearing a lanyard, same as everyone I'd spoken to over the past four days.

"Hi, I'm Bill, from Vancouver..." I said with a smile, extending a hand.

"Hi, Bill!" she said, shaking my hand. "Really nice running into you!" A momentary pause, then, "Gosh, I have to apologize, I don't remember where it was we first met."

It was then I realized I was no longer at a convention. Just an effusively friendly weirdo at the airport. To which I said, somewhat ashamed, "Oh. Yes. Right. Well, in fact, we haven't actually met. I've just come from a conference and was on autopilot, meet-and-greet mode. I apologize."

To which she laughed, relieved. "Thank goodness for that!" she said, "I pride myself on remembering people I meet. You see, I'm Lieutenant-Governor here, and I admit I fall into that trap too sometimes. But it was lovely to meet you, Bill. Have a good flight."

Which I did, chuckling most of the way.

From a pad of convention centre stationery:

Dans la belle province, pratiquer mon français.

A jaunt west by northwest takes us to Quebec, resting in part on Atlantic shores via the Gulf of St. Lawrence. I'd use snippets of middle school French to which locals would invariably sigh and speak English. This experience occurred repeatedly across the province.

Four-hundred-year-old Quebec City is a piece of Old World placed neatly into the new. Architecture is sturdy, solid stone. Cuisine is rich, regionally unique and prideful. The distinct pocket of Canada felt far from my west coast home and fuelled a passion to keep our country intact that surprised me in its intensity.

In Montreal it was a get-together with friends for drinks and a wet walk to Old Montreal, where we descended stairs to a warm, candle-lit restaurant furnished in deep-grained, dark wood. One friend ordered rabbit and when it arrived I suggested he send it back, as there was a hare on his plate. I laughed enough for everyone.

Next day the weather changed from bleak to bright, clear sky and pleasant heat with low humidity. We traipsed around Mont Royal and Beaver Lake, past Outremont to the Plateau for smoked meat sandwiches at Schwartz's Deli. Following this we ate Basque pintxos. We wandered through Old Montreal, an informal walking tour, in and around Notre Dame, the original Bank of Montreal, historical sites and statues, up and down the pedestrian-friendly slope of Place Jacques-Cartier and along the St. Lawrence to Atwater Market, completing an exploratory loop around downtown. The Musée des beaux-arts had a Dale Chihuly travelling exhibit – roomfuls of inspirational colour and design, expressed through his unmistakable medium of hand-blown glass.

The previous time I'd been here I was on my own, a warm, sunny autumn. I was playing hooky from another conference, unwilling to bind myself once more in a suit and tie and instead embraced the liberation of truancy. I hung out in Parc La Fontaine, socializing (in a manner) with squirrels, before delving into the shops of Marché Jean-Talon, making a picnic of local red beer, strong Oka cheese and herb-crusted Mediterranean herring. At the market, a busker sang and played a beat-up classical guitar, seated on an upended apple crate. A beefy, dust-covered guy, he finished every song with a theatrical *"Merci, merci!"* which he lisped heavily ("Mer-thea, mer-thea!"), and I added to his upturned hat.

"Merci! Merci beaucoup," he said, *"Je m'appelle Sylvain."* ("Thillvan.")

He proffered a meaty hand that felt like grabbing a well-oiled catcher's mitt, and asked where I was from. I told him my childhood home.

"Ah, *oui*, I spent time in the Okanagan," he said, nodding. "In Naramata, picking fruit." He laughed. "I played a cowboy bar there. In Oliver. Real cowboys!"

Y

CARIBBEAN

From a stitched Moleskine, one of a packet of three, with a rigid cover in navy blue, the size of a driver's licence, paired with a tiny ballpoint pen that did nothing but blot in gloopy octopus strings:

I sat near a crumbling concrete seawall in the shade of seagrape and a tall casuarina, gnarled and twisted from a lifetime of salty sea wind. I'd pulled a chaise longue over grass toward the water, angling the recliner to optimize sun and shade. And grinned, remembering how we struggled with the pronunciation when Dad first brought home one of the nouveau contraptions with the comfy cushion and confusing name: shays-lounge, chays-long and cheese-lozenge were amongst our bastardizations.

With a lag to the south, let's head toward Central America, where we jumped in a cab before realizing we couldn't speak the language. The driver asked us something in Spanish. I fought the urge to use my Catalan lisp and replied with a few *¡holas!* and *¿cómo estás?* doing my best to emphasize inverted punctuation. Together we bumbled through pidgin and managed to communicate that we wanted to have a meal and explore the island of Cozumel.

The car took off along the coast, ocean breeze gusting through open windows. Tourmaline sea broke on bright sandy shore. We squinted in glare off the water, and afternoon heat had my head bobbing with fatigue and contentment. The water was busy with tourists on jet skis, but before long there was nothing but towering breakers offshore, their sound a deep and constant rumble.

After a while, the driver pulled off the road where a simple restaurant was comprised of a tilting hut of metal and wood on the sand.

We stepped into pressing heat, air blowing off the water like a radiator. Someone wandered out from the tilting shack and set up a table and umbrella that also leaned like the building – a series of Pisa towers. We jammed plastic chairs into sand and our place was set.

With smiles, pointing and a series of hand gestures we managed to communicate we wanted beer and food, please and thanks. A bucket of icy Sol was clunked onto our table, tilting it further to one side. Despite the beer being wrong, we'd slid into a Corona ad, gazing over blinding sand to turquoise water. And after a short while, two slender guys hauled a platter of food to our table. There was lobster, squid, octopus, conch, a whole fried snapper and prawns on a mountain of rice with onions, tomatoes, avocados and honeydew melon, all slathered in fresh floral olive oil – a beachside feast for too little money.

We were exploring the Caribbean by ship. Not a square-rigged tall ship with bloodthirsty pirates, but a gleaming ocean liner with overfed tourists. On Grand Cayman, we wandered streets filled with banks – small doors with brass signs embossed with names of banks I was certain didn't exist. It felt like a Hollywood set – expensive facades. A hurricane had blown through and every financial institution reported that everything was fine, not to worry. And, no. No one was allowed inside.

Meandering through a mishmash of tourists and locals, we explored Key West, which struck me as hinterland, a last resort for American misfits unable to flee any farther. Walking past one of Hemingway's homes, I squinted through palms to white sand and teal water, imagining Santiago hauling in his mast and sail after another unproductive day. *A guy could get awfully comfy here*, I thought, *writing; your only company a case of whisky, six-toed cats and imagination.*

Across the Gulf of Mexico on the Yucatán, we hiked overgrown trails, explored Aztec and Mayan ruins and climbed a pyramid for a sweeping view of sprawling jungle. The previous time I'd explored the country I landed in Sinaloa state, west coast, the water dark and rough. Half-submerged at a swim-up bar, I was a gangly youth drinking Tecate and visiting with a friendly local enjoying his vacation in a motel. He had a Pancho Villa moustache, a Lucha Libre physique. We toasted something, I quaffed a tequila and strolled to the beach where someone bound me in a harness, hooked to a parasail. A burst of incomprehensible instructions followed and a speedboat tore away from shore, pulling me into the surf.

The parachute billowed behind me, filled with air and hauled me into the sky. Mazatlán Beach shrank as the boat headed north, following the coast. Away to my right a scattering of mid-rise buildings, to the left, open water. The connecting rope was long, and from my high vantage point ocean sounds muted and waves seemed to slow as they pushed at the shore. Distance dampened senses until all I felt was the rush of high breeze. Sun danced on choppy water and the lush green lump of Isla de Venados rose in the distance. The boat thrashed about beneath me, another world, while I drifted through clear sky, the only interruptions an occasional creak from the harness and swirling gusts of wind.

I parasailed again, another day, the rope much shorter, the experience entirely different, one of speed, the roar of the boat and crashing breakers rushing past below. My confidence grew and I worked the lines hard, veering over the beach and racing past buildings. My imagination thrust me into a Bond caper and I envisioned my parachute adorned with a Union Jack, setting me down on skis to race away from snow-suited Russians, poorly aimed Kalashnikovs spitting bullets at my feet.

From the same blue Moleskine:

Mick Jagger's "God Gave Me Everything" puts it perfectly,
a single grain of sand conducting the essence of everything,
and the gratitude that can accompany that realization.

Let's conclude our tour of the Americas on another island – Barbados, a short distance from Bridgetown – a fitting pin on our map, as it is itself a bridge, a blend of Caribbean and Atlantic, and a bridge to our journey, which will take us viking once more across the pond. But, before that, let's enjoy here – a place of good people, food, rum, beauty and warmth.

Morning breeze rippled water in front of our rental apartment, while beyond that a line of jagged waves broke where Atlantic and Caribbean meet – wild horses on the horizon. We'd arrived with two dozen family and friends to celebrate a wedding. The island's popular for nuptials and I liked the analogy ocean and sea provided – two bodies of water meeting in frothy aquatic matrimony.

We rang in the New Year on the beach, fireworks bursting in the distance. I dove into black, nighttime surf, an exhilarating, frightening activity I hadn't done since I was a teenager in Hawaii, embracing life and trying to impress two women from California.

In the midday Bajan heat, we jumped aboard a small public bus, one of a number of independently owned shuttles that sped along the main road crossing the island. Each bus was staffed with a driver and a hawker who'd lean out the open door of the bus and holler at pedestrians, demanding people get aboard and discrediting all competitors.

Heckles and insults were hurled between operators as buses passed. Shouting seemed essential as each bus pounded reggae, calypso and hip hop at full volume. It was friendly, efficient, deafening and fun. It struck me as an odd combination of Adam Smith and Charles Darwin – free market survivalism – only the fastest and loudest seemed to thrive, steered by invisible hands, as drivers looked everywhere but the road. Heads bobbed to thundering tunes while warm air rushed through open windows. Passengers were a mixed bag of all ages and, aptly, all ages carried mixed bags – everyone toting food, shopping and anything portable. Our bus slowed in thick traffic and I watched a tiny stray puppy play with a bottle cap the way a regular-sized dog would grab a Frisbee. It was kind of cute but mostly heartbreaking and I wished I hadn't seen it.

After choosing a stop somewhat randomly, we made our way to a small fish market where we bought a bag of fresh flying fish and a stick of garlic butter. The fish wings were clipped, making preparation easy. We hauled the wet plastic bag to our unit and fried the lot in the seasoned butter, enjoying a sumptuous, simple meal before joining a few others watching the sunset at the beach in hopes of seeing a rare green flash in clear equatorial sky.

Next morning a shimmering sun peeked from the horizon. I was up before everyone, warming the previous day's coffee on the stove. I filled a mug, went outside and wandered down the beach, clutching the latest Deepak Chopra like a Gideon salesman. A half-hour and half a world away, I settled in, wiggling myself an ass-sized crater in the shoreline sand, still damp from receding tide and overnight humidity. Within a short while, I had a visitor. Someone I'd like you to meet, named Keith.

"My name's Keef," he said with a smile, ambling toward me.

Keith was barefoot, wearing a thin singlet and loose shorts. He had an athlete's muscles and the look of someone who didn't eat. His eyes were a little red, a little yellow. He'd just gotten up as well, his bed a *body*-sized crater in the sand. He settled in next to me and we talked. Mostly I listened. Keith spoke passionately about the world, his wonder at it all and our interconnectedness with nature. He showed me a grain of sand in his palm to make his point; that there was a world in there, like we were in here and so on. *Cosmic Russian dolls*, I thought.

He explained quantum mechanics with exquisite simplicity, despite lacking the terminology, and had a remarkable handle on the workings of the universe. His thought process flowed seamlessly between the hemispheres of his brain and, like the surge of surf, conversation washed from science to music. He explained Bob Marley was his favourite artist, feeling the lyrics spoke to him. And as we sat together, comfortable, gazing out to sea, Keith sang "Buffalo Soldier," his voice gravelly and slow like the tide, the waves his metronome. ("Woi-yoi-yoi-yoi-yoi-yoi-yo-yo.")

Keith was content, enlightened, eager to share but not force it on anyone. He was genuinely happy and positive. Despite seemingly having nothing, he possessed what most of us aspire to and in that respect had everything. When Socrates said, "He is nearest to God who needs the fewest things," he could well have been describing Keith.

As Keith spoke, I figured I was hearing much the same thing I would've read in my Chopra, but with a Bajan accent rather than Indian. Having heard Deepak so often on TV and audiobooks, in my head it read with his accent. But when I tried it out loud it sounded like a poor rendition of Russell Peters mimicking his dad. Deb felt my Scottish accent sounded much the same.

I told Keith I wanted him to have my book, as he was figuratively on the same page as Deepak. Keith explained that he hadn't learned to read – remarkable given his knowledge – so I said in that case it was something he could work toward, if he so chose. Plus, the fact he couldn't decipher the words didn't really matter. *Nobody* understands Deepak's books.

We shook hands warmly, Keith giving me the caring politician hand-and-forearm clasp, holding it for some time. I felt we each got a new friend. He caressed his new book, holding it to his chest with both arms like a school kid.

Later that day our extended family got together for lunch – pepper-pot stew with rice and peas. One of the group said she'd seen some "crazy guy" on the beach, and described Keith. "Waving some book around," she said, shaking her head. "Like a preacher."

Good for you, Keith. I smiled to myself. *Too bad she didn't hear what you had to say.*

UK AND EUROPE

∫

BRITISH ISLES

From my last artist's postcard, a packet of 25 ingenious blank
cards I shared with UK friends, pre-stamped and addressed
to me. The request? Put a little something – anything – on
this card if and when you're so inspired, then drop it in a
postbox, please and thanks. These would be my mementos of
this particular tour, what I'd receive being more than I ever
could have imagined. I gave out 24 of the cards. On the one I
kept for myself and brought home sometime later I wrote:

*It was morning where I was, overlooking Canada's west coast,
evening for pals in Europe, and teatime for buddies around the
UK. Together we were recreating, virtually, a literature festival
held in Britain each spring. This partial iteration took place
via Zoom, a collection of artists with one librettist, the man
we love who began this years ago, the in-person version.*

Which, along with the rest of this particular experience, appeared in
Write, the magazine of the Writers' Union of Canada. Now, imagine,
if you will, a group of creatives along with our inspiration, the librettist, gazing into monitors from living rooms, kitchens and, in my case,
tucked in a Harry Potter-like closet off our entryway, clothing pushed
out of frame. We lived, you see, in a space the size of a hotel room – not
in London or New York but anywhere else – a queen-sized bed, bath
and my closet-cum-conference room/performance space. I had earbuds with the mic on, my feet wedged amidst out-of-season footwear,
ready for a lit fest like no other. My friends on GMT, most of them,
had their G and Ts, while I, at 11 a.m., not wanting to feel excluded,

clutched a juice glass of morning Malbec. Prior to this I didn't know such a thing existed. Turns out it does and may, I suspect, catch on.

Normally, these events occur in Cornwall – England's southwest corner, near Penzance – the end of the line for rail, bus and, obviously, where pirates come from. Each day for the duration of the festival this eclectic group converges for evening readings, while daytime features public events in a tiny park called Norway Square, a pocket of wind-swept greenery with peekaboo views of the Celtic Sea. I'm one of a number of "regulars" who hail from everywhere, descending on this destination to share, perform and socialize with fellow artists. The energy's relaxed and inclusive. Something hard to find, at times, elsewhere.

The online version kicked off with our spoken word guru, a mentor to most of us, akin to an endless dock where eager boats berth and then launch into surf without a compass, just intuition and trust in a guiding North Star. In this case, our polar sensei's name is Bob. Bob, you see, *knows* his work. He's learned it. Different than memorization. We can rattle off a national anthem, or perhaps recite a prayer without inherently knowing them, lacking the ability to breathe fresh nuance into each performance based on room, audience, accompaniment. *That's* knowing your work. With Bob's guidance, encouragement and a few hundred hours of effort, I now have a few compositions of my own – prose, poetry and spoken word – under my belt. Work I'm proud of that's fun to share. One of these was my contribution. Our collaborative showcase – the equivalent of a small portion of the usual festivities – played out in a lively if somewhat displaced manner, that fascinatingly weird way online get-togethers simultaneously connect and dislocate.

There's a host or moderator, but of course in an online group of any size invariably someone overrides their mute and we find ourselves listening to a poem or passage overdubbed by the unending crinkle of a packet of crisps. To which I hastily type my thoughts into the chat stream, having learned from my tour in Seattle (*Hey pork rind, shut the fuck up!*), before deleting it all with a sigh and instead say nothing.

The alternate locale traditionally holding this festival is a venerable wood structure leaning slightly over the ocean. The building is St Ives Arts Club. The water, St Ives Bay. The first time I entered the venue it was a miserable, late winter night – dark, cold, wet. I'd made some perversely discomfiting commitment to myself I'd read my poetry in this special place, the way some might vow to one day grace a stage at Carnegie Hall. Deb accompanied me, because she's kind and supportive. So rather than spending a cozy evening in front of the purr of BBC TV – country getaways or titillating murders – we instead braved the elements to see who knows what, plus me reading newborn writing, ink still damp on paper.

There were six of us: Deb and me, librettist Bob, an actress from the continent, someone from across the peninsula and a man named Shanty who delivered 15 exceptional minutes of *Beowulf*, which he did not read, leaving me somewhat weak-kneed. The man *knew* his *Beowulf*. Still does, I'm sure. And could, no doubt, do the entire thing given the chance. But all I knew was an artistic bar had been set. The people – strangers at the time – welcomed us wholeheartedly. Yet I felt if I were to *truly* fit in, I too needed to *learn* my work.

Perhaps what I loved most – above and beyond the kind-hearted people and their significance to my growth as a writer – was the venue itself. This unassuming structure was where the very first motion picture was played. Before Edison was ripping off copyrights across the pond, here in remote England some guy in the late 1800s played a film of a galloping horse on the wall of this building. History in real time, albeit jumpy black-and-white vignettes.

Bob addressed the room, explaining that, given the architectural limitations of this ancient structure of resin-soaked timber with a lone stairwell and emergency exit ladder dropping to seaside rocks, in the unlikely event of a fire, to please ensure we've made the most of the evening! And with an uncomfortable laugh and glances at each other (*surely I can reach the ladder before the septuagenarian with a dodgy hip*), we got on with the show.

I'd been coming and going from the UK quite a bit. A privileged position, I realize, yet a challenging one as well – a blend of work, research and vacation melding into an amorphous goo of happiness, challenge and guilt. Happiness because I found myself doing things I love – trekking, performing and socializing with friends. Challenging because much of it was hard work. And guilt because once more I'd become part of an establishment that both gives and takes from people who live and work in scenic, economically challenged locales where others (like me) breeze in, drop a modest amount of money and assuredly harm the landscape – social, political, economic – as much as we add to it.

Without ever, ever forgetting that fact, let's jump a train (no longer virtual but *actual*) from Heathrow to London, then south and west back to Land's End, in part for *Gone Viking* research and also for a series of in-person gigs – sharing music, poetry and spoken word.

BBC journalist/explorer Simon Reeve, on travel:

"People are essentially warm, friendly, and
welcome. Avoid the dodgy salad at the buffet,
always wear a seatbelt, and you will be okay."

A few of us were visiting over beers on a seaside patio. One of the group seated at the picnic-style table was Renaissance man Gray Lightfoot – author and poet – a bus driver the rest of the week. I referenced Lightfoot being a bus-driver-slash-poet. The others sniggered, thinking I just called him a piss poet.

"You don't get the joke, do you." said one of the middle-aged adolescents.

"Of course I do," I replied. "I just don't have time for gutter humour," I added indignantly, raising a hip to break wind.

Lightfoot, a UK resident, had British roots running a long way back – to the 16th century to be precise – his Cornish ancestors being mustered to keep the Spanish from landing (and, no doubt, beating them at football). A creative split personality, he divides writing time between fantasy-mystery novels and contemporary poetry that's insightful and funny. He started the conversation, claiming he has a hard time communicating with people.

"What are you talking about?" I demanded.

"See what I mean?"

We arranged to meet again at his traditional place of work, and a few days later I found myself at sunrise, bleary-eyed, in Penzance. Naturally, I kept a watchful eye on the sea for pirates, and unwelcome Spanish footballers.

Like the coolest carpool ever, Gray pulled up in a bus. I got a welcoming smile and thumbs-up from the poet behind the wheel.

"Permission to come aboard?"

"Granted."

I clambered in like the touring rock star I imagined myself to be, and Gray changed the sign to indicate the morning's terminus. Others boarded and greeted him by name. He responded in kind; regular passengers on regular routes. From the bay, St Michael's Mount watched us like the viking ground zero at Lindisfarne. And as a train glided from Penzance station, we did the same from the portside bus loop.

This day we were in a pristine, closed-top single-decker still smelling new-car fresh, or, more accurately, new-bus fresh. Behind the wheel it was high-tech, and a dashboard terminal pinged with incoming driver emails as we followed meandering road bordered in hedgerows, visiting as best we could.

It was surprisingly busy given the hour, the start of the Penzance–Pendeen run. I distracted Gray and he forgot to remind a travelling couple to disembark. Instead we made a new stop, Gray providing tour-guide instructions that not only got the two where they wanted to be but did so in the most agreeable, scenic manner. Their modest detour became a highlight as they carried on with thanks.

An older passenger, impeccably dressed and using a cane, asked for another customized stop to get him closer to his destination. Gray made it happen. This was a community service in the truest sense of the word. I was torn, loving being witness to it while getting angry remembering dickhead bus drivers back home. Not all, of course. Just some.

Standing next to Gray while he drove, I stepped aside as he made change for passengers paying with cash. Then I looked at the interior screen, indicating where we were, which read, "This stop is Cemetery." Fighting the urge to check my pulse, I remembered something Gray said previously. We were discussing mortality, as middle-aged writers do.

"When my time comes," he said, "I want to go peacefully in my sleep. Not screaming in terror like my passengers."

Gray and spouse Wendy moved to the West Country from Sheffield, which, he explained, "Felt like coming home." After a year dedicated to writing it was time once more to incorporate traditional work. What were the opportunities in the area? Driving bus – rotating routes and times. Training followed and a driver-slash-poet was born.

I'd seen Gray perform at St Ives Arts Club. Yes, the place with a questionable exit and where the very first movie was played. Someone had ingeniously climbed the wall of the old building and removed the T from "Arts," so at the time it was an Ars Club. (I admit the seats were comfy.) On stage, adorned in a small-brimmed, upturned fedora, his tone and cadence were reminiscent of punk poet John Cooper Clarke. Not mimicked but comparable talent from comparable experience. Gray even performed the "Bus Drivers' Haka," terrifying as a Māori warrior. He admitted at one show he actually sprained his tongue, unexpected workplace hazards for a performance poet.

"Try claiming *that* on the disability insurance!" he laughed.

As the morning route came to its (first) conclusion, we made a tight turn on a side road and Gray had a moment's break before continuing. He pointed the way for me to carry on, down a narrow lane to Pendeen Lighthouse, where I'd trek the Coast Path for a few undulating miles to Zennor, a medieval pub, and another bus to deliver me to my own Ars Club performance.

"Alright, mate," he said. And I realized this was our chance for a hug, as we wouldn't visit again for some time. It was a scenic spot to part ways, a stretch of serpentine road cutting through bucolic fields and lonely moors with sea views. Hiking away, I found myself composing, and began writing this piece, called "South West Coast Path."

Tread along the coastal path
footsteps carry on
crunching shingle, pebble strand
beside rock cliffs and dunes

Golden scoops of silica
heaped desert on the beach
slicked-down marram blown askew
in need of cut or comb

Rolling bluebells, heather, thrift
foxgloves, fragrant gorse –
scent of summer, South Pacific
ripened peach and coconut

Heartbeat of a raven's wings
pumps through veins of wind
penetrating jackdaw's gaze
a solitary chough

The bay becomes a palette
green, blue, aquamarine
fired in a wash of sun
extinguished by the rain

Gusty squalls of spindrift
strafing salty spray

surf – a metered metronome
percussion on the shore

Cadence of the wind and waves
pulsing melody
every step harmonic fugue
as the chorus; the chorus carries on...

This poem, which appears in Silver Bow's *Forever Cast in Endless Time*, was the first I eventually wrote collaboratively, in a class at the university I'd later work for, those classmates and teacher–mentors now friends, while my visit with Gray was also published in *St@nza* magazine.

I was looking at photos of that UK trip, that tour – performing, socializing and goofing off with artists I admire and continuously learn from – when, as I'm prone to do, I meandered down a rabbit hole of recollection and memorabilia. The next thing you know, I was into a box of wine (you heard me) watching a full AC/DC concert on YouTube. The concert, if you're interested, was from the mid-noughties, the band performing in Buenos Aires. Which, as all rock fans are aware, is one of those places you go (that, or Brazil) to set Guinness records for concert attendance. Their football stadia hold upwards of two hundred grand (with the floor turned into a mosh pit). I believe KISS held the record for a very long time, with a quarter of a million collectively fist pumping and, needless to say, "Shouting It Out Loud." No matter.

Brian Johnson says to the throng in halted Spanish with a thick Geordie accent, "Good evening! Thank you! I apologize, our Spanish ain't great, but we ALL speak rock 'n' roll!" To which I chime in, with 200,000 new friends, Yeahhhhhhhhhhhhhh!!!"

Beside me on the sofa Deb looked over, askance, providing me with my first opportunity to accurately use the word, while she, on another device, watched something with subtitles.

Having rocked to the extent I'm able to (on a weeknight), I went back to travel memories, and by that I simply mean memories, as each one, in its way, is a voyage. Now I'd like you to meet Firoz. I liked his perspective, insights, all of it a reminder to never judge. And his story was a good one, grabbing my attention even before details of his three-way in Burma. A lean Fijian, he had worker's hands and hair coiffed with just the right amount of scruff. He was a professional golfer and played in Southeast Asia, Australia and New Zealand. His winnings weren't enough to get him through the year, so he lived and worked in Canada during the off-season, working on homes. That's how we met.

"Two dates, I banged her," he said with a nod.

"Ah," I replied, which seemed as suitable a response as any.

He'd been talking about life and relationships with open, coarse, unfiltered honesty. He was describing his girlfriend, and I learned much about her anatomy and sexual aptitude, not that I'd asked.

I smiled. "Will you ask her to marry you?"

"Oh sure," he nodded. "She's great. But if I was ever unfaithful to her, she'd chop me, you know?" He sliced the air – a guillotine motion. "That time in Burma?" he said, making it sound like a question. "It's near Thailand, you know? That was before we met. It was after a tournament. I did well."

"Did you get a trophy?" I asked.

"No, just the memory of the women was enough," he said, gazing into the past.

I'd meant the golf but liked the notion of him getting an award for his orgy. I mentally wrote an acceptance speech, grinning stupidly.

"It's true, you know?" he said, thinking I was smiling at what he'd said, which I suppose I was, tangentially. He went on. "But how much can you really do, with two others in bed, you know? Just enjoy."

I remembered a Sinhalese friend telling me about the time he'd watched Tamil Tigers training. He said they'd take turns carrying three other soldiers – practice for when comrades fell in action. He'd explained it was a combination of strength, balance and endurance. *No shit*, I'd thought. I almost gave up trying to hoist our IKEA futon into our vehicle, kicking it to death like a lumpy Swedish corpse, never mind dragging around a pile of people. Sure, you might think, Tamils are only 50 kilos each, but so was the guy stacking them up to complete the task at hand. Funnily, that memory popped into my head, having drawn, I suspect, some parallel between the demanding military drill and my new friend's sexcapades in Myanmar.

Firoz was about to go back to Asia. The tour started in Singapore. "Twenty-one tournaments," he explained. "One a week."

I asked him how he did.

"Oh," he shrugged. "Some good, some bad. Some win, some lose. But, you know, if you're good at something, you don't want to live life and wonder someday, you know...maybe."

"Firoz," I asked, "what's the meaning of life?"

He didn't hesitate. "It's about doing good for people," he said. "No problem. They don't even need to know it, you know? Just do good." He paused, then added, "Life's always turning. Sometimes left, sometimes right. Sometimes right, sometimes wrong. Always turning. But you do your best, you know? No problem."

A short while later we were in the parking lot of our apartment building. I'd walked him out to his van. It was mud-splattered white – an ugly Dalmatian on wheels, with faded graphics peering through the muck. He fought a little with some cords that wouldn't coil, then picked up as though the meaning-of-life conversation hadn't been interrupted.

"It's a jenny, you know?" he said.

"I'm sorry?" I asked.

"Life, you know? It's a jenny. No problem. I'm not sure how you spell it." He furrowed his brow and said, "I think...J-O-U-R-A-N-A-Y. Jenny."

"Thank you, Firoz, I *do* understand," I said and smiled as he hopped into the van.

"Thank you too, buddy," he said, and drove away with a honk of the horn and a wave.

Scribbled in ink on a glossy page torn from *The Rough Guide to England* – "When to Go and 30 Things Not to Miss":

A small domed helicopter droned past the London Eye, the cityscape a bell curve – a normally distributed timeline – Saint Paul's and Westminster bookending the view, while the Shard stabbed the sky, centring it all with modernity.

Bill Bryson wrote of Great Britain, "What a wondrous place this was – crazy as fuck, of course, but adorable to the tiniest degree." I was still exploring the wondrous place by way of trail, train, performance gig and rowing gig, with time perhaps to formulate my own evolving notion of life's significance – inserting oddly shaped pieces of clarity to the overall puzzle. Rather than taking time off, I'd simply handed the keys to my theoretical shop to a colleague, once more flipping a sign on my imagined storefront to indicate I'd "gone viking."

I'd trained to Paddington, arriving early in the afternoon. Days were lengthening, giving me time to drop pack and duffle at my lodging and get back outside to enjoy a few hours of springtime sun.

Arriving at the hotel, I was helped by a pretty and monumentally effeminate man with purple eyes and hair like a mop. He gave me my key and a restaurant voucher, explaining, "Breakfast service begins at half six."

"So...at three?" I said, thinking that was awfully early. I'd been in the same dilemma when someone told me to meet them at "a quarter of eight"; I got there at two.

I asked him for a pub recommendation and he suggested the Victoria, a few blocks away. I went, curious as to what type of place he felt suited me. It looked decent – traditional, small and dark, but on a gorgeous afternoon I couldn't imagine ducking into a pub. Not yet.

Sun shone, brightening Hyde Park in shades of peridot. I strolled toward Notting Hill, decided it was *now* time for a beer and stopped for a sleeve of London Pride at the Churchill Arms – a proper old British pub, serving proper old British beer to proper old British patrons. Teeny grey-haired men were wearing a great deal of clothing, which I suspect never changed, irrespective of the season. There were a couple of younger guys in suits and a pair of long-haired guys wearing sweaters, but the rest of the punters were rheumy-eyed, tweed-wearing, solitary drinkers, mumbling and shaking as though touched with the palsy.

One barrel-chested patron reached over the bar to pull on a draft tap. The barkeep grabbed the customer's arm and bit his hand until he let go with a yelp. I went back to my journal and tried to look well behaved.

The old establishment was a storage closet of epic proportions – small but packed with a cornucopia of eclectic stuff you'd only find in a rummage sale or on *Antiques Road Show*. Hanging from the ceiling were a shiny baritone tuba, brass pots and kettles, wicker creels, railway lanterns, an accordion, milk jugs, bellows, billy clubs, collectible plates with paintings of RAF planes and dozens of photos of Sir Winston Churchill looking like the jowly, poker-playing bulldog.

A particularly tiny old man wearing a flat hat walked in with purpose and stopped abruptly behind the stool where I was seated – empty seats left and right – looked me up and down, and began mumbling and shaking his head to clearly convey I was in his spot. Recalling that visceral experience I penned a few lines to express it in verse: "And now I've pissed off Andy Capp, standing by the seat I've chosen / tiny ancient man in ancient tweed, actually huffs despite a row of empty stools, I've clearly chosen HIS so I take the low road and ignore him / immerse myself in an imperial pint, then snap newspaper in front of me, international sign for DO NOT DISTURB / a further awkward pause…Andy lets out one last huff, and finally fucks off while I pretend to understand the cricket scores." (A variation of this appears in *Forever Cast in Endless Time*.)

While I flipped through the *London Evening Standard*, an angry woman plunked down next to me and struck up a monologue, complaining about McDonald's, Americans and child obesity. I didn't disagree, but after a while nodding became boring. So I feigned something urgent, glanced at my watch, which was eight hours off, and excused myself, making my way to the blue neon glow of the Electric Cinema, a 100-year-old Notting Hill theatre, where a few moviegoers had begun to queue.

The theatre featured squishy leather chairs and ottomans, hot food and bar service. My plan was to pay to see the latest *Pirates of the Caribbean* and settle in for an indulgent sleep. Although venues varied, I'd enjoyed wonderfully satisfying sleeps through each of the previous hundred or so *Pirates* films.

Back in my Paddington hotel, I was planning my route from London to Cornwall, looking at train connections through Truro, when Deb texted from Vancouver. She'd just received the latest phone bill, which included a short period of out-of-country data roaming, for 500 dollars. The note was brief: "OMFG. Last text for month. Regards." Or something quite similar.

It was now morning. I sat down to breakfast and was served by Manuel from *Fawlty Towers*. I ordered full English, eggs fried. Manuel gazed into the middle distance for a remarkably long time, leaving me curious as to what I'd get for my breakfast. Then he slunk away and timidly recited my order to the manager.

"No such thing as *flied* eggs!" the manager scolded.

Manuel shrank and stammered, "Eh-eggs?"

"It's *FRIED. FRIED* eggs!" the manager shouted.

I was certain he'd punctuate it by thwacking Manuel in the forehead with a spoon. If he did, I didn't see it, and eventually got exactly what I wanted: eggs, not flied but fried, with streaky bacon, baked beans, toast, tomato, mushrooms, sausage, blood pudding and bubble and squeak. Culinary perfection.

I'd been up since 5 a.m. and was the first one in the restaurant, where Cold Play purred softly from a sound system. Across the street, sunlight crept along a Georgian building and thickly vined maples in tiny Norfolk Place Park. Cold Play melded into Paul Simon, calculating ways to leave his lover. As I mopped my plate with toast, *Band on the Run* began to play. I chuckled, remembering a line from *The Simpsons*. Homer was speaking to a music industry executive who, in recounting his accomplishments in the business, said with pride, "I was the one who convinced Paul McCartney to leave Wings," to which Homer replied, "You idiot! He was the most talented one!"

Back in my room, lying in bed and reading Bryson's *Notes from a Small Island*, I had to bury my face in the pillows, afraid my guffaws would wake the neighbours, having multiple pillows to oneself a distinct benefit of travelling solo. I eventually checked out, astounded that my purple-eyed, mop-haired friend was still working reception, as though 36-hour shifts were the norm. I made my way to Paddington Station, clicking a selfie of Paddy and me (the statue of him in bronze) before boarding.

I settled into the train and the interior hummed to life, purring like a happy kitten. A friendly steward placed cardboard menus on the seats and an angry little grey-haired woman shoved past, sending him teetering like a punching clown. She was pacing up and down the car, ramming aside everyone she passed and studying seat numbers. I offered to help the nasty old thing find her seat.

"I'm looking for my *seat*!" she barked, effectively telling me in one simple, declarative statement, "I'm not dead yet," as well as "Fuck off" and "Fuck *you*." She lowered a shoulder and made another drive up the middle, but I dropped a hip, giving her a solid and satisfying body check as she passed. (Price of a one-way London to Truro: 50 quid. Hip-checking a senior citizen: eternal damnation. Beating up a bully: priceless.) It turned out she didn't have a seat in the car.

The conductor's whistle blew, doors slid shut and we began to roll. We rattled out of Paddington and a BBC voice came on the PA: "For those of you who don't travel with First Great Western that often, please read the safety instructions. Unless travelling in Car D." Leaving me to assume Car D was a lower-fare, buffer car that would crush or explode in the event of emergency, effectively damping the impact for those of us in full-fare cars. I liked to believe that's where the bully was seated.

Once more I opened my Bryson and ended up reading in Reading, which I found pleasing, despite mispronouncing it for years playing Monopoly. And again I had to fight to contain my laughter, lest I become the passenger from *Mr. Bean*, forcing passengers to stuff their ears with socks and used chewing gum to drown me out.

The steward came by, nodded and said, "Yuh' rye?" This is a potentially confusing salutation to which a response is not only *not* expected but, if one's offered, confuses the enquirer, like "How ya' goin'?" in Australia or "How'zit?" in Hawaii, which I only learned after years of prolonged and awkward interactions with strangers.

I ordered a bacon baguette.

"Yu' wo' sorce?" he asked, which could mean anything from HP to malt vinegar, mustard or unsweetened ketchup. I declined.

He passed me my sandwich, "Yuh' rye?"

"Cheers," I said, feeling I'd managed to get it right in ESL English.

I looked around at fellow passengers. A young mom weaved up and down the aisle with two excited kids – cute, pumpkin-headed bobble toys – happy little lower-case i's. An old man's obesity and osteoporosis left his chin resting improbably on his sternum. He sipped a lager directly off his chest. He became progressively louder as he drank his beer and shushed his wife in a nifty pentameter, "*Sh-sh-sh-sh-sshhh... sh-sh-sh-sh-sshhh.*" Their conversation carried on, then I realized it was a sort of speech delimiter.

"Well, I don't understand the situation in Spain," she said.

"*Sh-sh-sh-sh-sshhh*, I have to agree," he replied.

A baby slept unattended in a stroller in the bending, rocking section between cars, leaving me to wonder where her parents were. The fart-like smell of hard-boiled eggs slithered through the cabin, indicating either someone was having a picnic or the baby was due for a change. I imagined the parents taking the infant to the "Baby Change

Station," signage that always amused me. If you were changing your baby, could you request one that was cuter, better behaved or hadn't shit their pants?

We rolled past boats tilted on muddy flats at low tide, pastures with Jerseys and Guernseys grazing on emerald grass, slopes of bright butter-cups, crumbling medieval churches and miles of neat, low hedgerows. Stone chimneys towered above industrial buildings while hawks cir-cled. Woolly black sheep in a paddock stood in a ray of sunlight, and blackbirds and starlings glinted on a phone wire. We passed steep streets of row houses in muted rainbow colours, crossed a high bridge in Plymouth and curled our way down to a muddy bight, the tracks sweeping along sandy shore and moored sailboats.

"Cornwall!" a little boy shouted.

"Not yet, love; it's Devon," his mom replied.

Samuel Coleridge was from here, a key contributor to my litera-ture-inspired dromomania. The Devon native actually got the seed of his *Ancient Mariner* material from Wordsworth, the two tackling the controversial composition together. Collaborative writing, however, proved unsuccessful and Coleridge completed the final draft on his own. He too was a traveller, his life an open-ended journey. In research-ing the man, Bruce Chatwin labelled Coleridge a stranger at his own birthplace, a wanderer, unable to sink roots anywhere. He compared Coleridge with Cain, and "the horizon-struck navigators of the 16th century," a line I love and plan on reusing, implying I wrote it myself.

Our train continued through Devon, stopping at Par station with connections to Newquay. Kids in wetsuits stood on the platform with surfboards. It could have been Australia had the weather been warmer (and the kids better looking). At St Austell a strong wind blew and a brown dove sat in the breeze, feathers askew, looking unkempt. The conductor came on the PA and asked for our patience. We'd be stopped, he explained, to wait for an ambulance, as one of the passengers had taken ill. I assumed it was one of the full-fare passengers and not one of the expendable ones in Car D.

BY SEA

Jotted on the fly-leaf of a paperback copy of *Death on the Nile*:

In "Once in a Lifetime," David Byrne poses the question,
upon realizing we're suddenly elsewhere, "Just how did we
get here?" A sentiment I could relate to, as I found myself
in unfamiliar waters, sailing back through time.

What follows was the germination of our *Gone Viking* undertaking, snippets of which I refer to in the *Travel Saga*. The full story, however – personal experience, sights, smells and sounds – I withheld for no other reason than brevity. But the encounters: land, sea, people, flora and fauna, offer a breadth of exploration and revelation in keeping with our current viking odyssey. As we continue beyond boundaries, let me share it with you now.

I teetered from Falmouth station, pack on my back and duffle over a shoulder, feeling like Ishmael on my way to find a ship. I needed a ferry to take me across the Fal to my lodging in St Mawes. I'd have a couple of days to acclimatize and then would return to Falmouth to board the pilot cutter *Abigail* for a week of sailing, following a slice of North Atlantic taken by Norwegian King Olaf Tryggvason (Olaf Crowbone) a thousand years earlier.

When I arrived it was Fal River Days, the town bright and festive. Coloured spinnakers were strung between buildings, hanging like garlands over Bar Terrace. Weaving my way along narrow road under the weight of my bags, I felt I was already getting my sea legs. Being in Cornwall, I stopped for an obligatory pasty and sat on a curb to eat. The pastry pouch was filled, I believe, with potato, carrot and julienned moccasin – not an unpleasant combination but one requiring a great deal of chewing before giving up and simply having to swallow softened strings of leather. As I gnawed like a cud-chewing cow, a chunk of masticated gristle fell from my mouth into my lap, leaving a grease stain spreading on my crotch that looked, at best, like urine.

I knelt to retrieve a map and the weight of my big pack pulled me over backwards, where I rolled like an upturned turtle for a few helpless, humiliating moments. Craning my neck, I saw a tall-helmeted bobby walk past. I wanted to holler for help, but pride and self-reliance won out, and after a brief struggle I managed to roll to the side and hoist myself to my knees. I then loosened the pack's straps to allow a more graceful escape, should I inadvertently be upended again.

While waiting for the ferry I amused myself in the Prince of Wales. And by that I mean the pub of that name, where I visited with Dave, the proprietor. He had to raise his voice, as Quiet Riot's Kevin DuBrow was screaming at us from the stereo, insisting that we join him and "Feel the Noize."

Dave shared stories of his travels in Canada: Capilano and Grouse mountains, Lake Louise, Banff, Jasper and Victoria. A similar story to exchanges with Monisha and my Greenlandic friend. It was a funny thing, being told where you came from was better than where you were.

At the pier, the little tugboat-like passenger ferry had been taken over by Lions for the day. Not the Serengeti type but the *truly* aggressive ones – volunteer fundraisers. I boarded and a burly Lion explained it was a five-pound donation, return. I explained I just needed a one-way.

"It's a five-pound *donation*," he said, like a mobster suggesting I do, in fact, require protection. I fumbled for a fiver before the price went up.

We trundled from Falmouth Harbour, where Pendennis Castle perches high on the headland, across the Carrick Roads toward the squat turrets of St Mawes Castle. King Henry VIII built the castles to protect the country's vital waterway. Despite Sir Francis Drake defeating the Spanish armada (the first time), solitary Spanish ships remained a threat, raiding the southern English coast. While Pendennis cannons could fire far out to sea, St Mawes cannons, low to the water, could skip cannon fire like stones across the water to punch holes in ships at the waterline. The two castles were a deadly combination but never saw much action and served primarily as military muscle flexing.

I spent my time on the ferry slinking around, avoiding Lions and further extortion. The boat bumped into a high concrete jetty and I jumped to worn stone steps that climbed steeply into St Mawes's village centre. Atop the stairs and a few strides down the pier was the village inn – my lodging. There was a good-sized crowd gathered around a group of men in tattered sailors' hats, belting out a chanty:

Pump, ya' buggers, pump
We got water in the sump
And fish heads cloggin' up the drain
If ya' wanna get to shore
Then ya' better pump some more
Or you'll have to start yer pumpin' once again

The chorus was repeated a few times and the rest of us joined in and sang along. I weaved through the cluster of folks and into the pub – the lobby of the inn. A guy pulling pints for a crush of patrons tossed me a key and directed me upstairs, where my room faced the inlet. I opened a window, sliding up a creaky old jamb, letting in sea air and the sailors' boisterous singing. It was part of the Fal River Days celebrations and added a fine, nautical vibe. Vocals were rough; simply men who sang and loved the sea and where they lived. What morphed into the Fisherman's Friends hadn't yet hit and it felt like authentic grassroots. I heaved my duffle and pack on the bed and went to join the revellers.

Moments later afternoon sun was warming the back of my head and glinting off a tall, cold glass of Carlsberg. My mind drifted like a sailboat bobbing past Roseland Peninsula, my view at that instant. Eventually motivated by hunger, I dragged myself away in search of food. I'd read good things about the hotel restaurant a few hundred metres away and made my way there for dinner. As I opened the door, an officious maître d' flitted toward me, fussing and clucking. I'd arrived at 6:28, which I now considered half six. Dinner started at 6:30.

"Am I early for dinner?" I asked.

He sighed heavily, "Yes, you are early." A dead ringer for Fredo from *The Godfather*, he was jittery under an exterior shell of Fawlty-esque pomp. I realized "Sleep Softly, Love" (*The Godfather* theme) was playing on the sound system, which probably contributed to him striking me as a Fredo look-alike. He let out another sigh. "And we are very busy tonight," he added. The enormous restaurant was empty, save for two women waiting in the lounge.

"I can see that...*that*...*that*," my voice echoed. "I could be out quickly if that helps," I added.

Sigh. "I will have to see," he said, and buzzed away like those odd little flies that only fly in short, straight lines, bumping around as though everything's a maze. After a while, he brought menus to the two women and me.

"Great," I said. "So you're able to seat us?"

Sigh. "Of course," he said, indicating my stupidity.

We were shown to our tables and he dropped a heavily starched napkin onto my lap. With a sigh he turned back to the other two diners, who had strong New England accents.

"Er, an' the courgette is...?" one asked as she looked at the menu.

"Courgette!" he raised his voice. "It's courgette. Courgette, the vegetable!"

I turned to the women and smiled, "Zucchini."

"Er, well-ah, thank-yeww!" they replied in Kennedy voices.

The place exuded futile aspiration – overdressed waiters serving underdressed customers. Eight of the 50 tables ended up having patrons. An older couple in jeans sat at a table next to me. The man pointed at me accusingly.

"You checked in at the St Mawes. The St Mawes Hotel," he said down the length of his finger.

"Ah, yes," I said. "I, uh, didn't see you there."

"Oh, we're not there," he said, and went back to his menu.

The starter was pigeon. Outside, they cooed and flapped about, strutting and pecking cigarette butts. I was uncomfortable on a few levels until I tasted the gamey, dark meat with accompanying sauce but then thought, *Oh, I get it*. And became an immediate lover of pigeon.

The next course was cod tongues. They reminded me of beef liver, the way Mom used to make it. That's to say, not tasty. As I chewed away on the rubbery little things, I realized I'd, in fact, eaten them before, in Halifax, possibly the very ones I was chewing on presently.

A mummified couple shuffled in, both so ridden with osteoporosis they resembled two question marks entering the room, their posture quite literally an old British stammer. "What, what?"

Then a lady entered who made the deceased couple look comparatively young. Passing my table, she said, "Good evening," in a lovely formal manner I quite liked, as I was unshaven, smelling of old sweat, in a tee-shirt and stained pants. She sat down with an elderly couple I presumed were her great-grandchildren. They were seated and then apparently abandoned.

"I thought they offered us a *drink*," the lady tsked. More time passed. "They *said* we would start with a drink," she repeated. It appeared to be a special occasion. Perhaps her great-grandkids were retiring. She carried on complaining. "Awful, just awful," she said.

Finally, a server arrived. "Yuh' rye?" he said.

"Yes, thank you; lovely," she replied.

I grinned. *The very best of Britain.*

On the walk back, live jazz drifted across the small bay – a man played guitar, chording everywhere on the fretboard while a woman soloed on a big upright bass. I wanted to snap my fingers like an approving beatnik. The bassist went on a bit long, but it was good music, played well. Then again, in soft mauve sunset shimmering on topaz water, everything seemed magical.

The next morning, Peter, the proprietor, leaned over my wobbly wooden table.

"Yuh' wo' meeook in yuh' co-ffee, squire?" he asked.

"No, thanks," I said. "So how are you today?"

"Unfor'chin-attly, I wuz on 'ee uh-vah side the baa las' nigh' so I don' fee-oo too good tud'eye," he said, managing a weak smile.

I made a sound of sympathy and tucked into my food. He looked at my plate of eggs, shuddered, and went back behind the bar, from where he seemed to run everything: checking guests into the upstairs rooms, serving food, pulling pints, greeting suppliers and making everyone feel welcome. He poured beer for two guys on their way to work, starting their day at the bar, making me want to apply for a job in this part of the world.

I ferried back to Falmouth to explore and buy some supplies. It was a short, direct route across the wide river mouth, but we veered sharply out to sea. The skipper came on a tinny PA: "We're going out of our way a bit. We've seen a seal ("see-oo") and we'll take you to see it; shouldn't add too much time to our trip."

A couple of big Atlantic greys lolled on some rocks jutting from the sea.

"Ooohhhhh!" the passengers said collectively, and rushed to the front of the boat.

"Loo'ah'tha' see-oo!"

"Loo'ah'i' – iss no' bovvered."

"Yeah. We like you to see-al you can," the captain said to chuckles and groans.

A tiny boy climbed the railing to look down at a black lab.

"Goggie. Big," he said, teetering atop the gunwale like a miniature Cirque performer.

"OLLY!!!" his mom hollered.

The boy hung for a moment before clambering down.

A small cruise ship – *The World* – was moored at Falmouth Harbour. Each cabin was kitted out as a full-service apartment for long-term travellers. The vessel was currently circumnavigating the globe.

"Tha's *The Worl'* I fink, yah, *The Worl*," Olly's granddad said.

"Yes, dear. Hold onto that child."

"We saw tha' in Monaco din' we? Yah. Yah, tha's *The Worl*."

"We saw tha' in New Zealand, in Milford Sound. Iss no' as big as the *Queen Mary*."

"Iss no' as big as the one in Italy."

"Yah, we saw a bigger one."

This carried on, long after writing it down had become about as interesting as hearing (or reading) it.

The dinner special at the pub was moules and chips. I liked that. Not *moules et frites*. Not mussels and chips. But moules and chips. A young family of four were winding down their day and going to eat at the pub. Mom and a little boy were at their car across the street packing up, while Dad and a small girl had gone into the pub to get a table and order dinner.

Dad popped his head out the front door of the pub and shouted across the street to Mom, "Aw'righ'?! I gaw'ya' a mule, aw'righ'?!"

"A wha'?!"

"A mule! Wi' chips!"

"Kye!"

I'd been reading *Game of Thrones*; characters were eating a lot of horsemeat, and that's all I could think of with respect to the mule and chips. In Reykjavík I'd indulge in that same heathen practice, enjoying medium-rare equine from a deli. Whether or not it was a mule, I can't be certain.

This time I'd ordered scampi and chips. And as I popped the last one in my mouth I realized I'd, in fact, eaten a full order of scallops. I wondered if someone else was making the same realization as they finished my scampi.

I took my beer outside and sat at a little round table tilted on sloping asphalt – the edge of the narrow main street. The peninsula across the bay – a mound of bushy trees – turned soft, watery blue-green, the evening light reflecting colours like a Renoir. The temperature, like the sun, eased downward.

I was joined by Robert and Linda, locals from St Just in Roseland. They pulled chairs to my small, leaning table. They'd spent the day fishing and had a sea bass and a mackerel to take home for dinner. Robert went to the boot of his car and brought back the fish to show me. The bass was ugly, the mackerel beautiful, gleaming like a sil-ver-striped tiger.

They'd sold their home in Milton Keynes and bought in Cornwall. Winged it, they said. Found jobs and made it work. I told them how Deb and I enjoyed real estate shows where people moved abroad, say-ing what courage it took to do what they did.

"Yeah, well," Linda said. "I wouldn't let myself think about it. Too scary. I'd talk myself out of it."

"We were real estate shopping and we'd borrowed a friend's van to sleep in," Robert explained. "A little one like that there." He pointed across the street at a compact car. "And that night I was scared, thinking, 'What've we done?' That was 21 years ago, now," he said, and they laughed.

"I got a job at a department store," she said.

"And I started my own business," he added.

Together we sipped our drinks and watched a gig glide past, high in the water. Six monsters were pulling six long oars while a coxswain sat astern, screaming at them like a Michael Palin drill-sergeant char-acter. Linda and Robert finished their small drinks, took their fish and made for home across the peninsula, waving as they went. I waved back, deciding they had it well figured out.

Next day I ventured out to explore the Roseland Peninsula, taking a ferry from St Mawes to Place, and hiked to St Anthony Head. The trail was a blend of thick forest and slopes of grazing cows, exposed to the sea. Wood pigeons broke through leaves, blackbirds strutted along the ground and yellow birds I didn't recognize sang beautiful, com-plex, jazzy songs reminding me of Charlie "Bird" Parker.

The trail passed through a cemetery, calm and still. A large Celtic cross centred the plot. Faded headstone slabs leaned askew and two mossy medieval caskets lay open in the bush like ancient stone bath-tubs. There was a small church of stone and wood with a high bell tower and narrow, stained glass windows. I twisted a big iron ring and pushed the heavy wooden door in with a grating creak. The little building was empty, the dimly lit interior cross-shaped. Statues stood around the small room; carvings of people not from the Bible but local women and men who'd passed away over the previous 200 years. The space smelled of old dust. Flies crawled thick and silent inside the windows like in *The Exorcist*. Outside a dog let out a moaning yowl. With a shiver I left somewhat quickly.

Back on the trail I tiptoed around cow pies past a bull the size of the ferry that had brought me here. A steep slope looked west to the castles. On the headland I passed an elderly couple, sitting, enjoying the view with a pug-faced dog that smiled with a gap-toothed grin. I offered them some local Hereford strawberries I'd purchased nearby, and it was as though I'd offered them a house.

"Ooh, how lovely."

"Quite nice; yes, yes."

"But no, I couldn't really."

"Oh, no, no."

"But lovely."

"Quite, yes."

"Well, maybe just one. Ooh, lovely."

"Yes, alright, quite nice, lovely, thank you."

"Yes, quite."

This continued for some time, all for two strawberries. *Again*, I thought, *the very best of Britain*.

I made my way to the low-tide ferry pier – a slab of tilting concrete crusted in whelks and cockles. Ferries ran every half-hour, give or take a half-hour. With my pack as a pillow, I dozed in the sun, waiting for the little boat back to St Mawes, while grey mullet thrashed and splashed in the shallows.

When I was picked up, we went out of our way to shuttle a couple to their mid-sized cruiser, anchored in the bay. They were sailing to France on their own, they explained, and were clearly scared, never having done it before.

"But we've got the charts," he said, nodding.

"And read all the books," she added, giggling nervously.

The ferry pilot shot me a glance, raising his eyebrows.

"Good luck," I said to them as we motored away.

They waved, tittering, and the ferry pilot shook his head.

Back in St Mawes, the Hotel Tresanton was playing a short film shot locally. It was being shown in a small multipurpose room. I joined a half-dozen other people for a matinee screening. It was a lovely, miserable film of an old man taking to the water in a sailboat, where I was about to do the same, but the film ended with his suicide at sea. There was no dialogue, and halfway through what I thought was a silent movie the person running the projector got the audio working, so we had sound for the second half of the film, which was nicely scored. It would've been funny, but the movie was on a loop and had been playing all day, with the same projectionist.

From Samuel Taylor Coleridge's *Rime of the Ancient Mariner*:

"Stay here and listen to the nightmares of the sea."

Our crew had agreed to meet at Falmouth's Chain Locker Pub. I didn't know where that was, but passing a store I browsed a swivel rack of postcards. One of the cards was a wide-angle photo of storefronts facing the harbour. I was able to make out the tiny sign of the Chain Locker Pub in the picture, and felt I'd discovered treasure, the postcard my map. (After the 500-dollar scare, I was afraid to use my cellphone – the first smartphone I'd had.)

The Chain Locker was a dark little pub with picnic tables out front. Nearly everyone sat outside in the sun. I wandered inside and was poured a Cornish Tribute – a local bitter. "Hallelujah" played on the sound system; a particularly slow, lamenting version by someone I didn't recognize.

I scanned the room, trying to figure out if anyone was the skipper or shipmates I was supposed to meet, and imagined myself nudging some eye-patched, peg leg at the bar.

"I be lookin' for Cap'n Paul," I'd say in a low voice.

"Who be askin'?" he'd say without turning his head.

"I be askin'." I'd slide the rummy a piece of silver, which he'd bite with his one good tooth, before tilting his head to a shadowy figure in the corner.

Yes, my mind had been wandering.

The group met outside. There were seven of us, plus Paul, the captain. We exchanged introductions, had a drink, made our way to the boat and pushed off, after a half-minute of orientation.

"Mainsail, staysail, topsail, jib, halyards, port and starboard," Captain Paul said, walking briskly around deck and stabbing a finger at sails and rigging. "Life jackets on. I'm going below deck to start dinner." And he was gone, leaving me to steer the 18-metre cutter out of Falmouth Harbour, picking our way between freighters, around the headland and out to sea.

Our dinner consisted of boiled cabbage and ham. At first I'd thought something had gone horribly wrong in the head (toilet), as the whole boat took on the smell of my Amtrak coach. And when the captain dished up supper, I half expected him to bang weevils from hardtack and slop out burgoo.

The ship was handsome, rugged and weather-worn. It was about 50 years old, built to the same standards as the pilot cutters that sailed 150 years ago. When the Bristol Channel was one of the world's busiest waterways, cutters would race out to pilot cargo ships in through the treacherous waters. Cutters are sturdy but built for speed; the fastest ships got the most work. It was a lucrative trade for skilled navigators, and cutter pilots lived well. The ships were comfortable, well appointed, often finished in teak and mahogany, and could be sailed, if need be, by one or two experienced sailors.

Sun set as we passed Lizard Peninsula, England's most southerly point, where the smell of sheep hung heavy in the wind. Somewhere beneath us, basking sharks were feeding. We caught our first glimpse of Land's End while a sickle moon rose in a coral-pink sky. Thirty nautical miles beyond that, somewhere in the North Atlantic, lay the Isles of Scilly, our destination.

The boat bobbed through growing swells, mainsail and staysail bent full in the wind. A northeasterly blew at 17 knots and strong currents shifted the big cutter around as though we were riding wet ice.

"Hook up your lifelines!" the captain hollered. "And haul in the staysail halyards!"

He may have said, "Haul on the staysail halyards," but I was focusing on connecting my stay-jack lifeline and not being thrown into the sea as the boat's pitching intensified. (The cutter had no railings, just a small wooden lip around the edge of the deck, ideal for tripping.) The skipper shouted again and I heaved on a halyard, which seemed to quiet him.

Three of us were sent below deck to sleep for three hours, impossible in the heaving ocean. I rolled about on a narrow upper berth, secured with a band of sailcloth, knees and elbows wedged into corners to keep me from falling. The bunk was adjacent to the galley and a small mesh hammock of produce banged around my feet – cauliflower, iceberg lettuce and tomatoes that gradually turned to paste.

We were called up at 1:30 a.m. and bumped our way on deck, where we hooked to lifelines once more and were buffeted around in a gale force five. The stars had disappeared behind thick, dark cloud. I puked over the side and then took the wheel, steering into a vast black void.

Lurching through the night, we crossed the Celtic Sea, bobbing and weaving like a weary boxer. The only lights were pinpricks of red hovering in the distance – lights on faraway freighters – with a soft pinkish glow of instruments at the helm and an effervescent trail of phytoplankton, twinkling like stars in our wake.

The bow rose and fell – two-metre undulations shifting the blackness. I worked the big wooden ship's wheel against wind and current pulling us, rising and falling, into the black. The wheel twisted hard and a spoke snapped my watchband, breaking it off my wrist. I overcorrected, the mainsail slackened and we lost the wind, the force five and the current turning the boat like a 40-ton cork. The only sounds were the flap of a limp mainsail, the *whhshhhh* of rolling breakers and agonized retching from Kevin, a fellow crew member clutching the stern.

"Make sure you're clipped on," Captain Paul's voice cut through the dark. He held a cup of tea that he sipped at an angle with each 30-degree pitch of the boat.

"Uunnngh," was Kevin's reply, as though Frankenstein had just awoken. Then he noticed the glimmering krill in our wake. "Uunnngh...something's shining in the water...uunnngh," he moaned.

"That'd be the contents of your stomach, Kevin," Captain Paul replied, and sipped his tea.

I heaved the wheel to starboard, slowly correcting our course, and the mainsail snapped to, bent full with the gale.

"Find a spot and stay true. You can't rely on that compass," Captain Paul said and hunkered down out of the wind.

"It's all black!" I said in a voice that struck me as squeaky.

"Use your intuition," he said calmly.

As the boat pitched, my intuition was to grab the anchor and hurl myself into the sea like the guy in the half-silent movie, or seize a halyard and throttle the skipper. But I fought the urge, as my intuition also told me I couldn't possibly overpower the captain. Mutiny was out of the question; there was no indication the old ox ever slept.

As the boat lurched back on course with a shudder, I realized a grisly death at sea probably wasn't imminent after all, but the mental snapshots of my life that flashed like poorly spliced film were mildly interesting and left me feeling I should've spent more time at the office. I took a deep breath, spat some residual vomit and muscled the heaving boat into the dark.

An endless night finally wound down. Sun rose behind us – a ball of gold easing from the sea as we approached Saint Mary's. Treacherous rocks awaited us. We furled the jib and staysail and fired the engine, which promptly died and refused to restart. A sharp northerly pushed us away from our destination. Fighting a strong current and using only the mainsail, we changed course and gybed slowly toward St. Agnes and Gugh, nestling the boat between the two islands that join at low tide.

Peter, another passenger, recapped the turbulent night: "They say there are two stages of seasickness: first, fearing you might die, and second, as it worsens, fearing you might, in fact, live."

We slept for a couple of hours, ate and went off on our own to explore St. Agnes and Gugh (rhymes with Hugh). Floral smells hung in the air, interspersed with sea. Herring gulls – black-backs and greys – cried and chortled in the air, oystercatchers peeped along the shore, a gannet smashed into surf and a puffin took flight with rapid, duck-like flapping.

Wildflowers in orange, yellow, purple and red clung to windswept rock. I hiked through massive sandstone blocks cut by weather like cornerstones, standing in fields of scrubby grass, gorse and heather. It looked like alpine terrain, but we were in the Gulf Stream and the occasional palm tree seemed out of place. I stepped around a couple of cows and tents pitched on a headland and gazed at the distant column of Bishop Rock Lighthouse towering from a craggy rock on the horizon, the most westerly point of the British Isles. A fellow passenger had said somewhat dreamily, "Beyond that, it's America."

Seals basked and dove in deep green water as we sailed amongst the Western Rocks in strong wind and bright sun. While I gazed into the water, an enormous sunfish rolled to the surface, the look of a sea monster. I fished for mackerel with a hand line and spinner – simple, fun and unproductive. I hauled up a green clump of sea asparagus and munched away contentedly, imagining I was keeping scurvy at bay.

Captain Paul, awake for two straight days, spent the next night drinking. Retired from the Royal Navy, he was tough as nails, a stern man of few words. Weathered and grizzled, he kept a thick wool beanie perched on his head. If you envision a salty old skipper, the mental picture you paint is Captain Paul. It felt safe on his boat.

He had an exceptional and eclectic music library and selected increasingly abstract tracks as he got progressively drunker. After play-ing the entire first side of the *War of the Worlds* soundtrack – industrial instrumentals with spooky voice-overs – we convinced him to change the music. He refilled a stoneware mug with rum and slumped down, let out an *arrghhh*, and slur-sang along with Aretha Franklin's "(You Make Me Feel Like) A Natural Woman."

Privacy was non-existent in the tight space. We put out lights for the night, and Peter got butterfingers. The quieter he tried to be, the more noise he made. A retired British schoolteacher, he was very proper, and very English. In the darkness, he fumbled for his torch, which rolled to the floor with a *clunk*!

"Shit. Sorry."

More metallic rolling, then *thud*!

"Aw, shit. Sorry."

Peals of laughter filled the dark.

"Sorry."

My giggles continued as Peter made his way to the WC, thumping about in the tiny space with an alarming amount of noise. Without thinking, a limerick materialized in my head:

A fellow passenger went to the loo
I deduced he'd gone for a poo
By the time he was done
He'd been too long for one
So it logically had to be two

We woke to an overcast morning at anchor. Captain Paul was snor-ing like a band saw, while outside, a cuckoo called like a disregarded alarm clock. I stood on deck, drinking tea, and watched birds bath-ing, fishing and combing the shore. It was like thumbing through an Audubon guide: in addition to the cuckoo, there were guillemots, terns, kittiwakes, fulmars, gannets, cormorants, shags, herring gulls, shear-waters and oystercatchers. The *Hinterland Who's Who* tune played in my head, memories of CBC programming.

After a breakfast of sausage, beans and stewed tomatoes, the skipper rolled from his berth and we prepared to move on to another island.

"Weigh anchor!" he shouted in a voice resembling his snores.

"About 50 pounds," I said, regretting it immediately, the skipper's expression affirming my poor choice.

After a few hours at sail, we landed at the island of Tresco, where I wandered through the tranquil Abbey Gardens – a tropical garden and forest – towering palms and tinkling fountains around the ruins of a 12th-century abbey. Birds swooped and sang. There were partridges, pheasants, wood pigeons and a golden pheasant strutting about like a peacock.

The Valhalla figurehead collection (another Viking touchstone) was situated in the garden, an open-air museum of ship's prows and figureheads from dozens of ships that had sunk on the rocks around the isles over hundreds of years. A massive stone plinth stood offshore, erected by locals years earlier, a tribute to the patron saint of shipwrecks. It was only after doing research that I realized it paid homage to the notional saint who *caused* shipwrecks, providing much needed supplies to the islanders.

I stopped to rest and flopped down, dropping heavily on some gravel. When I got up, there was a mouse under my ass, flattened like a tiny bearskin rug. I assumed it was like that before I sat there but wasn't certain.

Back onboard, I scribbled notes in my journal and systematically worked my way through a *Lonely Planet* book. Space was at a premium, so as I finished each section of guidebook I tore out the pages to recycle and free up precious room in my pack. My shipmates were confused by the Canadian shredding his books.

"You're writing a book?" another crew mate asked.

"I am."

"I tell you what," he said. "I'd like to buy one, and in your honour, I'll tear out the pages as I read it."

We listened to shortwave radio for the weather advisory and storm reports. We'd tuned to Radio Scilly in time for the news and in the slowest, lulling monotone imaginable, the day's top stories were read:

Todaaay's...headlines...on...Rrrradio...Scilly......Lynn...has lost...a...bluuue...jumper......If...anyone...has seen...Lynn's... bluuue...jumper...please call...55...24......1.........8. That's the newwws...on...Rrrradio...Scilly.

After tendering to shore, I went to the Tresco pub for a carafe of coffee and sat at a window looking over New Grimsby Harbour and the isle of Bryher. After a few days on the boat, everything swayed when I sat. Walking was the only relief. Sun gradually broke through the cloud. I finished the coffee and went exploring.

A trail ran around the island, following desolate beach where pheasants nested in sand. A large green egg sat on the trail. I wondered if it belonged to a pheasant and, naturally, wanted it with ham. I climbed a steep, narrow side trail into thick, shoulder-high greenery – juniper and rhododendron, and came across a rough little fort built in a gnarly pine on a bluff. Fishnet had been strung about like fencing. A rope swing with a plank seat hung from a thick branch. Sun sparkled on the bay, turning the water from green to gold. A white lighthouse stood on a distant headland, and below me in the bay a seal popped its head up and stared, making me feel like the boy in *Waking Ned Devine*. I swung on the swing and stared back at the seal, the two of us the only living souls around.

I crossed the small island and climbed to the ruins of King Charles's Castle, which crests the highest peak on Tresco and looks down disapprovingly to Cromwell's Castle on the rocky shore. The cry of gulls and throaty chortle of pheasants drifted over windswept grass and rock, creating a desolate musical score. To the northeast, water crashed into Hell Bay, sending plumes of foam high up the cliffs of Bryher. Scrambling over low, crumbling walls, I peered through a small, square cannon hole, across the water to Man o' War – a ragged rock where puffins live – and beyond that to nothing but curving blue.

We sailed on to St. Martin's, another sparsely populated isle. Our group dispersed, scattering around the island to enjoy some exploration, dry land and privacy. Beachcombing on a wide sandy beach, I found a fist-sized piece of cuttlefish bone, then climbed a high pile of boulders, squinting to see Land's End, barely visible on the horizon.

As I walked to the village among low, unmortared stone walls, a tractor rolled past, the only motorized vehicle I'd seen. I happened upon Peter standing in grassy dunes on a Caribbean-looking beach. He was watching a group of young rowers launch a huge wooden gig. I stretched up to see better and he grabbed my arm.

"If they see you, they may expect us to help," he said.

I nodded and shrank down beside him. The boat looked like something a hundred Egyptian slaves would haul to lever pyramid stones.

"They look young and fit; they should be fine," I said.

He nodded, and we backed away through tall grass.

We met up with Captain Paul near the jetty where he'd dropped us.

"We have to go," he said. "Leave the islands. There's a force eight coming at us. We'll do our best to outrun it; head for the mainland."

A force-eight gale was meaningless to me.

"What's the scale?" I asked Mark, a recreational boater.

"It goes to nine," he said, raising his eyebrows. "After that, they give it a name. Like Hurricane Andrew."

We loaded up and set sail. A northwesterly pushed us along the front of the massive storm. Severe wind grew throughout the day. The gale gained on us as we passed Land's End. Steep waves broke across the bow, washing the front half of our ship with frothy sea. We clipped on lifelines and took turns working rigging.

Something high on the mast creaked alarmingly, then snapped with a sickening crack, and the topsail dropped, limp and useless – a lethargic white flag, as though we'd surrendered. The storm was gaining, winning a race I no longer wanted to be in. We hauled in the useless topsail, letting the bulging mainsail and jib yank us forward, climbing breakers and rushing down increasing swells.

"Stay back, and stay clipped on!" Captain Paul hollered from the helm.

I hunkered down on the starboard side, wedged between some sacks and Kevin, whose eyes were wide, and we let wind, sail and the captain do what they could to speed us around Lizard Peninsula toward the relative shelter of Helford River.

Despite the heaving carnival ride and intense wind, the sun shone, bright and warm. My energy was draining from an exhausting ten hours of sailing and I simply sat, listening to the grinding groan of stretching ropes and watched growing waves heave past. I closed my eyes, soaking up hot sun, until I heard Kevin's voice. "Je-*sus*!" he hissed.

I opened my eyes and saw nothing but water – a wall of it, rising three metres above our heads. I stared open-mouthed as the watery wall eased along the side of the boat, then slid beneath the hull, raising us up and sending us racing forward down the slope of the wave. This carried on for another two hours, becoming remarkably methodical and mesmerizing.

Rounding the Lizard, we veered north toward Helford, a sailors' safe haven for hundreds of years. We dropped all our canvas and fired the engine, which Captain Paul had jerry-rigged on Tresco, but were still blown around as though our lead-ballast boat were a toy on a pond. The storm whipped in behind us and we struggled to moor at a submerged buoy a short ways from shore, the only available moorage. All we could do in the rough water was lash two lengths of rope to the buoy in a series of ugly knots and hope it would hold. The worst of the weather raged in our wake, the open water we'd just left behind.

After a day of hard sailing to outrun the storm, all we wanted was land underfoot and hot food. We bumped our way to shore in the inflatable dinghy. I was clutching a rope that ran round the outside of the little boat, and as we bounced over a wave my middle finger dipped into water so frigid I was struck with an excruciating ice-cream headache. I expected the digit to simply drop off, frozen, and float out to sea, flipping off passing boaters.

We tied to the jetty, getting reacquainted with dry land on wobbly legs. Fat grey fish darted beneath the pier.

"Those fish are shy," Kevin said, peering into the water.

"You mean *koi*," I replied, indescribably pleased with myself. (Needless to say, it's a joke to be spoken, not written, but here we are.)

We climbed a steep hill to the Helford sailing club, which was the local pub and restaurant. We took advantage of coin-operated showers, scraping off salt, sweat and sunscreen, before pints of beer and fish and chips, which we ate at a long communal table.

I went to the bar to fetch the next round. "Another tall whisky, Captain Paul?"

"Yeah, go on, then."

Morning broke undecided. Helford River's little church advertised Sunday service, cream teas and Wi-Fi, which I found progressive, and made my way there along a tree-shrouded section of the Coast Path through honeysuckle, foxgloves and wild strawberries. A squirrel loped ahead of me on the trail and a myriad of side trails branched out like spiderweb. I detoured past Frenchman's Creek, where Daphne du Maurier set her novel of the same name. She wrote, "Still and sound-less, surrounded by the trees, hidden from the eyes of men," and I felt I'd wandered into the pages of her writing.

Helford's main road was tidal, crossing a tributary of the river. A narrow truck careened past, splashing through the creek. I crossed a little footbridge, climbed a hill and entered the small church, which had arching wood beams and simple leaded glass. It was dark but airy; door and windows ajar. I was served coffee and the woman working there turned on the Wi-Fi.

Another woman came in and ordered at the cash register.

"Um, a sarnie."

"Brill."

"Guess who I sore las' ni'?"

"Say wuh'?"

"Guess who I sore las' ni'?"

"'oo?"

"Jor-leen."

"Say wuh'?"

"Jor-leen."

"'oo?"

"Jor-leen."

"Ya, know the noim, jus' no' the pursun."

"Ya, 'ad a dring wiff 'er, we did."

"Oh, tha's noice."

Our last night aboard *Abigail* we were moored in Falmouth Harbour, and our little group seemed determined to finish all the booze in existence. Early next morning, I staggered to the train to make my way to meet up with Deb and start the next leg of our journey, together. Piecing together foggy mental snapshots from the previous night, I remembered Captain Paul finishing a pitcher of gin, then dancing the hornpipe, and I believe I led the group in a song with a great deal of profanity.

Time passed, enough to allow me once more to wax poetic, doing my best to grasp that time asea, chipping away at the stone of our saga. A version of these verses is in *Forever Cast in Endless Time*:

FORCE EIGHT, *ABIGAIL*, AND CAPTAIN PAUL, OUR AHAB

Aboard a pilot cutter, *Abigail*
fifty-four feet of wind-powered teak
reinforced steel
struts, strakes and keel
race ahead of force eight

gale on our tail
heave up, heave over
twelve-foot swells, that break
in icy froth of spindrift
strafing face
in saline sting of airborne surf
buckshot cut on skin
whipped water – black and blue to white
beaten, tethered, lifeline, cleats
deck-tacked, sufficient play
to make my way, midship to stern
our huddled hands hang on
waves thrash
submerge by half, our ship diminished
merciless Atlantic, Celtic Sea
dilutes the fear, leaves me bereft
the feelings that ensue
post grief and trauma

penetrating calm

leaves one accepting
grounded, finally rounding home
olly-olly-oxen, free! we all
come out from hiding
real selves emerge, after the storm
as newborn nautili
shell-less, drifting on a tide

above, beyond, hang herring gulls
fixed-wing as kites
while gannets plummet, suicidal
gold tipped meteors
smashing in the sea

now, Captain Paul was always
testy, crusty, so it seemed, disliking us
for reasons we won't know
then realized we weren't a threat
in fact respected him
to which he followed suit, one night

the sound of seven thirsty sailors
sopping up each bit of booze
a song by Great Big Sea
our drunken crew joined in the chorus
captain quaffed a vase of gin
danced hornpipes as we clapped and laughed
respectfully
a modern eighteenth century crew
but scurvy-free

later, liquor lingering
as lazy as a tapeworm
another stretch of silent shore
sea-wobbled legs find focus
like a roll of Polaroid film
blurred memories emerge, in chevron wake
storm-riled ocean, chased by rage, the gale
gripping mane-like crests we rode
each plunge of bowsprit a harpoon
spear plankton-sparkled waves
through endless, endless night
relentless steersman at the helm
our Ahab, Captain Paul

Ashore for the foreseeable future, I finished eating hake and chips
from a Rick Stein's takeaway and jumped a train from Falmouth to St
Erth with a transfer to St Ives, skirting Mediterranean-looking beaches.

Onboard there was a one-eyed dog named Wink. At least that's what I named him in my head. He was lying down and when he got up I saw a handle on his back, giving him the look of a one-eyed Seeing Eye dog, or a single-Seeing Eye dog, I suppose you could say. Wink pressed against his owner and rolled onto his side. His owner reached down, giving him an affectionate chest thumping that sounded like a bass drum – *toom-toom*.

I got off the train at St Ives – the end of the branch line – a scenic fishing village and artists' Mecca, surrounded by golden sand beaches. This stretch of English seaside is known as the Cornish Riviera, catching the warmth of the Gulf Stream. I stumbled from the station, my legs still reacquainting with land, and walked to Carbis Bay to meet Deb, where I checked into a room facing the water.

Godrevy Lighthouse stood on the headland to the northeast while breakers crashed at its base. Gulls mewled and cried, floating on air. Stubby, wind-blown palms framed my view of the bluff, and fishing boats in yellow, blue and white bobbed at anchor in the lee of the bay. Pigeons on the roof cooed, blackbirds and sparrows chirped from trees and a train rolled past with a shuddering *ka-chunk, ka-chunk, ka-chunk*.

I made my way to the lounge where George, the innkeeper, puttered behind a small bar overlooking the water.

"Evening, George."

"Evening, Bill."

It was our first night there and I liked that very much. Unfamiliar space in a foreign place and I felt entirely at home.

A few more days of exploring and hiking ensued, interspersed with fish and chips – pollock and cod, served with mushy peas. We trained to Penzance and walked the four miles to Marazion, where we checked into a room smelling of 50 years of saturated cigarette smoke. There was a large wooden deck – a refuge of fresher air, where we enjoyed a supper of antipasto and watched ebbing tide reveal the cobbled stone path crossing the bay to St Michael's Mount. A family played cricket on wet sand while gulls stood on shore, calling like fans at a stadium.

The game wrapped up, the family went in, sun dipped and gulls disappeared. Everything was still and quiet.

We left the door to the deck open. Ocean breeze and rain blew in. It was early summer and sky stayed light late into the evening. Girls ran onto darkening beach to play and all we heard was "Finn-Finn-Finn!" followed by peals of laughter.

Next morning vicious weather blew in. We breakfasted on instant coffee and biscuits, bundled up in waterproofs and technical gear, slung on double packs and set out along the beach, heading west. St Michael's Mount disappeared in fog. Tide was low and the stone path was empty, curving out into a cloud of grey. Wind howled off the water, driving pellet-like rain that saturated clothing. Within minutes my feet were squelching in socks like soaked sponges in my "waterproof" boots. Each squishy step sounded like a disapproving *tsk*, *tsk*, *tsk* to the manufacturer. The wind buffeted, pushing us off balance, front- and backpacks acting as sails, turning us as we walked. The temperature dropped and rain stung exposed skin like hail. It felt like being stoned (*not* the good kind). Bent forward, we struggled on in the frigid, nasty weather. Soaked and near freezing, I began to worry about hypothermia. We sloshed our way to a seaside hotel and called a cab to haul us the last few miles to our destination of Lamorna Cove.

Our apartment had a crooked little hallway connecting rooms like an afterthought. It messed with my equilibrium and made me feel I was back aboard the *Abigail*. Getting from the living room to the kitchen was like walking through a Miró, Picasso or Dalí – surreal, cubist and abstract. I kept expecting the kitchen clock to melt off the wall. I tucked into a window bench and watched leaden waves crash into the bay. A squat little stone house was nestled at the base of a quarry that looked like a scab on the cliff. Smoke from a peaty fire wafted in the air – earthy and comforting.

Weather changed in true maritime fashion and next day we ventured out around a steep rocky headland, following the South West Coast Path, literally south and west from our lodging. Across Mount's

Bay was Lizard Peninsula, where a speck of lighthouse blinked through morning haze like a star. A gangly heron flapped past. We crossed a farm where a hawk swooped over huge boulders of sea-smoothed granite. Passing Tater Du Lighthouse, we cut overland to an ancient burial mound and the Merry Maidens, a Bronze Age stone circle.

From the trail we heard scuffling in hedges and undergrowth – ground birds, mice, voles, and Cornish Oompa Loompas, I suspect. We walked farther down the road and leaned over a fence to view the Pipers stones, erected around the same time as the Merry Maidens, likely by Druids for reasons long since forgotten.

We carried on to the Lamorna Wink pub, something I'd wanted to do since reading the Martha Grimes novel set there. The "Wink" indicated it was smuggler-friendly, providing a discreet haven for contraband exchange. It had been in business for 250 years. I stepped inside. Heads turned like sleepy cows watching a car pass. The aroma made our stale hotel room seem springtime fresh. The Wink was a tiny ancient pub filled with tiny ancient people and the dank, musty smell of two and a half centuries of spilled beer and cigarettes. I scanned the room, checked something off an imagined list and then left for a pint at a lounge up the road.

Sipping Cornish ale, I watched waves thrash the promontory. Plumes of spray leapt up the shore like white-clad flamenco dancers spinning from the sea. *Scillonian*, a ferry serving the Isles of Scilly, slid past the mouth of the cove, where water changed from turquoise to purply-blue. The TV was on, and from across the room I heard an announcer bark, "*Embarrassing Fat Bodies* at nine, on BBC Four." Chuckling, I changed channels to where a young woman was being interviewed. It had the look and feel of a sombre documentary.

A soft voice off camera asked, "And what do you like to do for fun?"

Her brow furrowed and she replied slowly, thoughtfully. "Hmm... dancin'...partyin'...takin' me boobs out."

Weather turned again, changing like double jumps across our maritime checkerboard, determining the season. *Clack-clack*. Winter.

Clack-clack. Summer. The swings were extreme. Two days after our near hypothermia, we were heading out to hike in shorts, tee-shirts and extra sunscreen.

From Lamorna Cove we headed east to Mousehole, following cliff-tops 30 metres above the sea, where it crashed onto ragged granite. We climbed through Monterey pines, cypress, vine-wrapped maples and wind-blown gorse under high canopies of ferns. Fat black bumblebees buzzed in fuchsia foxgloves and orange butterflies fluttered over the trail. In the distance we spied St Michael's Mount, a sharp image in clean air and bright sun. The trail meandered toward the water and we strolled into Mousehole – a pristine fishing village; an inn and pub at the quay, whitewashed stone cottages and Cornish flags flying proudly – a white X on a black background. Two artists painted at easels on the beach. Tide was out and a fleet of brightly painted boats – skiffs and dories – stood leaning, beached in the sandy harbour.

We explored tiny shops on winding, cobbled streets and ate fried cod, with a glittering sea under brilliant sun. We left the county early, training from Penzance to London. The sea shimmered in morning light. Scruffy clouds spat some rain, precipitation almost uncertain.

For six hours we rolled through emerald pastures and vibrant green hedges. Crows hopped in fields amongst cows, sheep and rabbits, while squat stone cottages stood like blocks anchoring the landscape.

Deb and I parted quickly at Paddington in a futile attempt to mini-mize sadness. She was due back at work and I was staying to attend a party in Belgium. Simply writing that I find myself disliking me. I suppose I could've just said attending a party. But then you might've mistaken it for an *enjoyable* affair.

She boarded the Heathrow Express and I stood on the platform, lumpy duffle at my feet, and waved as she boarded, feeling somewhat sorry for myself. After shuffling about aimlessly, I decided moving on would be better, despite lacking a destination. I took the tube to Tottenham Court and walked through a tunnel that seemed to go for-ever without passing a soul. The city bustled high above, but the only thing I heard was a raspy tenor sax echoing through the tunnel from somewhere in the distance.

Above ground, music flowing through earbuds kept me company. I clocked up miles, crossing the city and drifting in and out of a mental soundtrack. I weaved my way through crowds on Oxford Street, along the glitzy curve of Regent Street and down Charing Cross Road, browsing pubs until finding one that was inviting. It was called the Pillars of Hercules. In Theroux's book of the same name, near the end, he explains he very much wanted to use the word "Herculean" but was unable. I tried too, unsuccessfully. Perhaps the task is too great.

I pulled a stool to a narrow counter across from the bar, under a black and white photo of the lumpy peaks that frame the Strait of Gibraltar, where Ragnar Lothbrok's boys sailed into the Mediterranean. I sipped a Wainwright and ordered a steak and ale pie, served by the Lucky Charms leprechaun disguised as a barmaid. She brought me food and insisted I enjoy free tasters of the ales on tap. This, combined with her calling me "dear," made me want to call Deb and beg, "*Please, can we keep her?!*" Going through customs, however, may have been a challenge.

"Anything to declare?"

"A wee, middle-aged barmaid with a superb accent. Go on, ask her anything!"

I thought better of it and left the leprechaun there, with thanks and a tip.

I went to the British Museum – overwhelming in its scope. I knew it housed the Rosetta Stone, considered one of the world's most significant finds pertaining to the study of Egyptology. However, I had no idea what it was. So I went to the information counter, not only for directions to the display but to ask what the stone was. Big posters announcing the presence of the stone featured prominently around the concourse.

"Can I help?" a woman asked from behind the counter.

"Please," I said. "I'd like to know about the Rosetta Stone."

"Oh, it's very important," she said. "Historically significant."

"Well, all right," I said. "But I must admit, I don't really know what it is."

"Right, well then," she said, and rifled through some brochures. "I know it's very important." *Shuffle, shuffle.* "Hmm. I suppose I don't know *exactly* what it is myself." Then she called over her shoulder, "David?"

"Yes, how can I help?" said a distinguished, cardigan-wearing man. David, I expect.

"Can you help us and tell this gentleman what the Rosetta Stone is, please?"

"Oh, it's very important," David said, somewhat gravely. "Most significant, historically." He punctuated this by dropping his chin and peering over his glasses, making anything he said irrefutable.

"Yes, so I've heard," I said. "But, I'm embarrassed to say, I have no idea what it actually is."

"Oh, well, yes, I see, quite," he said and stroked his chin.

The three of us looked at each other, nodding thoughtfully for some time. Finally, David sighed and spoke up, "Well, to be *perfectly* honest, I must say I'm not *entirely* sure what it is myself, but I *do* know it's very important; quite significant."

I thanked them both and found a thick museum map, hoping it would unravel the mystery. It turns out the Rosetta Stone is a slab of smooth, brown-grey granite. On it is written a decree by the king from Memphis. Not the one with the glittery jumpsuits from Tennessee, but Ptolemy V from Memphis, Egypt. The main difference between the two kings, as I understand it, aside from geography and time, was in the facial hair. While the more recent American king had meaty mutton chops, the earlier Egyptian king sported the then-popular shoe-horn beard, like Steve Martin's funky King Tut.

King Ptolemy's decree was written on the stone around 200 BCE, and the same message was written in three languages: Demotic, Greek and Egyptian hieroglyphics. The stone, therefore, provided historians and linguists with the first template to effectively translate hiero-glyphs – an ancient language dictionary of sorts. Did I mention that makes it very important and historically significant?

Out front of the museum, I saw a guy in the crowd wearing a Vancouver Canucks jersey (my hometown hockey team). It was Stanley Cup championships, the final and deciding game. The guy wore massive, Princess Leia hair-bun headphones, his head bobbing rhythmically. I smiled and raised my chin to him, the international sign for, "I intend to talk to you, so..."

He slid the butterhorns from his head, and I asked if he'd found somewhere to watch the game. To which he made the oddest geometrical shape with his hands, an inverted here-is-the-church, here-is-the-steeple.

"You know where Piccadilly Circus goes like this? And there's a museum, right? Well, around the corner and down a bit, there's a sports bar, I think," he said with uncertainty.

I furrowed my brow and nodded, the way I did with my college professor when he'd show us how to derive calculus equations. He was a kind man who tried very hard to educate me and I never had the heart to say, "No. In fact, it couldn't be *more* unclear to me." I did much the same to the guy in the Canucks jersey, bobbing my head and making an *ahh* sound, simply waiting for him to finish his confusing directions so I could go find a pub.

A short while later, having settled into said pub, I ate crisps, placed an open book in front of me, and eavesdropped on six guys seated at the next table:

"Fuck off. You know wha' I mean?"

"Iss ly', I keep 'at off, an ly' – fuck off you, righ'?"

"S'nowt on telly, yeah?"

"Fuckin' telly, yeah."

"An bowff an all – fucka!"

"Sry bubbly nah – two an' a 'aff quid?"

"Two an' a 'aff, yeah."

"'Ow can 'nat be righ'?"

"Fuckin' 'ell"

"Inna fuckin' middo."

"Yeah."

"Righ'."

"Yeah."

"Udder blokes – they pay an' all."

"Fuckers, yeah."

"Shit brains."

"A bundle a' scores."

"Ne'er 'erd 'uh 'at."

"Rye'doh!"

"Find yer way ou'."

"Streets, yeah."

"Fuck."

"Fuck."

"Fuck."

And with that, my entertainment exited the pub.

Eventually, I found the sports bar in Piccadilly Circus – an inviting, two-storey pub that remained open, serving, as long as a big game was on. Stanley Cup Game Seven aired until 4 a.m. local time. The only thing I hadn't thought through was my attire. I was wearing a yellow jacket, which made me look like an idiot. That is to say, a Boston Bruins fan. But it didn't seem to matter. The place was packed with jovial expats, most of whom were Canadian. From a scrum-like queue at the bar, a good-natured guy at the front passed me a pint over people's heads. I passed him money for the beer and he shoved it back with a "Cheers."

In a boisterous cluster of a few hundred strangers, we belted out "O Canada" like it was the most important thing possible, which it absolutely was at that moment. Despite our effort, Boston thumped Vancouver, leaving me feeling as though I'd been dumped. I hung my head, defeated Charlie Brown music playing in my mind, and walked across London back to my hotel. It was the longest day and the 4 a.m. sky was aglow, the streets still and silent. It was surreal, this city of eight million people seemingly to myself. Just me and my stupid yellow jacket.

Following a three-hour sleep, I went to Islington for breakfast at Jamie Oliver's Fifteen Restaurant. Dark cloud rolled in, unleashing a deluge, the weather reflecting my gloomy mood following the disappointing game. The restaurant fit the day – food prepared without care and served with disinterest. A pound was added to the bill – not optional – for some charity, no doubt a trust for Jamie's children. Full and fully dissatisfied, I shuffled into the rain, defeated Charlie Brown music resuming in my head.

I went to the Dominion Theatre to watch Ben Elton's *We Will Rock You* – the Queen musical. The theatre seemed filled with young and boisterous Glaswegians, an incomprehensible din. Then two middle-aged couples walked in and sat ahead of me. The man seated in front of me wore thick-framed glasses, his hair short and neatly parted – the look of a 1950s G-man.

"Sorry 'bout this," he said, turning around and smiling at me, and then said some more in English I couldn't understand as they settled into their seats. The theatre was full, but he still went through the apology routine as his seat was in front of mine. I liked him immediately, figuring I got the gist of what he was saying.

I smiled back and said, "No problem at all," which I'm sure he didn't understand either.

At midnight, following the show, I took the tube from Baker Street Station. Wisps of fog blew through the dark, swirling around the platform like a dream, and somewhere behind me a man softly whistled Gerry Rafferty's "Baker Street." I prefer not using the word "perfect," but that's precisely what it was.

I meandered around Hyde Park and read a news story I quite liked. Sting had been here recently, on his own in the park. An older couple approached him and asked if he'd be willing to take a photo. "Of course," he said and leaned toward them. They passed him their camera and backed up, standing together and smiling, waiting for him to take their picture. According to Sting, he then realized what was happening, which he rather loved as well. So he took their photo and passed back their camera. They checked the picture, thanked him, and carried on with their day.

On another occasion, back in the city with Deb, we were at our hotel, at the east end of Westminster Bridge, across from the Parliament buildings and Big Ben. Two storm troopers walked purposefully through the lobby. Not the Luger-toting kind in black à la Hitler, but the laser-toting kind in white à la Lucas. (It turned out there was a *Star Wars* convention in the adjacent conference centre.) I descended a wide flight of marble stairs leading to the riverside, where a resplendent Darth Vader stood on his own, admiring the Thames. We looked at each other. He nodded. I did the same. Apart from the Death Star thing, he struck me as perfectly pleasant.

The night was cold and wintery. Deb and I walked the South Bank, past the Tate Modern and Shakespeare's Globe Theatre, then made our way back and bought street food – lamb curry and potato-bacon-cheese goo. The vendor was closing for the evening – a French woman who pretended not to speak English. I was tempted to speak slower but then realized I may be falling into her trap. She gave us a ridiculously large portion, to clean out the tray I suspect, but we were happy to have a giant tub of warm, fatty food on a cold December night.

Back in our room we lay in bed digesting lamb curry and potato-bacon-cheese goo while listening to our neighbours have loud and seemingly quite satisfying sex. After a while, I'd given them names – Virile and Shrieker. Had I been a member of the Academy, Shrieker would've assuredly received my vote for best actor in a supporting role. It became difficult to read as our headboard vibrated rhythmically and

I found myself tapping along like a Gene Krupa drum solo. It finished more like a thumping taiko drum and I wished I'd packed my samurai headband to get into character. My tummy settled down about the same time the neighbours did – them with a yell and me with a soft fart. We finally dozed off; that is, until they started up again.

From a shiny black Moleskine with a yellow piece of Lego attached to the cover (for Lego aficionados, a flat, two bump by four, the kind to anchor a wall or the undercarriage of a Jeep), I copied this from a tourist brochure:

Bath is the largest city in the county of Somerset, named for its Roman-built baths. Bath is in the valley of the River Avon, west of London and southeast of Bristol. The city became a World Heritage Site in 1987.

Bill Bryson whispered in my ear, telling me I was enjoying one of the world's finest views. I was taking the audio tour with Bryson's spoken commentary. I stood against a stone wall, at a blackened hearth beside an open-air pool. Roman emperors and generals in stone gazed down from an overhead walkway – solemn faces reflected in calm jade water. Setting sun struck the abbey tower and flags waved in a breeze as sky shifted from orange to rose, glowing like soft embers. I stood a long time in the tranquil space, burning the image into memory – an emotional photograph, before finding my way through damp stone passageways.

As I emerged from the subterranean space into dwindling sunset, an unusual little band of buskers played in the central town square. An old guy shook a rattle, while two young guys played guitars and sang Tears for Fears – the band from Bath – a slow, heart-rending version of "Mad World." It echoed, haunting, through the square, as though summoning ghosts to harmonize.

BY LAND

I suppose it would be unfair to leave you hanging regarding the Belgium side trip. Fact is, that was one of many experienced over a few years. Like UK trips, a blend of exploring, socializing and *Gone Viking* research. One of those trips to Belgium – home to more Vikings than I'd realized – took place over Christmas, providing me the opportunity to live out a quirky but profoundly fun experience.

Growing up, one of my favourite bands was Men at Work, the Aussie band with a Glaswegian singer-songwriter. Hearing the man speak only confused me in my youth as to what an Australian accent was. Australia's AC/DC, also (more or less) displaced Brits, did nothing to help me figure it out until many years later. However. The first big arena concert I went to was Men at Work (Vancouver's Pacific Coliseum, 1983, *Cargo* tour). With a plethora of "G'day!" and "Bonzer!" in a Glaswegian accent, it made for a superb evening.

I felt I grew up (to a degree) alongside Colin Hay (said Glaswegian, who you met in the rainy tent on West Cracroft Island). He remains one of the finest songwriters and continues to impress and influence me as a writer. In his megahit "Down Under" (a song I've sung countless times in the shower, car and on stage), he refers to Brussels, the bread he bought there and the man he bought it from. On this particular trip to a Brussels suburb it was my job to do just that, go to the baker and pick up Christmas day bread (baguette, *pain au chocolat* and a cake). This allowed me to live out a simple but satisfying lifetime achievement, as to my delight I was *actually* – on Christmas Day, no less – buying bread from a man in Brussels. His name was Koen, by the way, pronounced midway between "coon" and "cone." (Alas, Koen was not six-foot-four and full of muscle, but, still, the whole thing was pretty darn good.)

From a thick, eight-by-five, no name journal,
written in mechanical pencil:

*The house was peaceful. Carols played softly, kids tinkered
with gifts, someone browsed a new book and someone napped –
the in-between lull of a Rockwell Christmas Day.*

I had the simple task of buying bread for dinner and strolled along a
winding street to the centre of town. Winter air was crisp and dry.
Sinterklaases hung from the occasional window ledge, poised mid-
climb, looking like festive burglars. Wide fields in fallow rolled in the
distance. Everything was quiet, content.

Passing a churchyard, I chuckled, remembering the last time I was
here. It was summer and a groundskeeper was mowing the cemetery
lawn, taking care around headstones. He raised the blade and I realized each headstone was bordered in tidy rows of flowering forget-me-
nots, beautiful and perfect. I watched him work, patient and methodical on the sacred ground. And then he stopped, undid his fly and
took a comically long piss against the church wall.

The bakery was open Christmas day, with shorter hours. The order had been called in, letting Koen the baker know what we wanted
and telling him to speak English to the poorly dressed fellow with a
foreign accent who'd be picking it up.

He bagged a round rustic loaf, some pastries and boxed a Yule log
resembling something I'd buy at Dairy Queen. In my mind it was a
Vegemite sandwich, of course. In fine holiday spirits, I took the long
way home, following a trail through a park and past a castle where
archery contests have been held for hundreds of years. A corridor of
tall, waving poplars met overhead, creating a natural latticed canopy
over the narrow, dirt trail. A light breeze gusted, a whisper moving
branches. When I was last here, trees were heavy with leaves and it felt

like passing through a Madison County covered bridge. Now-bare branches reached up like Grinch fingers – long and spindly and surprisingly spiritual – the whole resembling a cathedral.

As I'd been doing throughout this viking excursion, once more I had an opportunity to explore, in my way, views on life's meaning. My friend sauntered onto his patio, where I lounged in a deck chair, working my way through his beer, cheese and cured meat. He settled in beside me with his own full-bodied Belgian blonde in a bottle. It was a fine evening, a clear, sunset sky. High overhead, vapour trails criss-crossed in a hashtag – jets coming and going from Brussels International.

I described a "Live Laugh Love" wall ornament we had in our home, a gift from another friend. The theme's been overused, but I like what it represents – a tidy synopsis of perhaps the most important things: experiencing life to the fullest, enjoying and sharing. I asked my host to tell me what it meant to him.

He thought for a while and then spoke of the value of family – his love for his daughters, what a blessing it is to spend life with people you love and fondly recalled visits with his grandma, someone who wouldn't say a bad thing about anyone. Then he talked about the joy experienced in his daughters' laughter.

"There's absolutely nothing better," he said, grinning. "Times I'd even tickle them 'til it drove them crazy, but the sound of their belly laughs was just too good." He smiled, remembering. "I knew I couldn't do that forever. But when the laughter's full on, it's infectious. Ebullient."

"Nice word," I said.

He gave a cheerful laugh, aptly enough, and I made a mental note to learn what the hell "ebullient" meant.

Comfy in every manner, we sat in the dusk, our conversation dwindling like the day. The sky darkened, as though a set director was dimming lights for the next performance. And, seemingly on cue, a crescent moon rose while a crescendo of crickets, night birds and frogs rose like an orchestra from a reed-filled lake just out of sight.

The following day, we explored Belgium's Flemish and Walloon regions, tramping around the foundations of a Roman villa, circa 50 CE. Lunch was at an outdoor space that struck me as a poster for European travel – a stretch of parked Fiats, Renaults, Peugeots, Mercedes, an Aston Martin and a pair of Vespas in a tidy row on a curving, cobbled street.

We strolled through an open-air market, buying fish and flowers and gawking at a chicken and chips vendor on wheels – a kind of food truck – the birds on a slow rotisserie, dribbling fat into a trough of roasting potatoes.

I carried on to Tervuren's Royal Museum for Central Africa, a collection of treasures pilfered from the Congo during the reign of King Leopold II. The exterior grounds felt as though I was strolling around Versailles. A huge white elephant stood out front, trunk raised, symbol of Africa and used as a logo on Côte d'Or chocolate.

Inside the museum sat an enormous dugout canoe from the Congo River, indistinguishable from a fossilized tree. Displays outlined European "discovery" of Africa, colonial expansion and Henry Morton Stanley's historic meeting with Doctor David Livingstone (I presume) on the shore of Lake Tanganyika in 1871. I caught myself listening for drums, imagining the vibrations of a riverboat, chugging deeper into the jungle like Conrad's *Heart of Darkness*, the bookend to this jaunt being my visit to South Kensington's Royal Geographical Society in London, where Livingstone's statue greets you at the entrance across from Hyde Park.

While in Belgium, we explored the EU capital, taking a train from Tervuren to Brussels. In addition to beer, lace, waffles, chocolate, mussels, frites and Jean-Claude Van Damme, Belgium is famous for its animation. The country boasts a rich history of cartoons, comics and an off-key humour, likely from years of being invaded and occupied by everybody else.

While we waited for a train, I walked the length of the long, enclosed platform. Concrete walls were lavishly painted in various scenes from Tintin's exciting, albeit racist, adventures. "Chanson D'Amour" oozed from a sound system and the drudgery of waiting vanished, the whole experience akin to a pleasant stroll through a colourful museum. I was surprisingly disappointed when our train arrived.

The ride into Brussels Central was quick and from there we made our way to the Grand-Place – a magnificent medieval town square that survived World War bombings. Figures in bronze gazed down from high building facades, rows of sombre metal faces adding a formality to the bright space, liberally decorated with planters of brilliant flowers.

It was hot and sunny and we arrived during a full day of live music – an array of brass bands playing successively in the square. Author Pete Brown wrote, "What I have always regarded as oompah music, a flatulent, cheesy racket, suddenly sounds so right." Which it positively did.

We took seats on a restaurant patio at the edge of the square and perused a phone book menu of beer. Other patrons were drinking a huge diversity of beers in exotic, branded glasses that could only be found in Belgium, arguably the home of beer. It may have been born elsewhere, but it grew up here. I'd read a quote from Belgian writer Georges Simenon in which he stated, "The smell of freshly poured beer is the smell of my country." Other than the flowers and a few hundred sweaty musicians, I could smell nothing else.

I looked around at the array of beers on other tables to get inspired. Two giants that looked like those enormous motorbike-riding twins were seated next to us. Both had shiny sousaphones and big, droopy moustaches that matched their big, droopy instruments and big, droopy bodies. I could've mistaken them for walruses had their breath smelled more of herring than hops. They seemed to do everything in tandem, like silent actors doing a mirror routine, and were working on wheat beer in the largest steins I'd ever seen. Our server arrived and said something in Flemish (Belgian Dutch), then French, none of which I understood. I smiled and pointed, indicating I wanted what the tuba-playing fatties were enjoying and got my own Fiat-sized Hoegaarden.

Afterwards we went to see Belgium's best-known landmark – the Manneken Pis – a small bronze statue of a wee gaffer taking a leak rather proudly and playfully arcing it, creating a narrow, sputtering fountain. It's hugely famous and hugely disappointing, but one of those things that has to be seen.

In front of the statue a street vendor was selling boiled snails in garlic from a tiny mobile kiosk. Feeling terribly Belgian, I ordered a dish of the rubbery little things that resembled something you'd scrape off a shoe. Sadly, they tasted like they'd been poached in the liquid the bronze boy was passing but with less character. I gnawed on a few before realizing they were quite unpleasant; had a few more, which got progressively worse, then ate another three before stopping.

We trained to medieval Bruges, capital of West Flanders and home to the port of Zeebrugge. Following supper and sightseeing, we settled into our room. By now it was late, or early, depending on your perspective, everything dark and silent. We'd be catching a train in a few hours, but sleep wouldn't come. I crept from bed and leaned out an open window. The canal was calm, a mirror reflecting dim yellow lights from an abbey on the opposite side. The air was cool, still and fresh. Someone buzzed past on a Vespa and a dog trotted across the road. A cluster of scrawny elms surrounded an old-fashioned streetlight like homeless around an oil can fire. A gust of wind made the trees whisper and I wondered what secrets they knew.

A plump, gibbous moon hung in starless sky and, looking left to right, I made out three towering cathedrals – differing shades of dark. There was a light in the central bell tower – a hollow, glowing archway 30 metres in the air. It looked like a gateway to another dimension – a one-way passage to the past. But in the timeless city it could just as well have been a portal to the present.

From a pad of hotel stationery:

Morning in crystal ball grey, murky overcast with streaky,
unreadable Darjeeling stains. An aroma of fresh tattoo, indelible
ink, anticipation, a whiff of anxiety. And the amenable hum
of artisanal focus, the whole wrapped in possibility.

Back across the channel, I was on a West Country mini tour around
the UK's Penwith Peninsula, where I watched friends perform on a
clifftop stage in Porthcurno and launched my first viking book by the
sea. An easy commute, really. Just a walk, train, flight, car, two more
trains, a bus, one more train, another walk and you're there! "Easy
peasy lemon squeezy," as globetrotter Ian Wright once said, leaping
between plinths of stone atop a canyon.

I settled in to dine at the Captain's Table, imagining myself pour-
ing brandy for Cook and Banks as we discussed the day's findings. I
had a window view over St Ives Bay, where fishing boats bobbed. Otis
Redding's "(Sittin' On) The Dock of the Bay" came through the sound
system, which made me smile, as I watched tide rolling away.

This is that week at a glance: socialize, pizza, sleep (a bit), eggs, gig,
socialize, sightsee, goat curry, concert, sleep, gig, socialize, read, drink,
gig, gig, rest, write, hike, sleep, gig, dine, socialize, rest, write, gig, exchange hugs, then take another sequence of trains going the other way.

The first of the return trains was a nine-coacher that rolled from
St Erth, Paddington bound, through every conceivable shade of green,
hues nuanced into mulatto foliage, yellow-freckled in dandelions and
portioned into fence-lined fields with songbird flits in hedgerows,
punctuated with exclamatory chimneys in brick.

I munched packets of barbecue corn chips, the taste and aroma of
preteen, after-school snacks. The steward in the Pullman car and I recognized each other – fellow musicians and kindred spirits connected
across the globe by steel strings and rail lines. He was playing with a
new band now, members scattered around London and Reading, not

unlike my latest song collaborators, pepper-dusted in the UK, Hong Kong and Bangalore.

In London I watched a jet hang languid in the mist while a rhythmic KISS cover oozed from a sound system, filtered through African drums. I sipped coffee the colour of the Thames and stared dreamily at one of the world's great cities.

I'd be reconnecting with Deb and, while I drank coffee, watching tide shift the river, I recalled my last time here, at the end of a literature festival and tour. I had an overnight in the city, a big hard bed in a small dark room in Paddington where I slept the sleep of the comatose.

Morning revealed a treed slice of London – bushy beech and a spiky-topped purple cabbage tree palm, the look of a 1980s punk rocker. Fresh coffee, stale clothes and I was viking again. With a travel guitar and a small pack, I sauntered through Heathrow awaiting my flight. It was still early, gift shops opening for the day.

"Oi! Love! Give us a song!" I heard from an impeccably dressed clerk in a high-end store.

I laughed and gave her a wave as I passed, then thought, *Well, why the hell wouldn't I?* So I unslung my guitar and strolled back into the store, serenading her like something from a Richard Curtis film. She let out a delicious, bark-like squeal and clapped her hands, and as I finished she said, "More!" As much a demand as request.

A couple of bemused customers were now lined up at the till.

"Excuse me," one of them said to her.

"Hold on!" she snapped at them, then beamed back at me, "Go on, love."

Once more an unplanned, impromptu encounter, now one of my favourites.

And, for reasons I don't understand, as I stared at the Thames my stream of recollections took me north, across the border to another great city, Scotland's capital of Edinburgh, a place where you can't help but go viking.

Alternating between Robbie Burns and the Proclaimers, I'd

hummed contentedly as I strolled along High Street following the Royal Mile from Edinburgh Castle to Holyrood Palace, the steely blue Firth of Forth in the distance. I made a wide detour, however, as I approached the Museum of Edinburgh. Previously, Deb and I'd explored the many floors of the fine old museum, enjoying the history and having the place to ourselves early in the day. We were in an empty upper room when we experienced a ghost – a voice, clearly enunciating unintelligible words. There was no audio equipment and no living person in any other room; I triple-checked. According to philosopher Michel de Certeau, "Only haunted cities are worth living in." I disagree.

During our stay we toured a small distillery; made our own custom blends of scotch; ate the best smoked salmon ever; tramped around the royal yacht *Britannia*, where we enjoyed sunshine on Leith (like the Proclaimers' song); and explored the National Museum of Scotland, the first of many encounters with the Lewis chessmen, recurring protagonists in our first wave of viking adventures.

Back in downtown Edinburgh, I meandered along Princes Street, under the rocky gaze of the castle, where the Scott Monument loomed like a skeletal, less-refined Eiffel Tower. The discreet entrance to Old Calton Cemetery caught my eye – an enticing, narrow set of stone steps leading under a canopy of leafy deciduous. The old cemetery was eerily silent, an isolated time capsule plunked in the midst of a bustling city. I wandered amongst old leaning headstones and monuments, reading inscriptions to people who'd passed away hundreds of years ago, including philosopher David Hume. At one end of the burial grounds, I was surprised to see an Abe Lincoln memorial, and later learned it was dedicated to a small group of Scots who fought for the Union in the American Civil War.

In our accommodation I spent time (in a manner) with Neil Oliver – my viking mentor – making notes while reading his book *Vikings*, his role as pivotal to our first viking expedition as the Lewis chessmen, burning boats and an ever-present creak of oars. Eventually sharing a copy of my book with Neil became a lovely touchstone, be-coming friends with another literary hero.

Beside me in that Scottish rental a shelf of Ian Rankin (also) kept me company, a proper Edinburgh author and favourite of my dad. A short while later I was delighted to see *Gone Viking* beside Rankin's latest on a bookstore shelf of bestsellers. And I thought of Monisha Rajesh saying with a grin that she, of course, like all auth-ors, would never, ever look for her own work in a store. While an-other one that made me smile was Bill Bryson recounting a story of being somewhere far from home, going into a bookstore and shifting his books on the shelf so they looked more appealing. I liked know-ing we're all the same.

There's a photo I love. In black and white. Deb and I sharing a moment, having a laugh. We'd just completed a marathon, our first. And we were sitting on a curb, exhausted, content, unaware our picture was being taken. You see more in the black and white. Depth of character. Emotion. Perhaps the same reason a book – black ink on white paper – conveys more, at times, than film. Although not recorded in a journal, that particular shot's on a digital frame, surfacing every thousand photos or so. For some reason, perhaps being in an ancient city, a place recorded so often in black and white, I'm reminded of that time together.

Reconnected in London, Deb and I explored the city on foot, me-andering past Christopher Wren's Saint Paul's Cathedral in time for a chorus of midday bells. Rich layered clangs boomed jubilation, and I expected to see a frantic, partially tuxedoed Hugh Grant, hair care-fully askew, dashing toward the church, eyes batting, nervously stam-mering something tender and frightfully witty.

We carried on for a leisurely visit through the Museum of London, built in the barbican centre against a high, thick chunk of Roman city wall, two millennia old. The museum is a favourite, tracing London's roots from prehistory. An aurochs skull greeted us near the entrance, a monstrous thing that looked as though it wanted to play fetch like the T. Rex in *Night at the Museum*. The regal mayor's state coach was on display, gleaming red and gold, along with informative displays of the city's guilds, history of trade along the Thames and a disturbingly detailed account of the plague and Great Fire of 1666.

There was an excellent walk along a recreated Victorian street, complete with 19th-century retail shops and services with a dizzying collection of Stone Age, Bronze Age and Iron Age tools and weapons, with models of the city as it looked during Roman occupation, as well as earth and mud dwellings of the hairy inhabitants that settled the bogs that became Heathrow following the last ice age.

During our exploration we met Londoners John and Helen, who told us the story of how they met. Their respective friends were getting married. Unbeknownst to John and Helen, who didn't know each other, the friends had decided John and Helen should be together.

John played piano and Helen played violin. The couple who was getting married told John and Helen they wanted them to play together at the wedding and requested a technically challenging piece, one requiring a great deal of joint practice. John and Helen began meeting to practise, and did so for three months leading up to the wedding. After a couple of practice sessions, John explained, the piece sounded good; they had it down.

"Mind you," he said, "I was quite happy to keep seeing Helen under the guise of practising."

They laughed, comfortable together. They'd been a couple for two years; their duet, a success.

From the eight-by-five no-name journal, itself now as
well travelled as an old steamer trunk, the only thing
missing being destination stickers and labels:

*No nightingale sang, but we enjoyed a leisurely stroll
through Berkeley Square en route to a London train.*

Watching the Thames slide by in dirty green-grey under pale blue sky,
pockmarked in dusty white cloud. We were aboard a mildly grungy
commuter train, rattling us along elevated tracks from Waterloo
Station east through the city past the glass and steel of Canary Wharf
to Greenwich.

The district of Royal Greenwich was the birthplace of Henry VIII
and Elizabeth I, Greenwich Castle roughly in the centre of town, and
where Henry stored mistresses for a time. The property then became
the home of the Royal Observatory – a neat, octagonal building top-
ping a rounded hill overlooking the river. The observatory served as a
centre for scientific research, astronomy and navigation and is the lo-
cation of the prime meridian. It was from here England set the world's
clocks, then left it to the Swiss to keep them accurate.

The interior of the observatory had, I felt, an intellectual energy,
the facility never having lost its sense of discovery. We lined up with
other tourists for a photo atop the meridian line, where you can't help
but ham, balancing on the line like a grounded tightrope walker.

Maritime history here's a rich mosaic, centuries of viking for king
and for queen. I wandered through the National Maritime Museum,
touted as the largest in the world. The library houses 100,000 volumes
of maritime reference books and features fine exhibits of Captain Cook
and Admiral Nelson, their logbooks monstrous leather-bound beasts.

One display explains how Nelson effectively utilized England's su-
perior technology (copper-hulled ships) to lead his outnumbered fleet
to trounce the combined armadas of Spain and France at the Battle
of Trafalgar in 1805, repeating Drake's work from 1588. The admiral's

coat is on display, the seemingly innocuous bullet hole that killed him visible through the shoulder of the garment.

"Oh, sod," I suspect he said, upon noticing he'd been shot, before commending the men on a job well done, going below decks to clean the blood from his jacket, enter the day's events in the ship's log, salute King George and then expire.

The small hole in a child-sized naval jacket juxtaposes the enormity of that turning point for much of the world, paving the way for the Duke of Wellington to finish off Napoleon's cannons once and for all at Waterloo with sound tactics, audacious courage and Irish infantry.

ASIA

EAST SEA

From a nondescript pocket-sized notebook with a coil
top, the kind you hold in one hand like a journalist,
press card in hatband, looking for a scoop:

*Half a world away, across not only Atlantic but
Pacific, destination planned but unknown.*

As we continue crossing borders and boundaries, let's go (perhaps) as
far as we can from the once-beaten track, beyond our *Gone Viking* trail
through Europe, the Arctic and New World, to Asia. Yes, we were here
with Varangians at Miklagard and Ephesus, but now let's tackle that
land mass from the other side, westbound from North America, over
Haida Gwaii touchstones and across Heyerdahl's Pacific, to where a
viking trail's not always what it seems.

It was dark by the time we arrived at our hotel from Tokyo's Narita
airport. We went for late supper to a minuscule restaurant furnished
in minimalist decor; soft light, warm pine, tatami mats, paper lanterns
and slow, dampened music – single note twangs and deep chimes.

We were in Tokyo for the first time, smiling, nodding and pointing at plastic food replicas with an excess of *arigatos*. My miso soup arrived, steaming, comforting and familiar. But when I stirred, it rattled
like marbles, literally rattling my confidence. It turned out to be clam
miso, the bowl lined deep with tiny clams. I kept my Japanese phrase
book close at hand, finding it an excellent tool for pointing when used
in conjunction with smiling and nodding.

It seemed we were the only ones dining this late and we were suddenly very tired. The service was attentive but leisurely, and as my head
began to nod I feared I was inadvertently ordering more. We left, a

little hungry, but big bottles of Asahi left me feeling somewhat full and tipsy enough to be content. I was still uncertain as to the currency conversion but believe my soup and beer cost somewhere between ten and 1,000 dollars. And while fatigue and beer rendered me incapable of math, it also kept me from caring.

While in Tokyo we spent time with friends, saw the Imperial Palace and went sightseeing on foot, where we walked through the futuristic Shibuya, what I thought of as Times Square squared. But, despite the intense density, it lacked the chaos of China's big cities, with a sense of order and respect for personal space.

We spent a night at a salaryman's restaurant, sitting in tightly packed, wooden booths with benches. Groups of men quaffed pints of draft beer and burst into song – exuberant and near hysterical. We drank Sapporo and chilled sake from small, white pine boxes, the size of a squat whiskey glass, drinking from a cube requiring concentration. Our hosts used their few words of Japanese, along with smiling and nodding, and we dined *omakase* (chef's choice), although I suspect it was dumbed down for us *gaijin* – a great many things in tempura. I enjoyed a large fried order of prawn heads – salty and crispy like pork rinds but with antennae that I crunched through like uncooked spaghetti.

Next day a bullet train rocketed us from Tokyo, south and west, past a foggy outline of Fuji in the distance. Following a couple of hours of blurry greens and misty blues we arrived in Kyoto, the former capital, renowned for cherry blossoms and geishas, time-warp individuals still shuffling through town with a clack of wooden joist shoes. But it was the greenness of the city that struck me – regenerating forest creeping from surrounding hills into seamless urban and suburban. We meandered through wooden temples of massive dark timber, enshrouded in silence and the heady smell of burning joss sticks, then checked into a traditional ryokan.

Our simple, elegant room had sliding rice-paper walls, tatami mats on pine flooring, a small cedar bathtub with slatted wood drain mat, flat art pictorials and a small bud vase with a single fresh flower. The room looked onto a central courtyard with a garden of leafy bamboo, green and purple maple and elm, sand raked into patterns, artistic lava rock and neat bonsai pine. The garden itself was as much a piece of art as the interior decor, a hum of serenity through it all.

Shoes were removed upon entering the building. The ryokan was a fair size – 18 rooms, but we were never aware of other guests or staff. The whole experience felt utterly private, secluded and personal, despite the inn being full. It was remarkable but an expected part of the experience – a peaceful encounter, simple yet luxurious. If we needed something, it magically appeared. Dinner was served in our room, at a low table surrounded by cushions; course after course of exquisite fare. And when we re-entered the room after brushing our teeth, the dining area had become our bedroom again, with a large, plush futon having taken its place. I imagined how easy it would be to simply live out one's life this way, never leaving the room, gradually morphing into some variation of Howard Hughes but without the Kleenex-box shoes or accumulated jars of pee.

This is what burbled to the surface of my recollective soup in the pit of COVID lockdown while living each day, all day, in our home. With Deb and I now living in a compact studio apartment, we were, in large part, living out what I once envisioned as perversely romantic. One year in, it was no longer as dreamy or aspirational as it once had been.

In the ryokan we were still using cameras (with film!) and went through roll after roll of celluloid, photographing meals in a stationary, culinary excursion. Seafood: raw, grilled, steamed and fried, with a dozen types of seaweed, mushrooms and twice as many pickles, sauces and condiments. Every dish had a method, a manner of eating, combining and accentuating each flavour. Patient servers walked us through it, while serving beer, hot sake and tea. (Break the raw egg over rice. Stir gently. Now pickle. Some salmon collar with roe. Now mushroom. Now more pickle.) We learned of umami – the fifth basic taste – savoury, protein-rich mouth feel. As I learned, I ate. As I ate, I learned.

The whole experience was beyond compare. And when the bill arrived in our room before departure, I realized why. I knew the place was going to be the most expensive accommodation we'd ever stayed at but decided, with trepidation, it'd be worth it – an experience of a lifetime – retirement be damned. And as long as we never had kids and stopped getting haircuts or using energy in our home, we'd get by. A friend had made the reservation for us and told me the price, so I was prepared, I thought. But when I opened the bill, I realized that exorbitant amount I'd been prepared for was, in fact, the cost per person! An actual sweat broke on my upper lip. Deb looked at me, eyes wide, as I turned the green-grey hue of an imminent coronary. My mind raced, calculating. The cost of our two-night stay, I determined, wouldn't be too bad if paid monthly and amortized over 25 years. Plus, I thought, as my panic subsided, we'd always have the photos, and a story I could forever embellish.

YELLOW SEA

In that same "journalist's" notebook, a blend of train-ridden scribbles and improvised shorthand, smeared in sake and soy:

Across the Sea of Japan and Korea, we head
toward the Chinese–Mongolian border.

Dropped on a lonely stretch of gravel road, backpacks stacked in the dirt. There were four of us, and we looked at the heap for a while – too much stuff with too few necessities – putting off having to lift it all and climb an unmarked track up a mountain. Everything seemed awkward and heavy (which it was). While we stood there, a tiny, wizened man in thick, baggy clothes appeared, making his way down the road toward us, curious as to who (or what) we were. He stared, pointing, gesturing, and we realized he'd never seen blue or green eyes before.

To get here we'd travelled back through time. Farmers had laid wheat sheaves on the road and the occasional passing vehicle, scrunching over the wheat, provided a preliminary threshing to save time in harvesting. It made a muffled dry hum as we passed, a sound like driving on thick, coarse carpet. From a blanket of "road wheat" the route became potholed asphalt, eventually giving way to gravel and dirt, then disappeared completely. The road had flooded, water covering the surface for 100 metres. As we debated how to proceed, our driver (the fifth person in the car) dropped the car into gear and drove into the lake, water splashing high up the doors. I held my breath. After an anxious few moments, crossing the halfway point, peering through windows we saw that the depth was dropping, and we were going to make it, emerging on the other side like an amphibious vehicle, water sluicing from wheel wells and from under the hood.

Now, with that tremulous car ride behind us, the old man at the side of the road gazed into our foreign eyes and let out a series of grunts. Our friend spoke to him in Mandarin, telling him where we wanted to go. Gurgling in his throat like a crow, we realized he had no tongue, and I didn't want to imagine how he'd lost it. Lowering himself to one knee, he drew a crude map in the soil with his finger, showing us how to get there. With *xièxiès*, smiles and nods, we hoisted our gear and walked toward an ancient village in China's Hebei province.

It was a collection of squat dwellings made of stone and mud stucco. Large, painted characters in chipped, faded red on a wall stated, "One child. No more." And from a small doorway a sparrow-like woman watched us approach. More smiles, nods, broken Mandarin, and she invited us into her home. Chunks of coal provided a cooking fire and warmth for the single-room house. There was a stone recess beneath a raised sleeping platform where another small fire could be lit in cold weather, warming the bed. After a brief, mostly silent visit, we thanked her and moved on.

In a few dozen strides we were through the village, into arid fields of waving grain where a butterfly fluttered, cicadas buzzed and a long brown snake wound past my feet. Land rose around us and we climbed a steep incline following a faint, overgrown trail through shoulder-high brush. Nettles and brambly greens grabbed skin and clothing, holding us back as though keeping us from something secret. We forged ahead, breaking through to see it loom in the distance – China's Great Wall, snaking along a mountain ridge that ran forever. Wisps of cirrus drifted in pale blue sky and the wall seemed to move, gliding over hills and growing as we climbed – a monstrous living thing of history and stone.

We made camp beside a crumbled section of wall – broken rock and mortar – on a sharp ridge between high round platforms that once supported guard towers. Our buddies had packed the gear and I took my first look through the supplies for the four of us: two single-person sleeping bags, two small tents, one thin cotton sheet, one toque, one pair of mittens, a great deal of booze, coffee, oranges, PowerBars, bread, salami, baguette, tomatoes and a one-kilogram hunk of raw, frozen chicken. For the duration of our stay the poultry remained a solid, icy brick. In all likelihood, it still is. Our friend rummaged through gear and found the world's dullest knife, and made chunky sandwiches with torn hunks of meat and ripped tomato – one of the best meals ever. We set aside wine, oranges and PowerBars for breakfast, made a vase from a can and filled it with wild flowers, then opened champagne to celebrate Deb's birthday as sun sank, lighting the wall like a cake-topping candle.

A full moon rose, the Milky Way emerged and tangerine light dawdled in the sky like a child struggling to stay up past bedtime. Wind gusted through steep hills and, with a soothing, shushing sound, slowly extinguished the day. The temperature slid toward freezing. We shivered and took turns wearing the toque and mittens. Our other friend, a Sherpa-like pack mule who hauled most of the heavy gear, had pitched the small tents, one held in place by rocks, the other by icy tins of Tiger beer and the lump of frozen chicken. Our pals said good night and wedged themselves into one of the narrow, single sleeping bags, having to join coitally, I expect, to fit. I gave the other slender sleeping bag to Deb and took the sheet, which felt like bedding down in a single layer of tissue paper.

The sound of the other three snoring in their nylon cocoons soon filled our camp, while my body began to involuntarily flex, stiffening to stave off hypothermia. I got up and moved around, rubbing my hands in the cold night air. The moon was near full, the colour of ivory, and hung directly overhead. Fluffy dark cloud raced past like time-lapse photography, creating a soft strobe in shifting darkness – surreal and dreamlike – shades of black, grey and pockets of moonlight glinting dimly off the wall. Then a break in the clouds offered a planetarium view of night sky and a quilt of a billion clustered, solitary stars. I thought about waking the others but let them sleep, keeping the scene to myself.

From a tiny journal with a ribbon attached, bought
on the street, the look of Mao's Little Red Book:

Back in Beijing, everything the colour of charcoal.

I stood on a little concrete balcony and gazed into the bank of cloud,
fog, coal smoke and industrial smog that made up the city skyline. The
temperature had dropped even further and I shivered, holding my coffee cup like a tepid hot pad, cooling too quickly. The deep *woo-wooooo*
of a train sounded from somewhere far away, and in the courtyard men
swept with twig brooms – *whsh-whsh-whsh*.

We went to explore the city, passing simple markets – hawkers
with piles of produce on tamped dry mud: oranges, kiwis, onions and
carrots. Chestnuts roasted over coal in steel drums. A man fried balls
of dough in a massive iron pan of sizzling, rancid oil, while flies crept
over everything. I fought the urge to bathe in Purell and eat nothing but Mars bars. Vendors howled at us as we passed. I went to buy
something, trying to look impoverished in a 40-dollar tee-shirt. The
vendor told me it was 20 renminbi. Another buddy, who lived there,
tried the same, using his few words of Mandarin. His price was 15. And
while we watched from a distance, our other pal flew at the hawker,
an assault of nasal diphthongs in passable Mandarin. Her price was
ten. The shouting continued a short while, the traditional manner of
concluding a mutually successful transaction, and then we moved on.

The city struck me as a human ant colony – seemingly chaotic, but,
in fact, highly efficient. A baton was being passed between generations,
philosophies, economies. The transition was everywhere; older people
in drab proletariat greens, while the younger generation wore two-piece
blue suits. Every worker I saw wore a two-piece blue suit – crisp ones
on office workers entering the high-rises, rumpled and dusty ones on
the workers building them. Across the city, more buildings were going

up. Construction was constant. Lashed bamboo scaffolding clung to towering new builds of glass and steel, holding the past to the future like a bridge across time.

At the Silk Market we joined a crush of people moving through the smell of living earth – compost, mushrooms and dank, wet rot. We dodged cyclists and idling cars that never seemed to move, and explored the Forbidden City, where Roger Moore described points of interest through audio tour headsets. The architecture was beautiful – carved lions, dragons, phoenixes, cranes and turtles marching along rooftops and gables – inanimate infantry, but despite vibrant golds and reds, it was dampened by soulless grey.

Wandering through a huge central Beijing park, we watched people do tai chi, dance, play netless badminton, fly kites from fishing rods and socialize. A congregation of men stood in a circle visiting, all holding cages of drab little songbirds.

We had a good, simple meal of duck, assembling wheat-flour wraps with shredded duck meat, julienned vegetables and hoisin sauce. Next day, however, we decided I needed a more adventurous culinary experience. My buddy who spoke the best Mandarin took me winding through hutongs, far from the ring road bustle, until we found a small, deserted eatery. An elderly woman said a few words in Mandarin and with that we were served.

A large bowl was set in front of each of us – viscous amber broth with chilies floating on a skin of oil. The surface moved as though never quite having reached a boil. *Might be poison.* Then a sizzling cast iron platter was placed between us, strings of gristle and sinew dancing in hot oil. It was served with spicy peppers and something gelatinous I was unable to categorize into any particular food group. Intermittently, it throbbed.

The tiny old server watched me, the way we'd scrutinize the kid on the playground after the dare before the earthworm was eaten.

"We call this one Cat on a Hot Tin Roof," my friend said with a wicked grin.

Definitely poison, I decided, eating enough to appear polite and hopefully just be sick and not die. That night, cramped and clenched, I tiptoed around snoring bodies in the small unit to get to the lone bathroom, where I did my best to silently facilitate the violent evacuation that ensued without waking those sleeping nearby on the floor. Interestingly, this event came to mind when Astrid the fortune teller told me to start ditching friends.

From the margin of *Lonely Planet: Destination China*, torn into three – Beijing, Shanghai and possible toilet paper:

A porcelain bowl of tea-steamed quail eggs was set before us with tiny pouches of sweet sticky rice wrapped in banana leaves, artfully tied with string. Black Darjeeling steeped in a pot and the chaos of Shanghai drifted away like steam as we nestled into a crimson pagoda to enjoy Chinese high tea.

We'd been whisked from Beijing to Shanghai. Not by a press gang but by our friends, to avoid the anniversary celebrations of communism back in the capital. The world media would be there and we'd anticipated even more congestion, the thought of which seemed unbearable. Ironically, we fled to the very city where the Party began, with Mao at that first meeting in Shanghai. We too started a party, drinking red wine until our teeth were pleasingly purple, before moving on to the rooftop of the Peace Hotel, enjoying the same view of colonial buildings Noel Coward, George Bernard Shaw and Charlie Chaplin did when they were here in the 1930s, in all likelihood behaving in a manner that helped fan the embers of the communist movement.

We joined the crush along the Bund on the Huangpu River, our walk a stroll through time. From the futuristic, smog-shrouded Jin Mao Tower, we made our way past the sweeping riverside curve of

Victorian architecture to a 19th-century expat pub, anchored by a long, polished bar in dark, lacquered wood. Vertical fans moved air like oarsmen from the ceiling. It was the kind of place, I imagined, where pith-helmeted men with mutton chop whiskers met, drank gin, swapped stories of the Raj and placed wagers on the next tea sailing of the *Cutty Sark* from Hong Kong to Bristol. The bar was an odd combination of being abroad, experiencing something new while remaining in insulated comfort; what expat bars the world over provide. It felt familiar, which was not why we'd left home.

Irrespective of the destination, our journeys were providing an opportunity to consider what we wanted, where travel was really taking us. And it felt as though we were finding a route, doing our best on an unmapped road. We'd been working hard to minimize things in our life. Simplifying, ironically, requires an enormous amount of effort. Like so many things, it's a process – the road travelled versus the destination.

One time Deb and I had hiked a faint desert trail in Arizona as clouds swirled around mesas and sandy buttes. We traipsed through palo verde, creosote and agave, spiky ocotillo, towering saguaros, strawberry hedgehogs bursting with fuchsia blossoms, brittlebush and jumping chollas. I had to step around a fat lizard that resembled a Komodo dragon strutting down the path like a leathery runway model.

We discussed our pursuit of less and obstacles that hinder progress.

"Glimpses of simplicity. That's what you get," Deb said, summing it up perfectly.

I nodded.

I'd read a small plaque by an ancient firepit where the Navaho would meet for prayer, meals and socializing. They used the term *hozho* – balance – to define the concept. While in Kyoto's temples, I'd thought of the Buddhist aphorism summing up the balance inherent in actualization: "Before enlightenment; chop wood, carry water. After enlightenment; chop wood, carry water."

Glimpses of simplicity.

Hozho.

OCEANIA

10

AUSTRALIA

From an invitingly new journal, pocket-
sized, with unbleached plain paper:

*Leaping the Date Line, thrust into the future. I think of the
Dave Matthews song "Crush," as he wonders, what with
the world being round, and us here, standing, or dancing, if
we're right side up, upside down or if all of it's a dream?*

From viking a sliver of Asia, we went back to routines of work, paying for travel, saving for travel, watching escapist TV and reading every
travelogue I could find. Before too long we'd saved sufficient funds
and time off to do it again. Wanting to delve farther into unfamiliar
terrain, we chose to explore Oceania – Australia in particular – from
a world map perspective, the antipodean antithesis to our original
Gone Viking trail.

Join me as we peel back the skin on a fresh wedge of globe – viking
in a manner I'd never envisioned before. Where we'll meet an array
of intriguing people – some lovely, some not, some funny, some not –
and a swath of the planet that remains as precious as anywhere. Let's
start with a carpool on a thousand-kilometre drive. One way.

The temperature *dropped* to 45 degrees Celsius. We'd been driving forever along Australia's west coast on a narrow band of bitumen,
a fine line dividing outback and ocean, literally the end of the earth.
One side was a sandy expanse of nothingness – arid infinity, while the
other was surging surf, inky indigo, glinting like gold leaf on the horizon. Steve Parish had been here, photographing kangaroos bounding
in surf – spectacular stuff that messed with your mind.

A small, unassuming sign marked the spot and we pulled over to where aquamarine tide washed against rocky shore. Dark splotches just beneath the surface were what we'd come to see – stromatolites – three-billion-year-old living rocks. Before there was much of anything on earth, these submerged rocks released minuscule bubbles of carbon dioxide, starting the process of photosynthesis, providing the oxygen and building blocks for all living things – a fly-leaf to Genesis.

We stood in silence at the edge of the ocean, a seamless expanse of space and time, peering through a watery window onto creation. Half a world away I'd be gazing at much the same thing – stromatolites, or thrombolites – on Newfoundland's west coast, near the top of the Great Northern Peninsula as we homed in on Leif Erikson's camp at L'Anse aux Meadows to complete the first *Gone Viking* odyssey. And in the same manner that Dave Matthews questions where exactly we might be, so too do recollections simmer, meld and solidify into an amenable roux.

Back in Western Australia, we were immersed in molten landscape. Heat waves shimmered and the air conditioner laboured as I drove, tentative, trying to keep our tires in disappearing tracks on shifting, blowing sand.

This was Nambung National Park on Australia's Coral Coast, the midst of the Pinnacles, clusters of tall and amber-coloured stone standing like faceless chessmen on a giant's board – a colossal, paleolithic Fischer/Spassky match.

We stepped from the car into a hush, and heat that was a punch to the solar plexus – UV index of 14 – surrounded by vast, stark beauty. Nothing but lapis sky, gleaming sand, brooding gold rock and penetrating silence. Far away, land became a violet-blue sea. We gazed, enthralled, until skin began to burn. Then we staggered back to the car, hoping tire tracks would still be there.

Lighthouse Family's "Raincloud" was playing in a loop on the stereo like a cruel joke in the expansive dry land. We made for the ocean, to the blinding brilliance of Shell Beach, an unspoiled swath of white, and were the only ones there. Walking toward the water, we sank to our ankles in coarse, bright shingle that creaked and grated underfoot. I dropped to a knee, cupped hands and scooped. Seashells spilled from my palms, running through fingers like a pirate rifling doubloons. The entire shoreline was bleached shells, smooth from the tide and magically intact, near flawless. I rolled and laughed, rattling in a vast, dry bath, the joy of playing in sand but nothing to stick, cling or chafe. The glare, however, was overwhelming. Too much even for sunglasses. Tired of squinting through tearing eyes, I dragged myself from the unusual beach, shuffling through shells that sucked like coarse quicksand, and laboured my way to the car.

The following day, a white pelican with black, yellow-rimmed eyes was trundling toward us. Its webbed feet thwacked on the sand like a diver in fins plodding toward the water. It stopped and looked up at us, reminding me of a *Flintstones* trash compactor. I wanted to scrape off a dinner plate into its dangling dewlap. It may have read my mind, and turned and thwacked away – a short, pigeon-toed Aquaman.

We were at Monkey Mia, Shark Bay, halfway up Australia's west coast. For 50 years, generations of wild bottlenose dolphins had been coming to these shallows, interacting with people. They weren't fed and there was no pattern to the visits. Morning tended to be best, but you never knew.

The park had just opened and there were already a dozen of us at the beach, mumbling in morning whispers. A game warden came by, looking the part in khaki game shirt, Stubbies and Akubra. The mumbles grew louder, anticipation in the air. The warden waded into the water and turned to us on shore. He spoke with the expected upturned twang, turning everything into a question.

"Now sonscreen, plies?" he said. "Iss stings thore oys? An' now pitting plies?"

I wanted to ask if that meant heavy petting, decided not to and made a mental note to not make out with Deb while we waited. We stood, gazing across the water, until someone squeaked, "They're coming!" And far out in the bay, three dorsal fins broke the surface. My heart raced from years of *Jaws* terror, until I remembered this was what we'd hoped to see and I began to breathe again.

The dolphins meandered into the bay, swimming in a wide, leisurely serpentine. We pressed out toward them, thigh-high in cool water. The *pffooo-pffooo* of their breathing grew louder – the sound of clearing snorkels.

"Thit's Puck?" the warden said. "The wun with the woit mack on 'im?"

The dolphins moved in and swam through our group. Puck pushed past my leg, touching my hand as he passed. The skin was rubbery, both smooth and coarse, and felt as though I'd been touched by something electric.

"Look!" someone said. And we realized there was a baby dolphin with the pod, a little further out. The adult dolphins continued interacting with us but kept between the humans and the calf, who stole the show, porpoising in shallow dives and breathing in gasps – an excited child at play. After a spell that felt both long and brief, the pod began a slow retreat out to the bay, the adults jumping and splashing, encircling the calf. They swam away in growing circles and with a final blast of *pffooo-pffooo-pffooo* they vanished, leaving us standing in the water, smiling.

11

INDIAN OCEAN

Tim Winton:

"There is nowhere else I'd rather be, nothing else I would
prefer to be doing. I am at the beach looking west with
the continent behind me…I have my bearings."

Perth, Western Australia. A broad beach of brilliant sand curved for
miles, fronting a deep purple sea. The Fremantle Doctor was ferocious, blasting shoreline with hurricane gusts. It was Christmas Day.
Venturing out in the violence, I was forced to cinch my cap until my
head resembled an hourglass. Offshore, the Indian Ocean bled like
squid ink, flecked with dancing sun.

In his book *The Coast*, Chris Hammer writes, "On the sand and
in the water, there is a sort of innocence to be found, where the arti-
fice falls away, where we are children again, playing in nature." On
this gusty holiday, there were only a handful of us at play. A group of
teens were running some sort of girls-versus-boys surf relay, riding in
breakers, dragging boards ashore, then tagging off while the next ran
into the water to do it all again. There was laughter and high fives; the
energy good, and the girls were clearly winning.

I sat on the beach, barely able to stay upright in the wind. Gulls
and songbirds were doing the same, hunkered in the sand. A sparrow
tried taking off only to be blown back 20 metres before giving up. A
little ways down the beach, a man sat just beyond the reach of high
crashing surf in a full lotus position, meditating. He radiated calm,
amazing me with his peaceful concentration in the midst of the gale.

Surrounded by an ocean beach postcard, I squinted into the wind
and wondered at its source. India? Arabia? Madagascar? The stuff of

National Geographic and childhood fantasy. I understood Winton's perspective.

From Perth we went to Rottnest Island on a fast ferry – a sleek white thing with the look of a *Miami Vice* gangster boat, except crammed with people. I made the mistake of suggesting the trip for the day after Christmas (Boxing Day), when all of Western Australia was there as well.

In Aboriginal mythology, the island's referred to as Wadjemup (place across the water) and used to be attached to the mainland. But a few thousand years ago the Indian Ocean seeped in, leaving quokkas here and not much else. Quokkas are furry little marsupials with teddy bear faces, squirrel-like bodies and tails like rats. When the Dutch arrived in the 17th century, mistaking the quokkas for rats, they gave this pristine spot its Dutch name of "Rat Nest."

Following a rough ride in the outsized cigar boat, we landed at the unfortunately named but picturesque island – white sand, indigo ocean, a handsome lighthouse and (approximately) a billion day trippers. We rode a rattling bus around the island, hoping some distance from the ferry port would thin out the crowd. Which helped, somewhat. I went for a swim in water that was nearly purple. A black lava shelf extended from shore, creating a long, wide platform to deep water. Ocean washing over the shelf was a metre deep, but at the far edge the ocean floor dropped away, providing convenient access for divers.

Later, on a plane, I visited with a woman named Paula. She had short brown hair, round glasses and a slightly pinched look about her. She was a teacher from Canada, on a year-long exchange in Perth. She said she didn't care much for the job, nor the house she was in, which was part of the exchange. And she didn't seem particularly enamoured with Perth as a city. The reason she took the job, she explained, was the diving around Rottnest. And, as she described it, everything changed. She relaxed, her face warmed. Even the space around her felt more inviting. Although not particularly talkative, her body language became effusive, radiating happiness as she spoke about the water, the ocean her internal geography.

We talked a short while, then I asked, as I do, what Paula thought the meaning of life might be. And it was as though I'd dragged a needle from vinyl – *brrzzzzptt* – conversation ceasing, a dead, silent stop. Everything about her shut off, a drawbridge slamming closed. I felt I'd yanked Paula from her happy place. But, despite the truncation of our visit, I suspect I glimpsed an answer, somewhere off the shores of Rottnest, just beyond that submerged lava shelf.

From a Hilroy exercise book (*cahier d'exercices*) half-plain, half-ruled, with a cover in yellow and blue:

If I forgot I was in a country far from North America, I remembered the instant I turned on a TV. There were six Sky channels: three were showing cricket, two showed Bollywood trailers and the final channel had basketball – all the players were white and, needless to say, not particularly good. I went back to the cricket and tried to figure it out.

To the unsuspecting North American, at first glance cricket can resemble baseball, but in fact is quite different. In baseball, the guy throwing the ball's called a pitcher. He stands on a mound and uses a rubber. In cricket, he's called the bowler and does not use a rubber. It goes without saying cricketers have more STDs.

Baseball pitchers rub the ball between their hands to wear it down. Cricket bowlers tend to rub the ball against their genitals, also to wear the ball down and, I presume, it feels pleasant as well. Cricketers may also itch more from the STDs.

Baseball pitchers remain essentially in one spot, other than moving to spit and realign their junk, while cricket bowlers run a great distance up the field before chucking the ball like a windmill. The distance each bowler runs varies, but I believe it's something like eight furlongs, or 12 stone, or ha' penny and a farthing.

While a baseball pitcher tries to throw the ball into a strike zone and get a batter out, a cricket bowler's objective seems to be throwing the ball as hard as possible at the batsman's crotch in an attempt to knock him down or break the wicket. The wicket, I presume, is a bone in the upper thigh region. Cricket batsmen wear helmets and faceguards that provide protection when they're knocked down by a successful bowl to their groins.

In cricket, runs are scored by batsmen running between stumps after a hit, or hitting the ball out of the playing area, not unlike baseball. But in cricket runs are scored in singles, fours and sixes. In cricket, "duck" is a term used to indicate that a batsman got no runs. The same term is used in baseball to indicate a ball is flying at one's head.

The duration of the two games can also vary greatly. In baseball, a game lasts nine innings, give or take, while in cricket, as I understand it, a match lasts until they break for tea, the solstice changes or the umpire reaches mandatory retirement age of 100.

(Side Note: There's a cricket match, I believe, called the Coronation Test that's been played continuously since Queen Elizabeth II took the throne in 1952. There are only four players still in the game, three living, not to mention two dwindling teams waiting to use the field.)

12

SOUTH PACIFIC

From another blue Moleskine, having gone front to back using
only right sides, now working back to front, writing on the left:

*The notion of living a life of travel struck me, first time I heard it,
as pompous. Self-aggrandizing. But the fact is, if I were drafting my
resume now, claiming a life of travel would be accurate. Metaphors
aside, we're all travellers, moving toward or away from things,
what we long for, what we fear. Doing so with a pack, passport
and open mind still strikes me as the purest form of pursuit.*

With a kangaroo-like bound, we find ourselves across the continent,
the opposite side from where we watched Indian sunsets. Now we're
viking in New South Wales, where sun rises from our old friend the
Pacific. We'd taken a westbound train from Sydney to Leura, a small
inviting town in the Blue Mountains, and had a bistro lunch under
a coolabah tree. I ate rabbit. A good-sized parrot flew into the tree,
sidestepped along a branch and shat on our table with a wet splat, a
hair's breadth from my hare. I couldn't decide if its aim was poor or
exceptional.

We found our lodging, checked in and I went to brave outback heat
and explore the Jamison Valley and Blue Mountains. Thousands of
hectares of blue gums exude a fine mist of oil, which evaporates from
the leaves and tints the valley air a hazy shade of greenish blue. An angled afternoon sun accentuated the effect and the forest glowed like
Avatar's planet Pandora.

Sticky, relentless black flies crept on my face – in eyes, ears and
nose, driving me batty in moments, but a strong breeze blew through,
keeping the worst at bay. Following a mishmash of narrow trails, I cut

through eucalypts and dry scrub into deep gorges, long-dry riverbeds and back along high cliffs of sheer sandstone. A pair of king parrots flew past, screeching – big birds in vibrant red, blue and green, and a kookaburra sat on a tall stump, laughing hysterically. I leapt between massive, coppery-gold rocks, worn from years of exposure, and crawled to an overhang with unobstructed views of the valley, stretched in a long, glowing *U*. Laying back on the slab, I imagined it may well have been there when the earth formed, the feeling one of timelessness.

As sun approached a treed horizon, I made my way back, finding a trickle of creek to follow and pushing my way through dense brush. A tiny, pylon-orange spider caught my eye, creeping along the ground, and while I couldn't identify it, I was certain it was one of the hundreds of things in the area that could kill me. I carried on, breaking through bush, following faint remains of a sandy trail. I'd been gone a few hours and was a long way from any signs of civilization when I spotted something deep in a thistle. I pushed back some twigs and realized it was a golf ball – Titleist Pro Tour (extra-long distance), which made me laugh. I imagined some hacker whacking through the tall thickets, golf bag over a shoulder, swinging a nine iron like a machete to emerge panting, doubled over, and croak, "Titleist?"

From another coiled book of A 4, recycled, lined paper with thick, hard cover, the look of a brown paper shopping bag:

A fat green lizard stared, unblinking, from across the living room, like a roommate who's called the big room, with no intention of sharing.

We'd just entered the place in Byron Bay, having seen the rental unit with the uninvited foot-long guest for the first time, and were driving back to town to find new accommodation about 60 seconds later. This was pre-smartphone and wireless data. We'd crossed the state line from New South Wales to Queensland, losing an hour with the time change despite travelling due north. By the time we got to the tourist office, we had two minutes to find a new place before they closed for the weekend. The woman behind the counter was friendly but clearly had no intention of staying late. After pleasantries, we had 90 seconds, and not a lot of options.

"How much is *this* place?" I asked, pointing at a photo of a house like Frank Lloyd Wright's Taliesin West. The woman quoted me the price of a car.

"Hmm," I said. "No last-minute discounts, if it's going to be empty tonight anyway?"

She made a call and the price dropped to a fraction of the quoted rate.

"We'll take it," I said, with 20 seconds to spare.

The sprawling home had a large swimming pool and Zen garden with manicured sand, lava rock, trimmed bonsai and high bamboo that provided privacy for open-air, outdoor showers. The house was beautifully appointed, but we were surprised to find the plush bathroom was equipped with an environmentally friendly toilet, essentially a high-end outhouse in which the user tosses in scoops of woodchips rather than flushing. A fat, hairy spider crept out and meandered away. We decided we could hold it for a day or so. Deb read the guest information book, which guaranteed, "With the earth-friendly toilet, no odour will be omitted."

"Do you think they meant emitted?" she asked.

I sniffed and was uncertain.

It was Saint Patrick's Day and our travelling companion at this juncture was from Ireland, inspiring us to party appropriately. There was a bottle of sparkling wine in the fridge that lasted about as long as Tom Cruise's Irish accent in *Far and Away*. We went out and brought back a great deal more liquor, getting into stereotypical character. Celebrations continued most successfully; later that night we all attended mass and became foul-mouthed Red Sox fans.

Next day we hiked clifftop trails around Cape Byron Lighthouse, Australia's most easterly point. Far below, pods of dolphins played in ragged surf rolling south to Broken Head. Later I went surfing. It hurt and I did it poorly. I was sure I'd been good at it in my youth when I surfed quite a bit in Hawaii. I didn't remember it being so painful, and convinced myself the equipment must've changed, or possibly the surf, what with global warming and rising ocean levels. Dragging my board across the beach, Deb snapped a photo in which I looked competent. I liked the picture and anticipated lying about it in the future.

It was late in the season and sun set early. The sky was a ruddy smear of rouge that softened to coral-orange and mauve as beachside trees – eucalypts, palms, pines and beeches – warmed in dampening light. Hundreds of rainbow lorikeets swooped through the trees in a shrieking swarm – a blur of colour and deafening noise – a wondrous, ear-splitting cacophony. I dropped the surfboard at our unit and went back to the beach, walking along soft sand, gazing out to the water and nearly tripped over a naked couple shagging on the beach. I felt I'd stumbled into "Pasolini's 'The Third Test Match'" from Monty Python – Terry Jones in a dream-like cricket match, leaping over a coupling couple to bowl. I felt awkward, happening upon them, then realized we were in the middle of a public beach and the display was probably the intention. I stole a couple of fleshy glances and decided I quite liked the Australian term for shagging – rooting – as though everyone's pulling for you.

Surfer shenanigans aside, I found this swath of country immersive in its natural beauty, once more triggering a poet's perspective. As well as appearing in *Forever Cast in Endless Time*, this piece was published in Australia's *Quadrant* magazine, inspired not only by the scenery and sentiment but by the words of W.J. Dakin in *Australian Seashores*: "We speak of course of that narrow strip of land over which the ocean waves and moon-powered tides are masters – that margin of territory that remains wild despite the proximity of cities or of land surfaces modified by industry."

FREESTYLE SUNSET

I drift, the direction of sleep, sound of surging sea, set
to birdsong score – rooftop ruckus harmony, cacophony
staccato squawks with whizzing gliss, acappella chirps
on bee-bop peeps with whippoorwill whines, lorikeet
prides in seven bands, glitter floats and dance halls dressed
in hanging mirror balls, spinning, radiating lightness
chorusing avian close encounters, extraterrestrial melody
sung to sun submerging, settling into simmering ocean swell,
and still the sail-like sweep of setting rainbow sings, sings, sings

Entered in Notes on an iPad; a cheap model
I'd lay flat and type like a keyboard:

*From a compact deck in a city apartment, an eclectic architectural
vista – brick chimneys, red tile roofs, sandstone facades and Victorian
terrace homes with ornate wrought iron on windows and doors.
Beneath massive old eucalypts were squat palms and bougainvillea
in purples and reds, the gums reaching toward salvation.*

Slumping into a patio chair, I opened a stubby bottle of Victoria Bitter
and watched the bottle sweat. A gust of warm wind shushed a leafy
green canopy over Bourke Street. Rainbow lorikeets swooped past with
a pleasing shriek. A koel bird sang its unusual song of heightening anticipation, inching up a scale in a flat, lingering crescendo, like building to a sneeze that never happens. We were in Sydney's Surry Hills,
a bohemian neighbourhood with age and character, rich diversity, affluence and grit, grown together like a reasonably happy dysfunctional
family. I felt entirely at home.

A cockatoo squawked as it flew over the Sydney Cricket Grounds and an ibis strolled along the grass beneath our unit, a million years out of place. Dark cloud rolled in and night fell early. The sound of cicadas faded and a dog barked, anxious. Bats filled the sky, nearly hovering in flight. And as the dark curtain fluttered past, the night exploded. Lightning bolts ripped through an inky sky and the coast surged in pulsing pink, the horizon a shudder of blood-like flashes.

Next day was calm, the city cleansed. Our lunch server was friendly, taking time to visit despite being busy.

"They had it right for 60,000 years before we fucked it up," he said.

We were across the street from our rental, seated at a sidewalk table in a funky coffee shop called Cowbell 808. Every table and mismatched chair leaned slightly. The food, coffee and service were exceptional. The place was named after the Roland 808, the first programmable drum machine from the 1980s. I owned one, connected to an electric piano and a Juno 106 synthesizer. The combination was versatile, enabling you to make any sound you wanted, provided you wanted everything to sound like Harold Faltermeyer, with cowbell.

Thirty years later it was retro chic, made cool by a 20-year-old, loosely scripted *Saturday Night Live* sketch with Christopher Walken and Will Ferrell that went on too long (as they do). Fashion comes full circle, looping back on itself like a four-measure bossa nova beat on the Cowbell 808. Maybe I should've hung onto it, following Dad's example as he did with neckties, keeping every one he ever owned – everything from neat slender ones to wide swathes of fabric that covered the chest like a colourful piece of lumber.

"They'll come back," he'd say. "Just you wait."

The conversation with our new local friend continued. We talked about the neighbourhood. It had been a number of years since Deb was here, travelling solo, and she described her experience.

"Yeah," he said. "Redfern was dodgy. You wouldn't wanna be there without a local guide. But after the Olympics, values doubled and things got gentrified. It's a good mix now – rich and poor, posh and cazh. It's like an extension of Surry Hills."

Surry Hills went through the same thing a hundred years earlier. It was a seedy downtown sprawl – brothels, drinking and gambling houses – essentially present-day Vegas but without the French Canadian entertainers.

"Yeah," he went on. "It used to be the non-Aboriginals just wanted to put the Aboriginals away; keep 'em down. But it's better now; it's gotten a lot better. People used to come and want to see the kangaroos. Now they come and want to learn about the Aboriginals, embrace the culture. It's better."

The following day, we woke to jungle sounds in the city, a mix of tropical birds and traffic. Bright sun began the day, then disappeared in dark cloud that covered the sky like a cast iron lid. We made our way to Paddington for the Saturday market, where warrens of stalls surrounded the invitingly named Paddington Uniting Church, a chunky sandstone structure under mottled green gum trees.

Entering the market was a pleasant nasal assault – fresh flowers, herbal soaps, leather, wood and eucalyptus – but the space felt congested, cut off from Oxford Street's refreshing breezes. Sun emerged, hitting the blacktop and making the market ten degrees hotter than the street a few strides away. Rhythmic world music played somewhere, segueing into reggae. This welcoming, colourful crush of sellers and shoppers could be anywhere in the world.

Paddington too was another bridging neighbourhood – high-end retail seeping into dirty storefronts with edge. All walks in a short walk. We left the market and made our way west and north on Oxford Street. Within minutes we'd left Paddington and entered the bustle of Sydney's CBD (Central Business District), the leafy swath of Hyde Park, the cooling splash of Archibald Fountain and serene presence of Saint Mary's Cathedral.

It was rainy when we left one accommodation for a few days in Bondi Junction to experience another neighbourhood. The heat and rain created a permeating damp like an endless steam room. By midday the shower was a driving, diagonal torrent. We climbed stairs to the Australian Museum, shook water from jackets and joined a short queue for an Alexander the Great exhibit, a travelling collection from the Russian State Hermitage Museum.

Alexander, tutored by Aristotle, built quite a resume, despite only running things for 12 years. His reign began in 336 BCE, when a bodyguard assassinated his father. Predictably, Alexander's first order of business was culling bodyguards, and anyone else whose loyalty was suspect. Alexander's expansion of power began with conquering Thessaly, when he took his troops over Mount Ossa at night, catching their opponents unawares. The brief history I read stated, "When the Thessalians awoke the next day they found Alexander in their rear and promptly surrendered."

As King of Macedon, he went on a series of campaigns and gradually conquered the "civilized" world, becoming king of Persia and pharaoh of Egypt, as you do. He had a remarkable public relations machine, espousing his grandeur long after his demise. "The Great" came later, record keepers effectively perpetuating Alexander's manufactured public persona. PR aside, he did manage to accomplish a great deal during his reign. In addition to plenty of killing, monumental consumption of drink, and sexual activity that would even impress Robbie Williams, Alexander brought the Greek language, science and philosophy to the Western world. Democracy, needless to say, came later.

Next morning. Cloudless sky, brilliant sun. The temperature dropped 15 degrees to a balmy mid-20 centigrade. We jogged to Bondi Beach, joined the coastal walkway and ran south through Tamarama and Bronte. Homes sat nestled in greenery, overlooking sun-streaked ocean and a jagged cliff of pockmarked sandstone.

Spending an afternoon strolling through Edgecliff and Woollahra, we shopped for books and food. We passed huge palm fronds, dry and woody on the ground, mauve-blossomed jacaranda and an Illawarra flame tree in full red bloom. Half the flowers had fallen, creating an illusory reflecting pool at the base of the tree. We traipsed through urban bush at Harbourview Park – stringy pockets of untamed outback tucked beneath the motorway, gazing toward the harbour like hermits with views of civilization, an unbridgeable distance away.

The low buzzing hum of a didgeridoo vibrated over the water, bouncing off concrete, brick, glass and steel. The white of the Opera House was muted under ashen cloud. Beyond Farm Cove and Mrs. Macquarie's Chair, gunmetal navy ships at Woolloomooloo mimicked a threatening sky. Yes, Woolloomooloo, where according to Pete Brown all the country's surplus *O*s are kept.

The city's vastness and thrum of activity, I suspect, dulls the senses, creating a kind of indifference. Sydney's heat, ironically, drains its citizens of warmth. But like any metropolis, it's an amalgam of individuals. Friendly interactions occur. And when they do, it's extraordinary – kindness a lifebuoy in the crush of a faceless city.

Local author Delia Falconer calls it a city of longing. And I couldn't help but think Sydneysiders want desperately to live in a worldly, European city. Determined to remain active, they live outdoors, making the harbour their personal play place. But the brashness and bravado often masks an underlying sentiment of sadness – being thrust into this enviable seaside resort, but now what? Like being granted your wish, only to realize at times it's a hollow blessing.

On my own I explored alleyways, worn stone stairwells and entryways, pondering long forgotten mysteries – from George Street to Pitt Street, through the Rocks, Martin Place and the Strand Arcade, along Chinatown, through Pyrmont and Sydney's Fish Market, and once more through Surry Hills, Paddington, Bondi, Tamarama and Bronte.

Together we browsed crafts and produce at Bondi Junction's market, bought food at Double Bay's organic market and picnicked on lamb and tabbouleh, watching ferries chug north to Manly, before walking beneath high gums, red-bloomed rata, rose hibiscus and bright white plumeria. Skirting Hyde Park and the Domain, we followed Macquarie Street, where bundles of wool were once winched onto waiting ships.

Outside the Museum of Sydney, the whispering poles – commanding and haunting – hiss secrets from the past (a mixed-media display with soft, haunting audio), the pocket of creativity a striking juxtaposition to the towering CBD. I was excited to finally get the chance to visit the museum, and now, of all things, the feature exhibit was a showcase of British Columbia, which made me laugh, some new faceless entity telling me where I came from was just as interesting as anywhere else. The feature included carved totem poles from Haida Gwaii, a unique contrast to the Aboriginal-inspired whispering poles, and felt like another nod to our continuing *Gone Viking* adventure.

We changed into running gear and jogged Centennial Park's Grand Drive, beneath raised cannons and a high bronze statue of someone important, standing proud, head drenched in bird shit. We ate at a couple of restaurants touted as fine dining. They were unremarkable. Yet, in hindsight, I realized the description was, in fact, spot on. They were fine. Not particularly good. Just, fine. The best meals we enjoyed were the simplest: slipper lobster at the fish market, a kebab at a ferry berth and lamb in phyllo from a farmers' market in Double Bay. A highlight from one restaurant experience was the weather – a spectacular lightning storm igniting the sky in explosive flashes like New Year's Eve. Thunder rumbled without stopping, sheet lightning pulsed and blue-white forks sliced over the Opera House, stretching across the harbour. Never before had I experienced thunder that boomed and rolled continuously, on and on and on.

Crossing the city by train, I watched an old man with close-cropped hair holding the overhead handrail. His sleeve slid down slightly, revealing a string of numbers, the unmistakable tattoo of a Holocaust survivor. Two muscle-bound guys seated nearby self-consciously held hands, awkwardly linking fingers. The one guy shot me an angry look. I smiled back, but his frown told me he may never be at ease. I can imagine but can't truly empathize, and felt I knew the city a little bit more. Sydney's Pride Parade and Mardi Gras celebrations are huge, with enormous participation, an encompassing snapshot of the city. There are bigots, like anywhere, but the majority does its best to quash hatred with humour and wit. I read of a graffito spray-painted on a

Sydney wall declaring, "God hates homos." To which someone added, "But he loves tabbouleh."

From the hardcover journal of lined A4, now a mash-up of doodles and geometric shapes, along with the longhand and prose:

> *Bottlebrush, banksia and kangaroo's paw lined the*
> *road as I ran to Bondi, then to Bronte and back,*
> *finishing with laps in Bondi Icebergs pool.*

I swam in the outside lane, fronting the ocean where angry waves burst over a breakwater in frothy blue spray. Back on the clifftops walkway, brisk walkers and joggers passed, huffing and puffing like fairy-tale wolves. One of the first Europeans to record their experience here in the 1840s called this beach a place of peculiar loneliness. The busier it is, the more fitting I find the sentiment.

Ancient carvings adorn the stone at the water's edge, interpretive art of the Aboriginal Eora. I sat in a nook in the sandstone carved by the elements, a natural bench with a jutting stone ceiling. Pockets of sandstone became faces, like pillars atop Gaudí's La Pedrera – Roman centurions staring seaward. Beneath me on barnacle-crusted rocks, silver-clawed emerald crabs crept beneath a wash of rolling waves. Down the beach stood the Bondi Surf Pavilion and Hotel, familiar landmarks, extensions of the sandy shore.

Early in the 20th century, the local executioner, affectionately nicknamed "The Gentleman Hangman," lived here, a solitary life in a shack on a hill overlooking Bondi. According to a historical plaque, he suffered a nasty accident later in life and lost his nose. "How did he smell?" you might ask. I know I did. But following the accident he stopped interacting with people, leaving us to wonder.

Another day, I jogged under intense sun, giddily running intervals up and down the Opera House stairs. Sulphur-crested cockatoos screeched from the trees, while ibises flew past, looking like Air France Concordes. I passed Mrs. Macquarie's Chair, past anglers fishing for bream, snapper and bonito, to the finger wharf of Woolloomooloo, and slowed to circle Harry's Pie Shop, a small trailer-like building that's a Sydney institution. Photos of celebrities who've eaten here over the past 60 years are tacked and taped to the exterior walls. There was one of Richard Branson, smiling and holding a pie he clearly had no intention of eating, and another of Elton John, face buried in his food. The picture was taken late at night and Sir Elton had the look of someone who's just left a club, lacking good judgment. For all I know he too has sampled the wares of the King of Donairs. There was also a photo of *American Pie*'s Jason Biggs, and to my inestimable relief he was eating his pie and not humping it.

Later the Opera House gleamed like conquistadors' helmets and the Harbour Bridge towers shone gold. A green and yellow ferry named *Friendship* trundled into Circular Quay, while a balloon drifted past, yellow and red – Aussie lifeguard colours. As sun set, flying foxes sailed from the Botanic Gardens through a gap between high-rises. Thousands of the huge bats flew past, immediately to my right, eye level on the tenth storey. As they flapped over the harbour, evening sun vanished and the city backlit their metre-wide wingspans, turning the skyline to Gotham.

New Year's Day. How this sneaks up remains a mystery. At least to me. The previous night was spent in a crush of affable drunks cheering at pounding music and fireworks exploding around Circular Quay, spraying from the Harbour Bridge, Darling Harbour, a floating barge and rooftops in Sydney's CBD. We'd seen it before but every year's better, the bar raised as the city continually outdoes itself.

(Side Note: The tunes are generally the same – proper Australiana – Kylie, AC/DC, INXS and Midnight Oil, but the song speed changes, getting faster each year, perhaps in keeping with tech and our outlook on life.)

We made our way to Bondi Beach while a kookaburra watched us pass and a spinifex pigeon sat on a wire, tufted feathers waggling atop its head. We accessed the coastal walkway, following a jagged shoreline offering views of Port Jackson to the north, Botany Bay to the south and a gleaming cobalt Tasman stretching east. Under hot morning sun we went to the saltwater pools at Bronte Park, naturally filled with cold sea water. I joined a handful of swimmers, slipping into the cover of a *Travel and Leisure* magazine, squinting against sun off a curving sea.

From there we sauntered through Tamarama, passing lifeguards leisurely starting their day, the morning after. Half-full beer bottles lined the seawalk. Then we realized they weren't half-finished beer at all but 12-ounce receptacles for urine. Perhaps Howard Hughes lived nearby. While we skirted the recyclable bottles of pee, a lifeguard whizzed up on a scooter, calling to his co-workers.

"Fahhhck boys, have I got a story for you!" he shouted.

Deb and I laughed. Hard. There was no need to hear the story.

When I went back to the beach another day, the ocean pool was closed. Thieves had dug out the copper pipe used for drainage, leaving a gaping hole. But I'd walked three kilometres to get there and was determined to have a swim, so instead I stood on the beach, facing towering breakers, debating my decision and steeling my nerve. A couple of diehards were in the water, being thrashed about in high, angry surf. The lifeguards were down the beach, preoccupied with pool repair and giggling, bikini-clad posers.

I once saw a CPR video of Bondi lifeguards bringing a guy back to life after he'd been floating dead for an uncanny amount of time. They were uncertain but figured he'd been dead for ten or 15 minutes. So I had confidence in the guys down the beach with their white noses and Budgy Smugglers, and ran into the surging wall of water. It felt like those fairground rides you see where someone (usually a kid) gets strapped into a taut bungee harness attached in a horizontal X between four tall poles, where they dangle above the ground. The operator tugs down on the kid and sends them flying into the air, where they bounce for a while, until someone yanks on their leg again, or the kid throws up.

I did much the same thing, letting the surf heave me up and down for a short time, enough to fill my ears with salt water, until I remembered former Australian Prime Minister Harold Holt, who'd come to a beach like this, ignored his companions' warnings and went for a swim just offshore, never to be seen again. So I scrambled to shore and futilely tried to remove water from my ears, satisfied I'd managed a swim and accepting the fact that I was now deaf.

From the back of a curled receipt – semi-glossy paper spat from a cash register – for two lamb gyros and a water:

Turns out zebras and giraffes get along. Who knew?

Apparently, this is common knowledge amongst zoologists and fans of the *Madagascar* franchise, but it was news to me. The two groups of animals shared a big space and were socializing when we visited Sydney's Taronga Zoo. Which reminded me of the time Deb and I went to a party where nearly all the guests – women and men – were basketball players. Next day we couldn't understand why our necks were so sore, until it occurred to us we'd spent an entire evening craning our heads back to converse with a roomful of giants. I felt an obligation to warn the zebras as they exchanged pleasantries with the giraffes.

After the zoo, we hiked gum-treed shoreline in Sydney Harbour National Park, which encircles the harbour in narrow swathes of forest, creating a natural wrap around the city. A metre-long goanna (monitor lizard) sunbathed on deep grass and watched us pass, the look of those poolside people who spend all their life in the sun.

We walked by a sandy swimming beach with shark netting – a semi-circular enclosure around the shore. The top of the net drooped well beneath the surface in a few spots and looked more like the kind of net used to lower live bait into a fish tank.

Exploring Sydney's north shore, we wandered around the surfing community of Manly. At Manly Beach a crush of would-be swimmers crowded the shore, looking out to the water. We learned there were ten or so mako sharks in the bay, like grazers browsing a buffet. Lifeguards roared around on jet skis in an attempt to herd the sharks out to deeper water.

The temperature was in the mid-40s Celsius, and there was a story in the *Sydney Morning Herald* explaining that ice cream trucks had stopped running. Their compressors were shutting down in the heat and mobile freezers were no longer working. It was too hot for ice cream!

Enduring extreme heat, we trekked around North Head with spectacular views across the water to the city. In 1860 a mortgagee's ad describing this area read, "The romantic loveliness of the situation must be seen to be appreciated – being immediately on one of those delightful jutting headlands, surrounded by wild, bold, majestic scenery, softened by the still, lake-like waters of Middle Harbour." Not bad for 19th-century ad copy. And, in fact, quite accurate.

We walked through the Sydney Fish Market, stocked with seafood in every size, shape and colour imaginable, reminiscent of my dripping pass through the market in Vancouver: countless round fish, flat fish, eels, bivalves, univalves and crustaceans. The wholesale market operates as a Dutch auction – prices start high and then decline until there's a buyer. Highly efficient, the method cuts auction time in half.

Amongst the displays, there was a side of tuna the size of a sofa and swimmer crabs the colour of lapis lazuli with a bold sign, "Handle at your own risk!" They reminded me of jumping crabs I saw on lava rock in crashing surf on Hawaii's Big Island. The crabs were the size of tennis balls, inky blue in colour, and would rocket a couple of feet in a single leap at blinding speed. It was something from a nightmare, creepy and fascinating – their movement almost quicker than the eye could process.

Weaving through fish market kiosks, I stopped to buy fresh kingfish, like ordering deli meat, sliced raw and served as sashimi over the counter and charged by weight, which I ate with a drizzle of soy and my handy travel chopsticks that collapse into a pen-like container. We browsed the stalls and assembled a picnic of papaya, cucumbers, avocado, citrus, a small mountain of Balmain bugs (slipper lobsters) and ate with a view of the harbour, the smell of the fish market and the ambient call of big healthy gulls.

In the green heart of the Domain, we stopped at the Art Gallery of New South Wales to see the travelling exhibit of Terracotta Warriors from Xi'an. The room had soft, stage-quality lighting and thoughtfully paired music, bringing the roomful of warhorses and soldiers to life. It was hauntingly real, as though we'd stumbled into a crypt like Howard Carter in Tut's tomb. Terracotta eyes followed us around the room as though we'd interrupted the warriors at work. Silent and patient they stood, waiting for us to leave, it seemed, so they could get back to guarding their emperor.

Early the following morning, we enjoyed breakfast at Bills (no apostrophe), part of a chain by celebrity chef Bill Granger. I bought two of his cookbooks, as much for their high-end photos of Sydney as for his recipes. This particular outlet was a stylish, converted old house in leafy Darlinghurst, where we ate sweet ricotta pancakes with honeycomb butter, the kind of meal that makes you seriously consider changing your country of residence to get more.

For a change of pace, we dressed like adults and went for high tea at Bennelong at the Opera House, where a symphony conductor played piano while a singer performed bits of opera. A colourful array of tiny sandwiches, pastries and petits fours were served, and we sipped pink champagne while sun glared off the blue of the harbour to the angelic voice of the diva, as sweet and satisfying as the tea. Another time we returned at night. Again I filled up on finger sandwiches, and we sat high in the wings as Stephen Merchant made us laugh on his Hello Ladies tour.

I took a day off from journaling. You missed nothing. The only notable event being a moment of joy as I watched NFL football live on a Monday morning. The Date Line remains a wondrous invention.

Back to viking. Circular Quay was a dazzle of sunlight and ferry traffic bustling through the waterway like characters from a children's story. We had drinks and food on a patio with a view of Harbour Bridge and the Opera House. Afterward we strolled along Writers Walk, reading quotations in brass by those who lived here, travelled here and wrote about the area. Despite being male-centric, the list of names was impressive: Arthur Conan Doyle, Joseph Conrad, Rudyard Kipling, Charles Darwin, Umberto Eco, D.H. Lawrence, Banjo Paterson, James Michener, Robert Louis Stevenson and Mark Twain.

We carried on past the historic Customs House, Cadman's Cottage and the old Sydney Sailors' Home, making me wish I had a hook for a hand and an eye patch.

"What happened to your hand?"

"Oh, a shark took that from me."

"And your eye?"

"Well, I'd just gotten the hook..."

Then we meandered through the Rocks – Sydney's birthplace. The weekend market was a bustling affair – an eclectic array of art and crafts – drawings, paintings and carved hardwood burls of rich jarrah and polished red gum amongst the usual array of tourist junk, postcards and tee-shirts.

It was here the First Fleet arrived and the convict–settlers disembarked: about 750 men, 200 women (all named Sheila) and some heavily armed British soldiers. Under the infantry's watchful gaze, the new immigrants set about chiselling away at the sandstone cliffs – still visible near the site of the weekend market – planting vegetables in dry earth, crushing rock for a road, constructing buildings and learning to drop their Rs and speak through their noses.

(Side Note: Watching local news each day, I'd have to look away, the violence and bloodshed too disturbing. But once Aussie rules football highlights were over, it was quite all right.)

When those first forced immigrants were here, during some recreation time, a group was playing football (soccer) when one of the prisoners got bored or frustrated with the pace of the game, picked up the ball and ran with it, much like that first impatient cheater in England who "invented" rugby. Back when I was on the playground, any kid who picked up the soccer ball and ran with it would get a penalty, or a new ball, depending on their speed. But here in the penal colony, ironically, no one was penalized. Instead, a new national game was born: Australian rules football (Aussie rules, or footy). Whether it was a desire to set themselves apart from the country that sent them here to rot, or simply the fact the rules were invented by convicts, the main rule of the new game seemed to be an absence of rules. They essentially took soccer's rule book and, rather than throwing it out, tore it in half and used it to box the referee's ears.

At the Rocks, the city's colourful history is palpable. The Gadigal of the Eora Nation were here, watching the First Fleet land. I strolled down Sydney's Suez Canal. One or two centuries ago I'd have been taking my life in my hands, the narrow alleyway a haven of brutal crime. Behind me rose a natural sandstone wall, chiselled by convicts and time, vertically striped – shadowy lines seeping from gold-coloured stone like tears, as though moved being in the midst of such beauty. At the end of the lane I faced Sydney's harbour and randomly opened Delia Falconer's *Sydney* and read her description of where I was standing, the exact view I was looking at, and wanted to cry like the sandstone.

A shallow store with a long display window drew us in – Ariel Booksellers. Despite its small size, the store offered a wide selection. The vibe was good; the staff cared. It made you want to read. I approached an employee who looked like a librarian from central casting.

"If I'm limited for space and want one book – pure Australiana – what would you recommend?" I asked.

"Easy," she said. "Tim Winton's *Cloudstreet*; required reading for all of us at school."

It was a good read, so I began ploughing through his stuff, including *Land's Edge*, one I love and reread regularly. Simply picking it up takes me back to the Rocks, to the peaceful interior of Ariel (sadly, now gone).

Years later I visited with Winton at a writers' festival, thanking him for instilling in me the courage to write *Wonderful Magical Words*, my first book, a bestseller that raised money for Make-A-Wish Foundation. And once more I felt it can be good to meet your heroes.

I shared some ridiculous photos on social media of small rubber ducks I carried around Oceania, clicking pics of the duckies as they visited scenic sites. One that I loved, taken on film, I learned after the fact was unusably blurry. It featured the ducks poring over a tourist pamphlet of the amphibious excursions called Duck Tours. This I wrote on that glossy brochure:

Rainbow lorikeets flitted about, giving everything the look of cartoons.

It was early morning and we were the first ones into the Wild Life Sydney Zoo. Hustling past a five-metre-long croc, a cassowary and a chubby wombat, we made straight for the koalas. They all had names: Jay, Jack, Charlie, Stu, Fraser and Moe. And they were all sleeping, as they do. All, that is, except Moe.

Moe had escaped, sort of. As he did every night, we were told. A cluster of workers had gathered around the base of a single tall eucalypt. It was from there Moe had launched his most recent escape attempt, beneath a high, net-like ceiling. Each day he'd go about his regular koala business, eating eucalyptus leaves and napping, along with Jay, Jack, Charlie, Stu and Fraser. But at night he'd creep away, like Tim Robbins slowly shifting soil dug from under his Shawshank cell out to the yard in the cuff of his pants. But rather than biding his time doing the warden's taxes, Moe was unceremoniously hauled back each morning, given, I presume, a stern reprimand from the screws and put back to the chain-gang-like routine of leaf eating and sleeping.

This particular morning, Moe had created yet another stir and appeared to be outwitting a growing number of worker/guards. Eventually, it was decided a rake was the way to go. One guy held the metal tines and, reaching up, poked Moe in the bottom with the handle. Moe simply climbed higher in the thin, wavering tree. The staff discussed some more amongst themselves and agreed on turning the rake around.

A taller guy took the rake and, holding it by the handle, tried to simply rake Moe down. Moe squeezed his eyes shut and pushed through the flexible metal tines, climbing to the uppermost part of the waving, pencil-thin limb where he swayed back and forth – a furry metronome in dire need of an ear-hair trimming. Had Moe's mother seen him at that moment, she would've surely boasted of his advancement to her friends. He was literally as high as he could go at the zoo and had nearly ten people working under him.

We watched for a while and then wandered away. But I liked to imagine that after we left some quantum leap of evolution would occur, like that first flying squirrel or feathered dinosaur, and Moe would leap from that high, skinny branch and soar! Up through the mesh ceiling he'd go and into the open skies, where he would live with his new friends, the lorikeets. Triumphant, Moe would pump a little fist and blow kisses, while far below Jay, Jack, Charlie, Stu and Fraser would cheer and wave, between naps.

I have some great shots of Lord Howe Island from the air, through the window of a turboprop, taken with a cool little camera the size of a packet of gum (sticks), the dimensions of four dice in a row. But when I had a story of our Lord Howe excursion published in *Travel Thru History*, my picture resolution was insufficient, so we were forced to use a stock photo. While the new photo was excellent, it wasn't my own. This, however, is what I scribbled in the margin of a *Daily Telegraph* on the plane ride there:

The flight aboard a roaring Dash 8 took us northeast from Sydney over the Tasman. Two hours of flying surrounded by nothing but blue – a bright cloudless sky and deep open water below.

The closest piece of land was a thousand kilometres east – Norfolk Island, former penal colony and eventual home of the Pitcairn Islanders, descendants of the crew of HMS *Bounty*. I gazed into the blue, feeling anything but, and thought of the story as we travelled the mutineers' route.

After serving as Captain Cook's master on the *Resolution*, William Bligh took command of the *Bounty*, his task to gather Tahitian bread-fruit – a cheap, plentiful food source to feed slaves in the Caribbean. Bligh was meticulous in his mapping and scientific research, an exceptional navigator and cartographer. He was also a skilled botanist and illustrator, displaying the finest traits of both James Cook and Joseph Banks.

The breadfruit work took only a few weeks, but the crew of the *Bounty* stayed on Tahiti for half a year. The time was productive. Bligh gathered volumes worth of scientific information but eventually decided it was time to leave. The rest of the crew, however, did *not* share the captain's sense of urgency, feeling their time would be better spent enjoying Gauguin scenery, eating roast pork and sleeping with dark-haired Polynesians. Who could blame them?

Fast forward a few hundred nautical miles. Whether your reference is history books or one of the films, you know what followed shortly after they set sail. The Tofua volcano was erupting nearby, adding an ideal backdrop to the violent escalation of tempers aboard the *Bounty*, a director's dream for graphic symbolism. Clark Gable, Marlon Brando and Mel Gibson all portrayed master's mate Fletcher Christian, the well-bred guy from a long line of sailors who led the mutiny, effectively giving the crew the choice of carrying on to England with the captain in a dinghy or joining him in taking the *Bounty* back to Tahiti, where they could live happily ever after. Ish.

And so the mutineers sailed back to Tahiti. Some stayed to live the good life and take their chances with the long but very slow arm of the law, while Christian and a few others hightailed it for anywhere else and ended up on Pitcairn Island. They promptly set about destroying everything, trashing Moai heads (viewed as false idols) and burning their ship, an oddly courageous yet moronic act that not only ensured they were all in it together but that the ragtag crew were permanently marooned on a small volcanic rock a thousand miles from anywhere. At that point, I suspect a few good months of hedonism on Tahiti before free passage back to England and a proper hanging may not have seemed so bad after all.

In a sad little museum in Oamaru, on the southeast coast of New Zealand, I saw the only Moai head that survived the mutineers ravaging on Pitcairn. It wasn't one of the monsters that litter Easter Island but a simple little guy the size of a garden gnome that got missed, overlooked or possibly hidden by some forward-looking, less puritanical member of the mutineer crew.

Eventually, the only ones remaining on Pitcairn were John Adams – the last survivor of the *Bounty*, along with a few dozen Tahitian women and a gross of café-au-lait children, all resembling Adams. Amnesty was granted and the sprawling family unit was moved to Norfolk Island to make a new home and add to the gene pool.

By the time Deb and I were in the neighbourhood, the only appeal to Norfolk Island was duty-free shopping in international waters. Which we were happy to bypass and go directly to quiet and isolated Lord Howe Island.

The turboprop banked sharply, giving us a steep view of Lord Howe – a narrow, curving atoll with a high, flat-topped mountain at each end, holding it in place like two craggy push-pins jammed in the sea. The Dash 8 needs about a thousand metres of runway to stop, we'd been told, while Lord Howe's bitumen airstrip was closer to 900, all that could fit in the tight space, requiring a strong headwind and a sharp descent to nail the landing. Plus, we learned, the runway grew in hot weather. I doubted it grew 100 metres and remained less than confident, recalling a Woody Allen line that rough flights made him particularly uncomfortable, being an atheist. The landing, however, was fine, the pilot nestling the plane between grazing goats and a couple of cows methodically munching grass by the runway like glassy-eyed, perpetual lawn mowers.

Accessing Lord Howe, a UNESCO World Heritage Site, was strictly limited. The number of guest beds – a few hundred – roughly equalled the number of residents. Kevin Wilson was the owner of the place we'd booked. Wilson was one of only a dozen surnames amongst island residents. He greeted us at the tiny, open-air shelter that served as the terminal, fronted by a low, white picket fence. In my mind he was a white-suited Mr. Roarke welcoming us to Fantasy Island, where Tattoo would take our bags and we'd have a chance to meet the other guests, most likely Sonny Bono and one of the earlier Charlie's Angels. But it was just the three of us climbing into his old truck. He tossed our packs in the back and we bumped across the island, where he parked at the store and waited while we bought overpriced groceries, then carried on to our lodging.

From our window we looked onto a horse paddock where two chestnuts stood nose to tail. There was a grass tennis court, playing on it a treat, as well as a concrete shuffleboard area, which made me feel we were aboard a hundred-year-old ocean liner playing with hundred-year-old passengers all dressed and talking like Mark Twain. After a few games we felt odd, new muscles straining in our sides, and gimped our way down to the beach before supper. We walked along the ocean and watched a leathery man standing in the sea, feeding dripping offal to a swarm of kingfish, thrashing around him like piranhas.

A massive Moreton Bay fig tree grew from the shore like a squat old castle. A knot was tied in one of its thick, hanging vine roots, which I was able to use as a stand-up swing and do an impersonation of Tarzan, albeit with more clothes and less muscle. As sun set we watched the ocean change colour like a watery rainbow.

We dined family-style in a casual eatery adjacent to someone's home: platters of salads and fresh fried kingfish. Enjoying the fish in this setting seemed a far cry from the violent display in the water an hour earlier. Following sunset, the island was cast in blackness. Generators stopped for the night. We left dinner and realized we couldn't see a thing, but a friendly local walked us back with his flashlight and we learned to always carry one to dinner to find our way home.

Next day we golfed. The island had a simple nine-hole course, every hole providing ocean views. The only structure was a small, open hut at the first tee with a row of loaner clubs leaning outside. There was an honour box for greens fees – ten dollars – and other than a guy riding a lawnmower up and down one fairway, we were the only ones there.

Later we trundled down the little island on ancient, single-gear bikes and made our way to secluded Lovers' Beach, where we lay in the sand and gazed at the Tasman. Norfolk pines threw some shade but exposed sand was scalding hot and I was forced to tiptoe-dance to the water. For ballet lovers, it was a technically perfect en pointe.

Deb read while I swam in an endless expanse of private water the colour of sapphires and freedom. At least I *thought* it was private. I splashed around, porpoising in shallow dives with open eyes, until a snake wound past, bobbing at the water's surface. It looked about a metre long, but with all the S-curves was probably longer. It had black and white bands striping it like a monochrome barber's pole, and an open, angry little mouth of teeth that made it look surprisingly dim-witted, like a small, mouth-breathing barracuda. I did my best to backpaddle, a graceless thrashing of arms and legs, the way I had when Deb and I were swimming in Okanagan Lake and a couple of deer emerged from shoreline trees to enter the water where we swam. We'd swum in from an anchored boat, enjoying the encounter with a real-life Robert Bateman painting, until the deer pissed in the water like garden hoses on full nozzle. The only thing impeding our rapid backwards movement was our laughter while trying to keep mouths closed as we swam back to the boat, heads craned up from the water like turtles.

Back in the Tasman, I managed to avoid the winding, bobbing sea snake and splashed my way to shore. The pull of the surf moved the serpent in a southerly direction and it seemed unlikely it would hit shore anywhere near us.

At a little beach hut down the road that rented out snorkel gear, bikes and beach paraphernalia, I asked the guy working there about the snake, describing what I'd seen.

He nodded.

"Are they poisonous?" I asked.

"Nah," he said in a soft twang. I was relieved. I wanted to get back in the water. Then he leaned in and added, "Not poisonous, mate. *Venomous.* You bite *him*, you should be fine, but he bites *you*, well, then y're fucked."

From the back of a boarding card:

I peered through a window, squinting at uniform cotton
balls dotting the ocean. The cabin interior glowed soft
blue, the comforting shade of Pacific far below.

We flew from Sydney to Honolulu, spent a night, had a sunrise ocean swim and headed to the airport to fly home to Vancouver. We caught a taxi to HNL and I heaved my pack in. It was a 75-litre bag in orange and grey with a dozen zippered pockets, bulging with electronics, books and weighty souvenirs. Some time later, one of the shoulder straps (tough, reinforced nylon) simply tore away, as though the pack said, "Enough!" This left me feeling both disappointed and irrationally proud, as though I'd somehow outlived my old partner.

Following a short cab ride, we pulled up to departures, got out, and our cabbie, a tiny man, ran around to fetch our bags from the trunk.

"That's alright," I said. There was a trick to hoisting it onto my back – technique and leverage more than strength, not unlike the Tamil Tiger trick. "I got it."

"Oh, no, no. I get," he insisted, and gently moved me away from the back of the car.

"Well, okay," I said. "Thank you."

He squared himself to the back of the car, facing the big bag as though it were an Olympic clean-and-jerk event, something you'd expect to see a hulking former Soviet do in a brightly coloured onesie. Planting his feet wide, he squatted, exhaling a few short breaths. "*Fff-fff-fff*!" And with a hearty grunt he yanked the pack from the trunk. But, like a planet dragging a moon, the bag's momentum carried on, pulling him wobbling into traffic. He tottered for a bit, gained control and pushed the bag up over his head, where it perched precariously like a giant stone cap atop a Moai head on Easter Island. Then the pack began a slow, irreversible slide down his back, making him look like Atlas, back bent, knees sagging.

"Ungh-urgh," his face screwed into a scarlet knot, the look of a constipated infant. "Oohhh," he said through clenched teeth. "Hay-vEE!" Panting, he teetered toward the curb and dropped the bag onto a luggage trolley, which creaked and bent slightly. Leaning over the handle, he caught his breath, wiping sweat from his brow. A small new appendage protruded from his inner thigh.

"Huh," he said, still panting, and poked it gingerly.

"Hmm," I passed him some money. "You're probably gonna want to get that checked."

"OK," he said, then shook his head. "Hay-vEE."

13

NEW ZEALAND

From another new, passport-sized journal:

I felt like Eddie Money, two tickets in hand, our destination paradise.

Things had changed since our previous South Seas excursion. Crossing the Date Line no longer required a puddle jump through Hawaii as a matter of course. Jet engine fuel efficiency had increased exponentially. Transpacific flights were the norm, and it was now simpler (and often cheaper) to fly directly from North America to Australia or New Zealand.

We'd put in sufficient time at work to not only clock up savings and vacation time but to convince employers (rightly or wrongly) that we weren't (as one might imagine) imminently dispensable. The oars I envisioned triggering our first *Gone Viking* departure had begun to creak in their oarlocks again, an anchor weighed and a square-rigged striped sail hauled into place.

A National Geographic hardcover atlas (the dimensions and weight of a table) had spent a number of weeks open, propped on the floor, a beckoning welcome mat. Two broad blue pages were permanently open onto Oceania – New Zealand, Australia and barrier islands – but this time our focus was on Maui's home. Not where he went in Hawaii but where he came from: New Zealand.

(Side Note: As well as hauling up tropical islands from the ocean floor, Maui had a line on the sun to lengthen days and delivered fire to humankind, something he brought back from the ends of the earth. Once more we find ourselves in the company of an exemplary travel-adventurer.)

It was nearly winter in Vancouver, but summer had just begun where we were bound, back to the southern hemisphere. That night (okay, the next morning) I was awake at 3 a.m., giving gear a final check, once more crammed into my trustworthy 75-litre pack: a few pieces of clothing, an excessive amount of books and journals and what felt like a ton of electronics, rechargeable batteries and adapters. And when Deb wasn't looking, I'd added my favourite ancient underwear. She'd insisted I throw them out, and I'd done some effective sleight of hand, like a three-card monte dealer, pretending to throw them in the trash. Then, ensuring I wasn't being watched, jammed them deep in my pack, grinning slyly. I'd grown particularly fond of my ragged stowaway. (Walmart, cotton, tagless, last survivor of a package of four: "Delicate as Belgian lace / two leg-holes with an outsized waist / the fly, a sideways happy face.")

We settled into the airport lounge in predawn dark. Wide blinds began to open, gliding up with a purr. A brilliant band of crimson – blood red – cut the eastern skyline, tracing the pyramid summit of Mount Baker and the dorsal fins of the Cascade Range. Black hung above the wound-like scene until a gently rising sun brightened it and a solitary, jagged cloud drifted like a double-handled lumberjack saw. Mountains and sky glowed burgundy and indigo with that indescribable slash of red. The blinds finished yawning open with a *hmmmmm-ka-click* – a showman's ta-dah!

We'd squirrelled away enough money to sit up front this time around, and I imagined the experience would exemplify refinement – dark, smooth liquor in heavy lead crystal, muted whispers and the occasional crinkle of a pink-tinged page in the *Financial Times*, while a tuxedoed string quartet played softly in a corner. I could not have been more wrong.

It was late December and the plane was pandemonium – running, shouting, squealing children, the anarchy of Christmas morning in Whoville – boom-clang of cartoomblers, carfinklers and zoo-zither-carsays. I expected a one-man band to go past, cymbals crashing inside his knees while a bass drum *thump-thump-thumped* on his back, ridden by a shrieking monkey.

Then a toddler waddled down the aisle, looked me in the eye and let out the same hearty grunt as our Honolulu cabbie preceding his dead lift. This was followed by the unmistakable wet raspberry sound of a diaper being fully loaded. Having deposited this gift at our seats, she scampered away, trailing a visible, tear-inducing cloud. It was then I realized I'd spent a year's worth of writing income for two seats on an airborne version of the Bajan bus ride we took to the fish market – the only things missing being someone holding a clucking chicken and wet laundry strung between overhead compartments.

I caught a glimpse of a flight attendant when he was unaware of being watched. He was scanning the cabin, the chaos, the screeching children, and the slump in his shoulders told me he was almost certainly calculating days left until pension.

Somewhere over the Pacific, at around 12,000 metres, we rang in Christmas. The flight crew was introduced and to my delight our captain's name was Dave Christmas. I wondered if we'd be delivering toys along the way.

Although we'd miss December 25th crossing the Date Line (we took off on the 24th and would land on the 26th), we still had a fun celebration. Flight attendants passed out small boxes of chocolates to everyone. A couple across the aisle carefully looked at their watches and then drank Baileys at the exact moment their friends were doing the same on the other side of the world. They did this every year – their Christmas tradition.

After a while I dozed, waking with a violent head snap. I mopped some drool and peered through a window at the night. The Southern Cross hung beyond the wing like a partial New Zealand flag, draped over stratospheric black. Smiling, I drifted off again and woke up two days later. We'd crossed the Date Line and all I'd seen was the back of my eyelids. I raised a window blind and squinted against the glare of a fiery sunrise. The eastern shore of New Zealand's Northland was bathed in orangey-pink beneath the fast-moving pillows of a long white cloud, exemplifying its moniker – Aotearoa, New Zealand's Māori name – Land of the Long White Cloud.

Our first morning was sunny and clear. We crossed Auckland on foot, winding our way toward a green hill representing another musical pilgrimage. Neighbourhoods were well treed – eucalypt, fern, evergreen and beech. Splashes of colour flitted between branches paired with organ trills of exotic birdsong. The land rose and we climbed through a park surrounding a volcanic cone – a high-banked, natural amphitheatre with steep, grassy slopes. Following a trail, we picked our way through bunchgrass, leafy trees and sleepy-eyed, grazing cows to summit Mount Eden.

We were in the heart of the city, with a panoramic Auckland view. Gulls wheeled overhead. A blend of smells hung in the air – dry grass, medicinal eucalypt, cows and the saltiness of sea. We squinted in gusting wind and the surrounding patchwork of greens and blues bled together – the lower end of the spectrum – the vibrating basso stuff you *feel* more than anything. Across three neighbourhoods stood the squat peak of One Tree Hill, my musical destination – same as the song by U2 – a twin turret to our vantage point. But instead of the tree that stood for years before being felled by a protester, a monument towered, a dull beacon on a lonely, urban hill. The U2 song is a tribute to their Māori crew member who died tragically, running some avoidable and mundane task for the band.

From a slim, unlined notebook, saddle-
stitch bound, with a burgundy cover:

Iron hooks the size of hams hung from the high ceiling of kōwhai
timbers, giving the room the feel of a medieval torture chamber. The
iron pieces had been forged into a cluster and lit, creating an unusual
chandelier. I realized each hook was designed to resemble a massive
fishing fly, and the whole effect grew on me – big, crude and beautiful.

We were in a lodge that catered to anglers, overlooking Lake Te Anau in New Zealand's Fiordland, a short distance from Milford Sound. We'd assembled for pre-dinner drinks with other guests before being seated as a group, and I was cornered by Arthur, an Australian Mr. Magoo type with thick glasses that made his tiny, blinking eyes dance. I warmed to him immediately as he told me in no uncertain terms that, as a Canadian, I hailed from the most beautiful place on earth. *On earth.* He repeated everything. *Everything.* Arthur told a story like James Michener. From the *very* beginning. He'd reached the point in his story when New Zealand broke off from the Gondwanaland supercontinent 50 million years ago, working his way up to telling me about what he did yesterday. Mercifully, we were called to dinner. Arthur introduced me to his wife.

"Hoi-ee," she said through her nose, in thick Australian. "Oim Julie."

"Hi, Julie," I said, smiling.

"Now," she corrected me. "Iss *Julie.*"

"Julie?" I said in a different tone.

"Now. *Julie.*"

"Ah," I said, to indicate I understood, which I didn't. It turned out her name was actually Jill. She went by Jilly and simply mispronounced it.

Reminding me of a time we were in Hawaii as a family on a sunset catamaran cruise. While the boat rocked its way around Diamond Head and Pearl City, Dad was filming it all with his ancient, eight-millimetre Kodak.

"Thet's an *all*-dee!" an Australian said to Dad with a smile, gesturing at the camera.

"It's a Kodak," Dad replied.

"Yee-ah, but eet's an all-dee," the Aussie said, nodding.

"No, it's a Kodak," Dad said in his loud voice, amazed at the man's stupidity.

In the Fiordland lodge's big dining room, our group was being seated and people were exchanging introductions around the table. Deb and I met Phillip and Carol, a couple from Perth. Phillip and Carol were from China but lived in Australia nearly all their lives and spoke with thicker Aussie accents than Julie-Jill-Jilly. Yet, with one look at Phillip and Carol, Julie-Jill-Jilly determined they were *foreign*, and spoke to them in that loud, slow manner certain people use when speaking to babies, pets, the elderly and servers at "ethnic" restaurants.

"HILL-OW!" Julie-Jill-Jilly shouted at Phillip and Carol.

They jumped back a little, and I watched realization dawn on their faces as they ascertained Julie-Jill-Jilly must be challenged. And so they responded equally loudly in slow, single syllables.

"HILL! OW!" they hollered back in unison, perpetuating Julie-Jill-Jilly's assumption they were ESL.

It was exceptional farce that showed no sign of abating. I topped up my wine and enjoyed the impromptu dinner theatre. Act II got even better as Arthur and Julie-Jill-Jilly got into the wine and not only monopolized conversation but simultaneously told the same story, both trying to drown the other out. Picking up snippets, I realized their respective versions of the same stories were vastly different. Scanning the table as they spoke, the two tried to force eye contact with the rest of us and win some contest only they understood. I realized we simply needed to choose one monologue and nod along lest we get caught in some unending left–right head snapping, like watching McEnroe–Borg tie breaks at Wimbledon. (Which is NOT an old pop culture reference, by the way. They show those on classic sports TV. So it's kind of, almost, current.)

One poor woman at the table made the mistake of trying to follow both sides of the Arthur and Julie-Jill-Jilly match point, and I was afraid I'd hear a wet, tearing sound as the hemispheres of her brain severed and she'd slump forward, drooling. The only person up to the task was a wall-eyed fellow from Canberra who I'm sure wasn't paying attention.

From a green journal, thin-covered and flimsy, that
could be folded in half to fit in a pocket if need be:

*As we rode through suburbs, the city was morning-time peaceful. Lush
palms, eucalypts and conifers lined the streets. Birdsong rang through
the open windows of our bus, and mynas hopped along the sidewalk
like early commuters. Sun broke through, brightening greenery and
sparkling water. Wherever land rose around any of the 50 dormant
volcanoes (in the city alone) you could glimpse the sea; whether an
inlet, lagoon or open water, it was there, close and welcoming.*

Reacquainting ourselves with Auckland on foot, we passed red-
bloomed pohutukawa, the dominating Sky Tower, through the neighbourhoods of Parnell and Ponsonby, past historic Symonds Street
Cemetery, along Tamaki Drive and inviting networks of trails in the
forested expanse of the Auckland Domain.

In the Auckland Museum we wandered through displays of
Polynesian and Māori artifacts – carved tikis, masks and a complete *whare* (house). There's a huge *waka* (war canoe), knives, fishing
hooks of stone, bone and wood, and slender paddles that served not
only as propulsion but combination spear, axe and war club. Māori
were skilled fishermen and aggressive warriors. Marvelling at combination fishing gear and weaponry, I couldn't help but think: *Give
a man a fish, he eats for a day. Teach a man to wield a club, he eats
whatever he wants.*

In the morning I woke surrounded by branches, sunlight shimmering through green, leaves twisting in a breeze. Waking from a deep,
12-hour sleep, I thought I was in a tree, but, sitting up, remembered I
was nestled in a bed by a window next to a big old beech, its branches
overhanging the apartment we'd rented in Ponsonby. Auckland's Sky
Tower was visible through the leaves; Christmas was approaching

and the tower was lit at night, glowing red and green, becoming a 300-metre-tall Christmas tree. Wind shifting greenery around our unit provided glimpses of harbour at Westhaven, a tourmaline I thought I could only imagine.

The neighbourhood was thick with trees and well-aged parks. Our building backed onto Western Park, Auckland's oldest at over 100 years of age. Unique birdsong rang through our room, an excited sound – something from a circus, under the big top – a sound to accompany a bike-riding bear (*deet-deet-deedle-eedle-eet-deetdee-dee*).

The apartment was situated on the slope of Freemans Bay, tucked between large old homes from the 1920s and '30s. Wealthy homeowners built on the slope for water views, while across Ponsonby Road workers' cottages stood tightly packed on small parcels of flat land. The next wave of building occurred in the 1960s – dull grey cinderblock apartments – where we were, looking out at grand old architectural gems, some lovingly preserved, others tired and worn.

Ponsonby Road boasted dozens of restaurants and a range of retail, with an earthiness that made it welcoming. After-work crowds buzzed on patios and terraces. We passed people sipping wine and mojitos and a pair of petite women sharing a three-litre keg of Asahi.

Sun defied a bleak forecast, breaking through fast-moving cumulus to make for a warm, bright day. We made our way to La Cigale, Auckland's French Market in Parnell, where we lunched on freshly carved ham-off-the-bone rolls. December produce was on display: peaches, apricots, nectarines, purple and green plums, strawberries, cherries and blueberries, along with colourful kumaras, courgettes, capsicums and aubergines – a summertime palette.

Auckland's known as the "City of Sails," but I renamed it "City of Parks," for Grey Lynn, Western, Albert, the Domain and nameless pockets of well-aged green. The sprawling network of parks provides miles of scenic trails for walkers and joggers. Joining locals for weekend runs, Chicago's "Saturday in the Park" and "Sunday Morning" by k-os played in my head. Moreton Bay fig trees with thick, splayed roots like Tyrannosaurus feet dropped ripe, sticky figs, smearing paths as though there'd been a fresh fruit food fight.

I watched sparrows nest, black thrushes hop through undergrowth and a tui hang beneath a branch with a quizzical, inverted look. Pohutukawa were in full bloom, bursting with red blossoms. Thick flax rattled in the breeze and the soft smell of jasmine moved through the air. I took a path that appeared to go nowhere, but carried on around corners and switchbacks, under cabbage tree palms and low-hanging pohutukawa, winding past three stone carvings of women hunkered around a non-existent fire. The carvings were crude, thick and feature-less, like trolls from *The Hobbit*, turned to stone at sunrise.

We went to a dinner party – friends of friends, people we hadn't met, and brought a couple of bottles of wine. We knew the address and the floor of the apartment. Our host buzzed us in. Taking the elevator up, it occurred to us there was no unit number, then we simultaneously realized the apartment was a whole floor of the large, posh high-rise. And we looked at each other, saying in unison, "We should've brought better wine!"

It was a nice evening – lamb dinner with a view of Auckland's Herne Bay and Westhaven. We were asked about where we were staying, which was a short distance away. I described the neighbourhood.

"Oh, that's where the girl from the Thompson Twins lives!" someone said, so irrelevant it became interesting.

During dinner an Australian guest explained it had been a special summer, as she'd put in nipple rings, and having them in for Christmas would be nice. She referred to the nipple rings again, saying how much people liked them. They were a great deal of fun, she explained. Deb and I didn't make eye contact.

When it came up for the third time, I figured it out. She'd been talking about *netball rings*. With a strong Australian accent – trust me on this – *netball rings* sounds indistinguishable from *nipple rings* ("nitt-ble rings"). Whether she, in fact, had nipple rings, we never did learn.

We ferried to Devonport on Auckland's north shore, hiking urban hills and following a historical seaside walking tour. Monarch butter-flies were thick in the air and tuis sang from podocarps. I was con-fused by the zones for bus fare, so asked a driver how much to get us across town.

"Ya' pie me innaff, all teak ya' inny-we'ah ya' wonna gow!" he said with a smile.

Another ferry took us to the north shore community of Bayswater, and we sauntered through Belmont, stopping for coffee and cake at the quirky Little & Friday bakery in Takapuna.

One morning we ducked into a Parnell restaurant as the sky opened, torrential rain that flowed deep down the street, spilling over the side-walk. Our server was a friendly, soft-spoken guy with short dark hair and a warm smile. His entire inner forearm was tattooed – tiny Chinese characters in neat vertical rows. I asked him about it and he explained it was a Buddhist prayer his mother read to him as a boy.

At Auckland's revitalized Wynyard Quarter we browsed food stalls, the Fish Market, saw the world's largest advent calendar and sampled local white wines, gurnard, tarakihi and fat fluffy chips. We window-shopped and noshed our way through Ponsonby and Parnell, eating tapas at Dida and walking around Saint Marys Bay and St Heliers with views of Waitemata Harbour. We hiked Mount Hobson and Mount Eden (again) – panoramic vistas of the city and both its harbours. The village of Mount Eden was a pleasant pocket of quiet retail and old architecture. There was a well-stocked book-store and I bought a pocket-sized, illustrated copy of *The Hobbit*, having seen the movie a few days earlier and feeling somehow closer to the source.

New Zealand has more bookstores per capita than any country in the world. We made the most of it with a steady rotation of books – buying, borrowing, selling and giving away, a combination of reading and gifting or selling to make a few dollars for bus fare.

It was Christmas and we walked up and down Franklin Road, ad-miring lavish displays of Christmas lights on homes under a canopy of tall gum trees. We browsed in a store while the radio played "Let It Snow," which made me laugh, as it was sunny and 25 degrees Celsius.

On an overcast Sunday we marched across town to Auckland's MOTAT (Museum of Transport and Technology), where a surprisingly uninteresting exhibit of Sir Edmund Hillary's South Pole expedition enabled us to kill a couple of hours on an uninspiring day.

Things picked up when I made my way to Auckland's Art Gallery to see historical Māori and New Zealand paintings. I returned for *Who Shot Rock and Roll*, a travelling photo exhibit from Cleveland's Rock and Roll Hall of Fame – familiar, iconic snapshots of Amy Winehouse, Jimi Hendrix, the Beatles, the Rolling Stones, Mick Jagger as a leopard, Sex Pistols, Ramones, Red Hot Chili Peppers with socks on their cocks, Tina Turner, Nirvana and Johnny Cash giving us the finger – walls of living and dead artists who helped shaped a half-century of culture through music and pageantry. But over and above the familiar images were intimate pictures that brought realism to the fantasy – a skinny, nervous Elvis tuning a guitar, a nerdy Jim Morrison being ignored by a group of young women at an early performance and haunting, candid photos of Paul McCartney taken by Linda around the streets of London.

There was a sign advertising a barber in Victoria Park Market. The ad was simple – a coloured, stylized photo (like a single panel from Andy Warhol's *Marilyn Monroe*) of a young Michael Caine. That was it. Just the name of the barbershop, the address and an orangey-hued, young Michael Caine. Needless to say, I had to go. It was a hot weekday afternoon and I was the only one there. The shop was run by a Korean man who'd lived most of his life in Auckland. He was an artist as well, his shop filled with lifelike pastels and charcoals of celebrities, some caricatures and original cartoons – clever and funny, revolving around a barber's life. He was an avid fisherman and ate most things he caught as sashimi, and described fish I didn't know. I enjoyed my time in the chair and forgot to ask about the ad. Afterwards I looked no more like a young Michael Caine than when I'd entered, although

I *did* find myself speaking out the back of my nose with a halting, breathy, East London accent. ("You were only supposed to blow the bloody doors off!")

11

TASMAN SEA

From the flimsy green journal:

I thought of the R.E.M. song where Michael Stipe declares the end of the world's arrived, as the land I was on simply ended, sputtering out in a handful of surf-encrusted islets.

We rang in the New Year on a quiet Auckland side street beneath old podocarps and pohutukawa with an unobstructed view of Sky Tower, glowing in primary colours like a vertical game of Simon. A full moon hovered over the tower like a flying saucer and, as midnight struck, fireworks burst like festive palm trees, lingering in the sky.

After a short sleep, we traipsed into town carrying packs and boarded a long-haul bus to wind our way north. The ride was a pleasant blur of greens and browns, flats, hills and steep volcanic cones, rimu, rata, totara and the occasional striped kauri, all set to the monotonous sound of a non-stop, four-hour soliloquy by a German woman nattering to her travelling companion. She didn't stop to take a breath. Not once. It was agonizing yet remarkable. Resigned to our fate, we settled in, fighting the urge to check our watches, and in a futile attempt to drown her out cranked earbuds until blood nearly seeped from our ears.

At our destination, our room looked over a road to the water of Horotutu Beach, our northerly view offering warm morning light and vibrant sunsets. I enjoyed a quiet morning swim, a half-moon hanging low in the sky while gulls wheeled past and a long-necked cormorant sat on an outcrop of lava rock. Sunrise glinted off the Paihia Maritime Building and far out in the Bay of Islands a tall and solitary rock stood like a sloop anchored on the horizon.

We spent a morning hiking around Te Ti Bay, following a dirt track past nesting cormorants and a long, meandering boardwalk through dense mangroves on the Waitangi River. Locals cast for fish at the mouth of the river. They had nothing but hooks and line. No rods. No reels. Just bait on hooks at the end of monofilament. They twirled line over their heads in tight loops like tiny lassos and then fed line out, the twirling loops growing until lengths of line were thrown into deeper water.

From Paihia we ferried to Russell, New Zealand's oldest European town. Kororāreka in Māori, the port offered safe, deep moorage and became a centre of trade for food and timber. Alcohol, firearms and whaling followed and before long the settlement earned a reputation as the "Hellhole of the Pacific," quite a feat given the depravity of 19th-century whaling ports. We familiarized ourselves with the town, admiring New Zealand's oldest church and lingering in Russell's compact museum. On the ferry back, we watched gannets soar, then plummet, smashing into the water like rockets.

Following a day's rest, we boarded a bus heading north, this one bound for the northernmost tip of the country. Partway along our journey, the bus stopped, parking near a shallow, sandy creek. Lugging boogie boards from the back of the bus, we climbed a towering sand dune, over 100 metres high, scrambling like Sisyphus for what seemed an eternity. At the summit, panting and on wobbly legs, our view stretched for miles to endless coastline and mist-shrouded sea. Behind us, the dune face dropped at an alarming grade, plummeting out of sight. Our driver led the way. Running at the precipice as though suicidal, he dove into the sky, board pressed to his chest, and flew from sight.

We knelt down tentatively, mounted our boards and pushed off. The ride was long and exhilarating but slower than we anticipated. But then rain began to fall, hardening the sand and increasing our speed exponentially. I made the climb twice more, getting more aggressive with each ride down, eventually hurtling past the parked bus and splashing headfirst into the chilly creek. As the rest of us towelled off and futilely tried to shake wet sand from everywhere, a lone speck made her way to the top of the dune for one more run – Deb on her fourth ascent, her excited grin nearly visible from where we stood, a very long way away.

Back aboard the bus, we sped along the sand of Ninety Mile Beach and on to Cape Reinga, the spiritual departure point of the Māori, where the deceased pass on to the afterlife, back to the underworld and homeland of Hawaiki. The cape is the tip of the Aupouri Peninsula, where the Tasman collides with the Pacific. It's an imposing land mass that juts into the sea in gangly steppes like an enormous, kneeling camel. When we arrived, land and sea were shrouded in fog, but as we walked toward the point, looking down at the 800-year-old pohutukawa – the only one of its kind that never blooms – beams of sun broke through, briefly illuminating the cape like a lighthouse.

In Paihia we celebrated my birthday with a patio dinner at a place called Alfresco's. Live music rounded out a fun evening, with two guitar-playing singers that could've been father and son, playing Men at Work, the Black Keys and Jack Johnson. Good music, wine and a covered patio created a cozy space. Across the street was the water, where a storm raged, which felt like a show on an alternate stage, immediately present but light years away.

From a back page of *The Rough Guide to New Zealand*, scrawled across indices:

I stepped between squat palms, down a grassy bank to the edge of the water. Water that was still a long way from the beach. It was a murky, natural canal that flowed like a slow-moving river between our rental unit and Northland's Ninety Mile Beach. The dark band of water seeped into the sea underground, somewhere north of

*us. I trudged into the canal, thigh-high in muddy water, my mind
flashing with images of thick, ugly eels that loved places like this.
But I emerged safely on the other side and walked across the broad
shoreline of flat, hard-packed sand that curved forever to the north.*

The beach was part of the national highway system, and the occasional
truck or bus could be seen speeding alongside the water. But this day
things were quiet. Calm after the storm. The previous night we'd witnessed a colossal thunderstorm, just sat in the house while it shook and
rattled, looking at the blackness explode as weather thrashed the sea –
ferocious flashes of sheet lightning with forked bolts that rent the sky.
I tried counting from the lightning burst to the thunder to determine
how far away it was, but the explosions of light and sound were simultaneous – completely upon us – frightening and wonderful. We scrambled to gather candles and flashlights, but remarkably the power held,
along with the shuddering old clapboard house.

The following morning, I sauntered along the beach where a couple
of guys surf-cast for snapper with rods like vaulting poles. People were
friendly, chatty and relaxed. There was a kind of relief in the air after
the violence of the previous night's storm.

Farther down the beach, a guy was hunched over a big air-filled
cylinder, like a blow-up oil drum. As I approached, I realized the
hunch was simply his stance – a stooped shepherd's hook. His hair
was a frizzy mop, popping out as though someone had jammed a fire-
cracker in there. He glanced up with a glint in his eye and struck me
as a cross between Jack Nicholson in *The Shining* and Bob Ross, the
Happy Painter. I smiled and his reaction told me he was painfully shy,
so I scaled down my hundred-watt grin to a more approachable 60-wat-
ter. (The 150-watt version might've killed him.) He smiled back with
a handful of crooked teeth like one of those inside rows you see when
a great white's attacking a diver's cage. In my mind I named him the
Happy Angler.

I asked him what he was doing and he walked me through it. He was long-line fishing from shore, going for snapper or anything else un-lucky enough to find its way onto the line. The big, inflated oil drum was the floater, and trailing from that was 15 metres of line, with 25 baited hooks, each spaced half a metre apart. The big floater had a kite attached to it, and the angler held a string that was also attached to the kite. To fish, he'd wade into the surf, toss the big floater beyond the breakers, then make his way back to shore where he'd get the kite aloft and slowly feed out the kite string. Prevailing offshore winds would pull the kite away from the beach, gradually dragging the floater and baited line into deeper water. The Happy Angler would then settle in on the beach, where he'd leisurely work the key end of the kite like a beachbum Ben Franklin. Every hour or so, he'd haul in the line to check bait and hopefully remove a meal or two. It was a unique blend of hard work, relaxation and play.

We swapped fishing stories and I spoke of catching snapper in the Bay of Islands, jigging for cod, coho and halibut off Pacific Rim National Park Reserve, and catching chinook salmon under Vancouver's Lions Gate Bridge. And I recounted a favourite experi-ence with my friend Doug (as referenced in our Hudson Rocks/"Rock Hudsons" story). Back in our kayaks off Vancouver Island, we were hauling in a shrimp pot. There were no shrimp, but it *did* contain a giant Pacific octopus. And, no, we didn't have to fight it off like Kirk Douglas in *20,000 Leagues Under the Sea* (although that would've been awfully cool). That just happens to be its proper species name – the giant Pacific octopus. The one in our shrimp pot was a baby, the size of a clenched fist. Doug held the pot aloft, wondering how to release this ball of slimy plungers and goo from the fine mesh of the trap, but, as we watched, it slowly worked its way through one of the tiny open-ings, living up to its reputation as an escape artist. It then lowered it-self by a stretchy arm as though rappelling, and dropped itself gently into the sea, where it squirted ink in our direction, the octopussy ver-sion, I suspect, of flipping us the bird, before propelling itself down, vanishing into deep purple water the colour of its ink.

Back on Ninety Mile Beach, it was time for the Happy Angler to haul in rigging and check bait, so I made to leave and wished him good luck. He flashed his warm, nasty smile and went back to work. I strolled along the beach and gradually looped my way to our rented house for lunch – fish and chips from a place we wanted to try, a short walk into the village. We were hungry and the take-away seemed exceptional. We agreed to do it again for dinner, which we did, ordering much more and enjoying it much less. That night we watched *Finding Nemo*, and the next day on the road we stopped at another fish and chip joint, where the daily special was dory, like the cartoon fish from the movie. Deb couldn't bring herself to lunch on the lovable character and changed her order to a burger. I sat on my own and ate two servings of dory.

Jotted on the back of a small local map:

Joni Mitchell (Counting Crows too) sang about something like this, gathering trees and stuffing them into museums.

We visited the Kauri Museum, a tribute to the massive, ancient trees, and although swathes of the giants were cut down over the years, the museum was positive and inspiring. From there we drove to the forest surrounding the looming kauri named Tane Mahuta – the world's largest living tree.

We parked the car and walked through dense fern on a trail leading deep into thick, quiet forest. The rustle of greenery broke the silence – a fat Pacific rat scuttling beneath ground cover. The trail meandered for a ways and appeared to end in a wall. Then I realized it was the tree. And only *then* did I realize it was still a long way away. We gawked, drawn toward it like gravity, craning our necks as we went. It hummed with energy, and as we continued walking it simply grew in front of us, impossibly high overhead, the sky nothing but leafy green. It was gargantuan. I didn't bother taking a picture, knowing it would be impossible to capture even a fraction of what the colossus was – living, breathing history, moving and utterly peaceful.

There was a small, rough bench and I sat for a long time. Deb wandered a looping trail where she met a Māori man who had planted his son's placenta in the sacred ground near the tree. It was the one-year anniversary of his son's life, he explained, and he was paying homage. He pressed foreheads with Deb, exchanging the shared *hongi* breath of life, then trumpeted a conch shell. I didn't realize the connection Deb was experiencing. Just heard the low, echoing sound of the conch moan through the forest, *wwhhhoooooooooo.*

From another pad of hotel-style stationery,
branded with a blue-green logo:

The punch to the face made a wet smack. The return punch gave a dull whump as a fist was buried in a meaty stomach. It started out like a well-choreographed western brawl. The only things missing were a chair smashed across a back and a breakaway railing. Haymakers went back and forth before digressing into scuffling, grappling wrestling. The two fleshy guys fell over a luggage trolley, sending it crashing onto its side, spilling suitcases onto the ground.

We were outside Kerikeri airport, about to load stuff into a taxi. The two guys had arrived to meet the same woman. As they fought, she wandered away, a blend of disgust, embarrassment and indifference. I was ready to jump in and lead the onlookers in a rousing chant of, "Fight! Fight! Fight!" but our cabbie was having none of it. He was a short, thick man and I saw him sigh, his shoulders sagging with a kind of resigned fatigue. Then he squared those same shoulders, pushed up his sleeves and waded into the melee. He was half the size of the fighters but grabbed each of them by the shirt and shook them both vigorously – rattling teeth and dissipating aggression. As the two big guys slumped in his grip, the cabbie looked like a kid at the fair, having just won himself two outsized stuffed toys. He made them shake hands, then shoved them off in separate directions, where they slouched away, pulling at stretched and torn tee-shirts.

The driver marched back to our car, tossed our bags in the trunk, gave us a curt nod that seemed to say, *Right, then*, *As you were*, and *Not on my watch*, all in one wordless gesture. I decided he could take us wherever he wanted.

We'd rented another unit in Paihia, looking out to the Bay of Islands. Marine wildlife was on parade as though attending a red-carpet gala: black shags with white masks like Venetian ball attendees and penguins going formal, as they do.

The hotel was built in a *U*, providing water views to most rooms around a central courtyard. The exterior wall of each room was angled, and large windows maximized sea views but made neighbouring units particularly exposed. A round, porthole-style window added a nautical vibe but directly faced the next unit's front window, effectively creating an outsized peephole into the next-door guest room.

Our elderly neighbours seemed to be of the "clothing optional" mindset, and began each morning with a series of stretches and contorting calisthenics while enjoying their water view. In hindsight I'd have gladly paid more for a blind view of the parking lot.

One morning, groggy and sipping coffee, I made the mistake of looking out the giant peephole when the neighbours were mid-workout. The convex Plexiglas created a kind of 3D magnifier, thrusting dangly bits my way. I sprayed coffee in an unplanned but flawless spit take. And, of course, I was caught, choke-coughing and staring. The naked pair smiled and called, "Good morning!" Leaving me no choice but to do the same. There was no need to say, "How's it hanging?" I knew all too well.

Later that day I was the only customer in a tiny fish and chip joint in a sad little strip mall. I ordered the seafood platter – a random assortment of deep-fried things that came from or possibly lived near the sea. While I waited, I watched the evening news on a small, grainy TV hanging from the ceiling. Over in Sydney, a four-metre great white shark was circling the waters of a busy urban beach, inconveniencing swimmers. It was inconvenient because helicopters were flying over, filming and disturbing the peace. Most swimmers were unconcerned. The issue was one of controversy. Conservationists were adamant about leaving the shark be, giving it the freedom to live its life and eat the occasional swimmer as they've always done, whereas another equally vocal group were in favour of going Roy Scheider on its ass. (For younger readers, this is a reference to the movie *Jaws*, which is like Blake Lively's *The Shallows* but with fully clothed old men fighting the shark, one of those being actor Roy Scheider.)

While I watched aerial footage of the real-life monster lurk through clear blue water, a bell rang and my order was up. At the till, I read a small notice: Opal, a black cat with a yellow collar, had gone missing. There was a phone number and a reward.

I hauled away my big greasy bag of chips and deep-fried ocean contents: tarakihi, gurnard, wharehou, snapper, dory, hoki and, if I wasn't mistaken, a loin of Ariel. I tied in to the life-shortening extravaganza and set aside some feijoa ice cream for afters. Working my way through the different lumps of batter, I had no idea what was tarakihi or wharehou. For that matter, I wasn't certain if either of those things were, in fact, fish. I did, however, bite down on something chewy and realized it was a yellow collar. I added salt and finished it, wondering if I could claim the reward.

An unlined journal adorned with a sailboat
and a cloud with a face huffing wind:

*Through morning traffic we walked along Quay Street
to a cheerful red and yellow ferry building, where we
boarded a boat that bumped its way into the Hauraki
Gulf, hauling us to the volcanic island of Rangitoto.*

Shags were fishing and black-backed gulls cried a welcome as our ferry reached the pier at Rangitoto. People dispersed and it soon felt remarkably private. Making our way from the little dock, we crunched along a dirt and lava trail, then began to climb. Bright pohutukawa stamen littered the trail like frayed red carpet laid out for us D-listers. Silvereyes, indistinguishable from waxy green, almond-shaped leaves, bustled about in low brush. Fantails showed off like vain little peacocks, flipping their tails like coquettish Southern belles, while a dun-coloured thrush crashed through low branches like an awkward teen. The sound of cicadas thrummed with a Cuban beat – the sound full and rhythmic; the only thing missing was a Brazilian drum leader's whistle punching out offbeats.

I took a side trail and broke through a cove of kōwhai, their springtime yellow blooms long gone, over moss-covered rock and dark, wet lava stone past well-hidden beachside baches. Swallows swooped over shoreline lava fields, struggling against strong northerlies. The screams of a gull colony on the headland carried over the water, which changed from turquoise to grey-green as heavy cumulus streamed past.

After about an hour's climb, we reached Rangitoto's summit, rewarded with sweeping vistas of Auckland and surrounding gulf islands. We took photos, capturing a surprising array of shifting greens and blues in the very same view as clouds swept past, changing light in the sky and on the water.

Ferrying to Devonport on Auckland's north shore, we climbed Mount Victoria on a steep, paved footpath. Flax rattled in sea breeze. Small, black-billed gulls squawked and chortled, while mynas clicked and snickered at some private joke. A tui chased a silvereye from the branches of a rata, the tui's song a complex hybrid of a Bing Crosby whistle and Herbie Hancock synthesizer. I read a book comparing the tui's call to R2-D2, a perfect description.

As we summited North Head, a fantasy-like rainbow drifted past – rosella parakeets swooping over gum and kōwhai trees. I wouldn't have been surprised to see a unicorn follow them through the sky. We looked back to the city, where Mount Eden and One Tree Hill stood like volcanic goalposts, proud and prominent across the water of Hobson Bay.

From a journal I bought while tailing Bjorn Ironside
through Tuscany, its cover a medieval map of Florence,
an envelope pouch inside the back cover:

We bounced from Viaduct Harbour into the Tamaki Strait,
waves dousing the ferry for a half-hour ride to Waiheke
Island, pink and white cloud drifting on curved horizon.

Disembarking, we shouldered packs and trudged up a steep path toward town. Great Barrier Island loomed in the distance and Little Barrier cut a uniform mound just beyond the bay. Wind in the trees mimicked the sound of waves. A tern wavered in strong breeze like a lopsided boomerang, while honeyeaters flitted through lavender.

We settled into a small unit perched on a hill overlooking Little Oneroa Bay. Our view included blooming lavender, bushy flax and beachside rata. Monstrous black bumblebees buzzed around the lavender, tuis fed on the flaxseed and thrushes hopped noisily through a hedge beneath the rata. There was a kitschy painting on the wall of cats sailing a large boat, which I found whimsical. And by that I mean stupid; their ability to sail anything bigger than a small sloop highly improbable. Don't get me wrong, I like cats. Just no one else's.

We pieced together a ploughman's dinner of local fare: olives, oil, bread, manuka honey, pecorino, Manchego and Camembert, all from

Waiheke – every flavour strong and floral. Our suppertime view was blushing blue sky and sun setting behind a volcano. Dessert was local cherries and juicy nectarines. The room was warm, the day's heat stored up in the small space and a floor fan whined in a futile attempt to move heavy air. Tide ebbed, low chop washed lava outcrops forming the bay and a scrawny Norfolk pine stood on a low hill like Charlie Brown's Christmas tree.

I decided to spend a day exploring the island on a scooter. Bruce, an American guy who ran the shop, made a serious face as he filled out my rental agreement.

"The roads are terrible and the drivers are nuts," he cautioned.

I smiled.

"No. I'm serious," he said. "Bad roads; crazy drivers." He punctuated it by passing me a stack of waivers to sign. After a brief lesson in a vacant dirt lot across the road, he gripped my shoulder, looked me in the eye and said flatly, "Have fun, but please, please be careful. These bikes are really expensive."

With very little confidence, I took off, flying along with suicidal traffic overlooking ocean views any tourism department would die for. My emotions zigzagged like the roads, flip-flopping between sheer bliss and abject terror, nothing in between.

We enjoyed supper overlooking Oneroa Bay, sun setting on moored sailboats. The Coromandel was a sliver of land on the horizon, barrier islands calming the surf. We'd spent a day hiking the northwest portion of the island, past a stoat and pukeko in a field, paradise shell ducks and oystercatchers on the shore, wood pigeons and lorikeets in the trees and gannets, terns and red-billed gulls soaring on open water. A square-rigged tall ship under full sail breezed between Waiheke and the Auckland skyline, the ship's mast mirroring Sky Tower, juxtaposing time.

The small kitchen in our unit was sparse and we ate most meals out: lamb kabob at Delight, Thai at Red Crab, fish and wine at the Shed in Te Motu vineyard, more fish at Oyster Inn and wood-fired pizza on the beach from Dragonfire.

One evening we dined across the island at a restaurant that offered one meal a day – a choice of two starters and a single entree, whatever the chef found or felt like preparing that day – an exercise in open-mindedness and trust. When we were there nearly all the ingredients in the entree were things we either didn't particularly care for or probably wouldn't order had we been choosing from a standard menu: duck, eggplant, green beans, Greek-inspired sauce – it made no sense. But put together with creativity and caring, the meal was exquisite – one we'll remember forever. We savoured, making a great deal of noise, took photos and did our best to make it last.

Next morning, gazing at the Hauraki Gulf. Sun peeked from the headland, illuminating a small church on a rocky hill tucked into spiky fern like a crown of thorns. Around the steeply sloping grounds, gnarly rata clung to cliffs fronting the sea. Tide was slack. Gulls splashed in tide pools at the shoreline, the occasional squawk breaking early morning calm. The gentle wash of surf was soft and lulling. Sky was chalky blue and sea wore away at wide sandy shore, rearranging speckled shells. A pair of rainbow rosellas flew over. Thrushes rustled through underbrush and mynas lighted in beachside trees, wings flashing white, black and brown, conversing in throaty coos and clicks I wish I understood.

I was on my own for a morning swim. It was just past 6 a.m. and sun was already high. The beach was deserted, save for the birds and a wet black lab playing in the distance. It appeared to be on its own. The sun, however, was blinding and the dog's owner may've simply been invisible to me. I piled shirt, cap and sandals on the sand, fingered my pāua-shell fish hook – safeguarding me from the sea – and entered the endless green water. A red-billed gull soared past and I scanned the surface for dorsal fins. The local paper warned of a few bronze-whaler sharks lurking a couple of bays over. The biggest was three metres in length. The news story explained they were mostly interested in snatching fish from anglers' lines, but one swimmer had been attacked and was quoted, "I just punched him in the nose – good and hard like – and it took off." The article concluded with general consensus that, if you saw sharks, get out of the water. I felt that was prudent advice but suspect I would've come to the same conclusion, my nerves still frayed from my unplanned swim with the school in California.

Standing in the shallows, surveying the surf, I felt a nudge against my thigh. It was the black lab, looking up, smiling and nodding at me, with a truncheon-like stick in his jaws. He dropped the wood with a splash and for a moment I wasn't sure which of us was supposed to fetch. But I took charge and threw the branch into the breakers. The lab plunged into the water, the same look of bliss that was on Sir Elton's face as he pounced on his pie from Harry's. But rather than fetching (to me), the dog returned the stick to its owner, a woman who'd approached through the gleam of the sun. We chatted a short while, but before long both dog and owner grew disinterested and wandered away. I believe I was mid-story.

The water was cool, as there'd been a few days of rough, churning weather. A gentle rip current pulled me out and I fought an underlying desire, or curiosity, to simply swim toward the horizon. Treading water, I surveyed the area. Fat white cumulus hung motionless in pale blue sky. Barrier islands were faint outlines on the horizon. A ray of sun illuminated the small church on the headland, its big cross glowing in the light. Both Catholics and Protestants worshipped here, weekend services alternating between the two.

A solitary man rowed by in a skiff. Beneath the church, greenery moved with countless silvereyes, the hillside rippling like a living blanket. A kingfisher swooped by, gleaming iridescent. After a while, tired and warm, I dripped from the water, grabbed my towel and climbed the hill to our lodging while a descending half-moon faded to blue.

From Oneroa we explored Onetangi, busing to the sun-drenched beach and visiting Waiheke Museum. We hiked trails that hugged steep, rocky shoreline and crossed farms, vineyards, forests and tussocky fields. A stoat loped across the path into a copse of trees. We passed a bench dedicated to a couple, the plaque reading, "May Cook, Stu Lamb."

I tramped to Fishermans Rock. A skink peered from the open bark of a tree. I climbed down to a rocky beach in a secluded cove beneath a massive old pohutukawa. Two gnarled trunks had grown together – a Māori double loop or lovers' knot. The woven trees had formed a horizontal portion of trunk, several feet above the ground. New trees grew from this level section of the knotted two in a high, tidy row – like children with parents – a posed family photo.

I climbed into the cluster of trees, an elevated bench with sea view. Beneath the trees, water swirled around outcroppings of old lava, crusted in barnacles and periwinkles. Flecks of abalone glinted in the water amidst shingle and coarse sand. A lone gull sat atop the Fishermans Rock pinnacle and a skeletal white tree crowned the headland like a lightning bolt. Puffy bands of cloud hung low on the horizon, frosting gulf islands. An oystercatcher flew past and a fat round fish leapt vertically from the water, landing with a splash. I eased into the lava cove and let current move me around, savouring chill water and the intimacy of isolation.

My writing partner Mala Rai and I have had a weekly ritual in which we take turns lobbing a prompt at each other – it may be visual art, music or something literary, the idea being we go to work for a while and write something that we exchange and critique. One of those prompts was this Truman Capote passage: "But the way to tame the Devil is not to go down there to the church and listen to what a sinful mean fool he is. No, love the Devil like you love Jesus, because he is a powerful man, and will do you a good turn if he knows you trust him." Thinking of that multidenominational church on the Hauraki headland, the seaside setting and incumbent spirituality, I came up with this, which appears in *Forever Cast in Endless Time*:

DETAIL AND THE DEEP BLUE SEA

I slid into that space, again
a comfy purgatory – prone
flat back, eyes cast upon a sky
where gulls and blue and cloud collide
adrift, as one, asail
as sheets and lines and knots align
and atmospheric surf breaks free
a spirit wave, it rises, curls, and rolls
to toss me in this state, aside to side
the pulse of tide and nautiluses drifting, drift, adrift
a forked expanse of blue, of you, of me, of sky, of sea
and all around this round of heaven, earth and water
glow, reflecting in our eyes each pulse, a pull of saline
stinging, singing, shoreline scalloped stairway, samphire
sand and grind of mollusk, mussel, oyster, clam
the colour of a thin blue line, above, below, dividing
joining, here and there, a present past, and you, and me
cast off, our company a two-toned hue of open sky
the detail, and the deep blue sea

We joined a steady stream of traffic making for the Coromandel Peninsula. An infrequent ferry crosses the Firth of Thames from Auckland, but like most travellers we made our way from the south, going east and then north onto the peninsula, skirting the massive Coromandel Forest Park to arrive at the seaside town of Whitianga on Mercury Bay. (*Wh* is pronounced like *ff*.) We'd come from Ahuriri, near Napier, enjoying a great string of driving tunes on the radio: "Everybody Wants to Rule the World," "A Horse with No Name,"

"Don't Dream It's Over" (used in New Zealand tourism ads), "Believe," and Tom Petty's "Free Fallin'." I couldn't think of a much finer play-list for a sunny drive at high speed.

We made our temporary home in a jettied unit on a lagoon that wound its way into Whitianga Harbour. Something like mullet thrashed in the lagoon, each splash like a paddle smacking the water. Every moored boat was pristine white and it felt like a miniature Monaco. The resort, however, was nearly deserted. In front of our unit, a Viking head sculpture sat in a garden. An alternative to a gar-den gnome, I suppose, and I took it as a good omen. A long-weekend crowd had just left, the town population having quintupled for the previous three days to 10,000, most of whom, we learned, had come to see the Doobie Brothers perform.

In 1984's *Romancing the Stone*, Michael Douglas, having been iso-lated in the jungle for an indeterminate amount of time, gets his hands on a current (1984) *Rolling Stone* magazine. Browsing a story, he ex-claims, "Aw, goddammit man, the Doobie Brothers broke up! Shit, when did that happen?" (At the time, the Doobies had been disbanded for years, making it a *very* funny joke.) When the band reunited, I was more disappointed than anything, as one of my favourite movie lines of all time no longer held true.

Later we would find ourselves in an airport waiting lounge with a group of loud Americans that defied physics, somehow taking up more space than they occupied. I scanned the departures board and deter-mined they were bound for LA. Their flight would leave shortly, giv-ing us some peace before we too had to go. Deb looked up something on her phone, smiled and passed it to me. The obnoxious group was, in fact, the Doobie Brothers. I suspect I was still angry they'd robbed us of the Michael Douglas line.

Still in Whitianga, I walked into town to explore the tiny but excel-lent local museum, chronicling Captain Cook's visit to these shores in 1769. While looking for fresh water, the crew discovered fields of greens they called wild celery. The captain had it harvested, boiled down to paste and served with every meal, keeping scurvy at bay. During their stay here, Cook observed the celestial transit of Mercury, determining longitude and enabling the accurate placement of Aotearoa/New Zealand on a map for the first time.

Back at our unit, I was outside, barbecuing a slab of lamb. Above the headland, a plump and gleaming harvest moon rose. As it reflected off the water, moored boats changed from white to gold, lighting the space like daylight and leaving me in a wash of weirdly bright night. I imagined I saw Mercury, hanging out there with the moon, and could almost hear Cook's ship straining at its anchor rope, the captain gazing at the same nighttime sky.

The following morning, on a ferry the size of a ski boat, we trundled across a narrow inlet to a trailhead at Whitianga Rock. A sharp ascent broke through shrubs and spiderwebs, leading us to a lookout and ancient Māori *pa* (fort) overlooking steep embankments of beech forest dropping away to the harbour. We crept back down, gripping roots and low branches, and made our way to Front Beach on Maramaratotara Bay, an immaculate strand of white sand and shade trees, our only company a nervous little dotterel and whispering sea. A short distance behind us, in the small town centre, sat what may be the world's cutest library, a square, single-room structure that looked like a frontier settler's cabin.

We spent the next day driving to Cathedral Cove, one of New Zealand's most photographed sites – spectacular shoreline rock carved by the sea into a wide, towering pass-through – a high-ceilinged, open sandstone cave. We cooled off with a swim in high breaking waves before a meandering hike back to the car. On the hot drive home, past winding water views and ancient seabed cliffs eroding in crumbling slips and slides, Paul Simon sang from the radio, aptly enough, "Slip Slidin' Away."

From the final stitched Moleskine out of a packet of three,
octopus pen long dead, I was writing with an Air New Zealand
rollerball, a four-sided pen that fits every hand perfectly:

*Descending New Zealand's North Island, crossing the Hauraki
Plains and stopping for a bathroom break. I'd been up for 32 hours.*

Paeroa. The town known as the birthplace of Lemon & Paeroa, a
Pledge-like soft drink with the fantastic tag line "World Famous in
New Zealand." We parked the car by a coin-operated public toilet –
a small, smooth-sided, shiny metal building in the shape of a kidney
bean. I found the right change and dropped in my coins. A door slid
open with a *whhsshhh* sound like on the Starship Enterprise. I stepped
in and the door closed behind me, *whhsshhh*. It was remarkably ster-
ile. I raised the toilet lid and heard a short *phhshht* behind me – lilac-
scented air spray. As I stood in front of the toilet to pee, instrumental
music began to play – Burt Bacharach's "What the World Needs Now
Is Love," which got me giggling, forcing me to concentrate. I decided
I liked the space very much – the fresh fragrance and soothing soundtrack – a private little spa with in-suite en suite. I wanted to get more
change, a picnic lunch and come back to spend the afternoon. But I
knew we had a schedule to make, so instead I did my business and
washed up, but waited for Burt to finish before leaving.

Pulling from the highway onto a long, straight and narrow road,
we detoured to Morrinsville, a sleepy farm community of 7,000.
("Nothing to do in these parts but farm, fart and fornicate," said the
preacher in an American dust bowl series I watched on TV. Which
flashed in my mind as we drove through town.) Our travel companion was going to a relative's house party. She explained how the evening would play out: boys play rugby in the yard, until there's a fight,
and girls gossip in the kitchen, until there's a fight. We wished her well
and went for a meal in town, "town" being the hotel across the street
from the gas station.

The hotel was built around the time of the last gold rush, its facade like a Hollywood prop wall that has to be filmed straight on. It was Sunday and a little chalkboard read "Sunday Roast Dinner." Inside, a few tables were neatly set with tablecloths in a long and cavernous ballroom-style room with a high ceiling and echoey hardwood. The place was empty, amplifying each step as we entered, and felt like a time capsule from a dusty past, a short-lived spate of affluence, long forgotten.

A buffet was set up along one wall – a table of steaming, silver chafing dishes. Other than Deb, me, and the sound of distant steps we presumed to be a solitary staff member, there was no one. We looked at each other, raised eyebrows and went to the buffet. Each serving dish was loaded with fresh, hot, excellent home cooking. Think of everything you'd want for Sunday dinner, then add a bunch more stuff and increase its volume to feed 50. Now imagine just two of us there to enjoy it.

It was supper hour, but no one else came in while we were there, just a pleasant server echoing around the periphery. Perhaps the town dined later and would arrive in a chatty clump after we left. Maybe the proprietor was overly optimistic. It was a mystery. But we enjoyed a good meal in the huge empty room, passing salt and pepper down the length of our table like Bugs Bunny and Yosemite Sam. We ate leisurely and left, still mildly confused but content.

From the same final Moleskine, written in four-sided rollerball:

> *Clear skies and a view of the volcanoes – Ruapehu,*
> *Tongariro, Ngauruhoe – Lake Taupō at their feet,*
> *a surface steam of geothermal energy.*

The lakeside town of Taupō, in the middle of New Zealand's North Island (Te Ika-a-Māui), is set between gently sloping hills to the north and towering volcanoes to the south. It was our home for a few visits, including a Christmas Day.

We sat down to dinner with people we'd just met, snapping open Christmas crackers, donning paper hats, reading flimsy jokes and laughing with new and immediate friends. A young Korean woman and her American surfer boyfriend were on their way to Wellington, where he was starting a job with Peter Jackson, paying homage to his father's love of *The Hobbit*. And a retired couple from New York implored us to make the most of life, to travel and treasure the blessing of health.

The next day, following a short drive from town, we hiked around the Waikato River and Huka Falls. Regal black swans glided on calm water just above the dam that powers much of the country. We had a picnic lunch and watched the reservoir gate slide open, gushing frothy water through a sandstone gorge and raising the teal river in spectacular fashion.

On another hike, farther up the Waikato, I veered from the trail to the inappropriately named Hot Water Beach, a sandy dent in the river. Pushing through shrubs and scrambling down a low embankment, I slid into the chilly green river, floating about like a gentle ride through a well-treed amusement park.

From Taupō, we explored the cave and thermal park of Orakei Korako, an unusual series of rifts exposing bubbling mud pits, geysers and steaming walls of mineral-rich stone and geodes in white, pink, coppery yellow, soft green and amethyst. To access the self-guided walkway, a small ferry crosses Lake Ohakuri – a short ride spanning 100 million years of geology. A low pier and naturally formed, terraced stone steps shrouded in mist greeted us like an elusive entrance to Jurassic Park.

The Buried Village of Te Wairoa is New Zealand's Pompeii, a short drive from Taupō and just beyond the sulphurous stink of tourist-popular Rotorua, the geothermal centre of North Island. A settlement of Māori and Europeans, Te Wairoa was a stopover for 19th-century travellers making their way to the natural attraction of the Pink and White Terraces. Caught unawares, the small community was covered in several feet of mud, pumice and ashy lava with the eruption of Mount Tarawera in 1886.

We arrived, sealed into our rental vehicle in a futile attempt to keep the rotten egg stink of Rotorua at bay. The Buried Village grounds provided a lovely park-like wander along a creek thick with spawning trout, down dark wet rock around a burbling waterfall, beside a towering wall of leafy hawthorn and poplar trees planted as a hedge 140 years earlier. A tall Māori man greeted us in song, playing a six-string acoustic guitar with a capo high up the neck, giving it a ukulele pitch, the sound distinctly Polynesian. He was our informative, friendly guide and walked our little group through the hard mud and pumice ruins. He spoke with pride of local history, his Māori culture and explained the oft-misunderstood tradition of cannibalism.

"You must understand," he said, "we were a nation of warriors. Strength came from victory, and with victory came the acquisition of your defeated opponents' *mana* – their life force, symbolically gained with their consumption." He met our gaze, slowly, until all heads nodded understanding. "Plus," he added, "it's an island. We didn't have a lotta protein."

I wrote this on a cocktail napkin. Seriously. I know it's a cliché. But I actually wrote it on a small, square, paper napkin I got on a plane and kept for reasons unknown:

Ian picked us up in a beat-up ute, towing a boat trailer, an inflated Zodiac tethered upside down on the trailer, looking like a fat grey tongue – something off a Rolling Stones tee-shirt.

There were five of us heading out for a day of fly-fishing on New Zealand's Mohaka River: a fat Texan asshole, his lovely Midwestern wife (an ideal sitcom pairing), a likeable Canadian named Bill, our Kiwi guide Ian and Ian's fox terrier, Trixie.

We headed out early, filled with strong coffee and a hearty breakfast prepared by Emil and Haimin, our hosts at the lodge. The accommodation looked down a slope to Lake Taupō, the handsome, volcanic lake perpetually dotted with waterfowl – ducks, swans and geese.

I asked Emil the significance of the country flags flying from the front of the lodge. They'd been changed since we arrived and, aside from the American flag, I didn't recognize any of them.

"They're for the geese," he said.

I nodded like I did back at Fiordland and so many times before, pretending I understood, which of course I didn't. It seemed like an awful lot of work to change flags for the geese (not to mention the ducks and the swans) and I wondered if the birds really cared. After a couple of days I realized he'd been saying *guests* ("geests") and had thought we were from a different country, otherwise I may have figured it out.

It was early and heads were bobbing in the vehicle as we drove to the river. Trixie sat on my lap, riding shotgun for the long drive (I suspect I was in her spot). Ian drove the boxy little truck like it was a Formula One vehicle, tearing along snaking roads at terrifying speeds, our trailer whipping behind us like a tail. He was friendly and talkative and spoke passionately about fishing, nature and the environment. He coached us on preservation and was adamant about treating the fish gently – nothing but catch and release, and explained the importance of care – the sensitivity of it all. We rounded a sharp corner and smashed into a songbird in flight, a fist-sized ball of feathers and guts exploding on the windshield. He gave the wipers a single flick that smeared the remains into a gory rainbow.

"Ye-ah," he said. "Delicate balance, the ecosystem."

We launched the boat and spent the day making our way downriver, stopping, wading in and methodically fishing a 12-kilometre stretch of the Mohaka. Using a double, two-fly leader line – one float-ing, one sinking – we fished for brown and rainbow trout. I caught a good-sized one of each – a highlight of the trip.

Sun beat down and a breeze gusted through the river basin. Hills enveloped us – a thick blanket of eucalypts and flowering tea trees with paddocks of sheep and deer. Paradise shell ducks flew in low *V*s and harrier hawks wheeled, fixed-wing, high overhead. We drifted past sheer banks of clay and sandstone, while pumice rock floated by on the river's surface. Petrified stumps poked from one earthen bank like candles on a lopsided cake. Smooth, grey river rock banked the shore.

"What's that stone there?" I asked Ian.

"Dun-ow," he said.

"Make something up," I demanded.

"Iss grey-stone," he replied without pausing.

"*That's* better," I said.

It turned out the obnoxious Texan was the worst fly fisherman in the world and managed to catch himself more than anything, even-tually throwing and breaking a rod. His wife, however, seemingly indifferent to the whole experience, caught fish constantly. This did nothing to quell his growing rage but was quite entertaining from a distance.

Trixie bolted after hares in the fields, nearly too fast to see, and rested with us while we lunched on sandwiches and fruit. She seemed to eat the most steak from the sandwich makings, but no one objected. She was working harder than any of us.

Back at the lodge, over communal dinner, rectal Texan monopol-ized conversation. As he recounted a grisly story of shooting and gut-ting something harmless on a hunting trip, I tuned him out. I was also concentrating on Haimin's cooking – an exquisite Korean pasta dish of spicy squid cooked in its own ink.

Texan wound the conversation around to include us in his mono-logue and posed the question as to why Canadians tend to be fun-nier that Americans, listing Canadian comedians to make his point.

I realized he was addressing me, and managed to turn my savouring *mm-mmm* into an *mmm?*

"I say, why'zit yew'all Can-ay-juns are all fuh'nee?" he asked. "Funn'yer 'an us Amer'cuns?"

"Well," I thought about it. "I suppose when you're next to a big country, you're not always heard, so wit or sarcasm..."

He interrupted with a new topic. "Yew know? As a kid, I had a dawg that cost eight-hun'ert dollahs. Wha' so much? Way'uhl, it was trained speh'shull for the airport; it was a buhm-sniffin' dawg."

"Hell, every dog I *had* did that!" I said. Everyone around the table laughed. Everyone, that is, except Texan.

"Bu' this dawg was trained speh'shull," he said, confused by the laughter.

Okay, I thought, *maybe unfair due to accents*. I laid it out for him. "Oh, *bomb*-sniffing dog. I thought you said *bum*-sniffing dog." More laughter around the table.

"No-o. This dawg was trained speh'shull," he said a bit louder, unaware he was answering his previous question.

This, I had no need to write in a journal. It's in my mind forever.

It was a good, albeit exhausting, swim with wild dolphins. This time well out to sea, in Whakatāne Bay, a vast crescent of land with orchards and farms and vineyards on shore, while the water offers up fish, cephalopods and cetaceans aplenty. Aptly enough, it's called Bay of Plenty. When I was first here, I was aboard a mid-sized boat, lumbering a handful of us skin divers from a pier, cutting through water that glinted like nickel and silver. Behind us, sandstone cliffs dropped into the bay, while on the horizon White Island (Whakaari) puffed smoke signals of angry volcanic steam.

Next time we were here, a short distance away, the island blew, killing two dozen people and severely injuring two dozen more. With the rest of the country, and much of the world, we listened to updates each day as the death toll rose. The most horrific news story, perhaps, was the government's plea for skin – they'd exhausted supplies for grafting onto survivors.

I could tell you more about the first time here – water like translucent jade, flying fish that soared over surf in 50-metre leaps, a bottlenose dolphin that gazed at me, eye-to-eye, for a timeless, timeless moment. Experiences I'll never forget, yet all of it irrelevant in relation to the eruption. The tragedy. And, yes, avoidable. The volcano had been threatening for 50 years. Odds got played. Dice, in a way, were being rolled. And tourist dollars tend to collectively turn a blind eye. Until our luck runs out.

From a JAM hardcover notebook with elastic band closure, in blue:

Crashing surf boomed through the black and sea lions yelped
from an aquatic park across the street as I peered through the
curtains of our little room to a cold, wet New Year's Eve.

You may've noticed many of our viking excursions taking place around the end-of-year holiday season. I hadn't put much thought into it as I recorded it in journals. But now that I see it in print I'm aware of some seasonal clustering. In hindsight, I suppose this was the time of year we could most easily get away from our day jobs. Plus, by timing it right, southern hemisphere weather tended to be agreeable, what with summer starting "there" in December. Of course, that's not always the case. This being a good example.

It was nearly midnight and partyers at the hostel across the lane were going hard in spite of the weather. The blue of the TV flashed behind me – a New Year's Eve countdown of what seemed like a thousand

Abba songs. We fought the urge to curl up under comforters for the remainder of the year and went out to brave the miserable night.

Just south of centre on New Zealand's east coast, we walked to Napier's central Clive Square, ringed in thick Norfolk pine and nikau palm. A stage was set up and would-be revellers huddled around the perimeter, avoiding cold drizzly rain. We did the same, but water trickled from high branches like glacial streams, finding exposed skin and making teeth chatter. We stepped into the open, finding it less unpleasant than the rivulets coming off the trees.

Determined to enjoy myself, I bought some fries from a mobile vendor. Then ate one and deduced the trolley was wheeled out annually, the vendor reheating the same chips he's had in the fat since he took over from his father, who likely retained the same fat and fries from *his* father before that. I wondered, when this batch finally ran out, if the owner would simply wander away. I made that face infants make when they first taste lemon, and kept gnawing on the world's worst fries.

A band walked on stage, we counted down to midnight and rang in the New Year like a muted trumpet (*wha-waaaa*). They kicked things off with a flat cover of GNR's "Sweet Child o' Mine." The dwindling crowd clapped politely. The rain picked up, we pulled our coats tighter, turned up collars and made our way back to our little room at the Motel de la Mer.

Morning, however, broke warm and promising, as though the season had changed overnight. Up early, I watched sun rise, amongst the first in the world. Beneath brightening sun, steep angry waves thrashed the shore. Each breaker reared high and black, sucking in basalt gravel, the sea foam dirty grey. A wide, curving walkway set back from the beach made for a beautiful run, distance hiding a surprisingly gritty shoreline of broken glass, rusty nails and nasty urban litter.

Napier was devastated by an earthquake and tsunami in 1931 and rebuilt predominantly in an art deco style. It felt like New Zealand's Miami, a miles-long swath of bright beach and pastel architecture, but instead of royal palms, the marine parade's lined with towering Norfolk pines. The town boasts an exceptional aquarium featuring tuatara – lizards unchanged for 150 million years, considered living fossils. Tanks of turtles swim and snap, colourful frogs climb and croak, bubbling tubes of seahorses float like question marks and dark rooms of hairy brown kiwis scuttle about as though pressed for time.

We hiked Te Mata Peak, through cypress and Monterey pines reminiscent of Northern California. And we experienced one of the highlights of our time in Hawke's Bay, a tour to Cape Kidnappers to mingle with gannets.

Squished into a little bus, we joined an eclectic group of locals and tourists and weaved along winding dirt roads, slowly climbing a high cape. We drove past helmeted riders in boots and jodhpurs riding speckled greys and palominos. They splashed through a stream, vanishing into a copse of flowering manuka, pohutukawa and white-blossomed jasmine.

The bus trundled over a wood bridge spanning a deep, narrow chasm and a muddy creek lined with bushy ferns. In the JAM hardcover I wrote, "Flowers resembling red hot pokers reached from the roadside like brands." Not wanting to guess at the flora, I made a point of tracking them down in a plant guide. Their name? Red hot pokers.

Pines clung to high cliffs, roots weaving from the banks, while fossilized whelks and cockles poked from natural walls of sandstone and clay. The Mohaka River had carved its way to the sea here. But, in 180 CE, a volcano blew from what became Lake Taupō, rerouting the river 80 kilometres away. When the massive volcano erupted, so much pumice and ash were sent into the stratosphere it blocked the sun, and was recorded throughout ancient China and across the Roman Empire.

The land was now an odd mix of arid and lush. High-reaching cabbage tree palms added splashes of green to brown landscape. We drove through eroded embankments and forests of poplar, eucalypt, fern and tea tree. Quail scuttled about with golf-ball-sized chicks, wild goats brayed and Perendale sheep grazed on rat's tail grass on steep hillsides.

In the distance we saw the rise of Mahia Peninsula, a swath of land jutting along the horizon, creating the massive crescent of Hawke's Bay.

The bus slowed as we passed a sheep-shearing station and a ring-necked pheasant crossed the road. Windows were ajar, moving warm air, and we heard skylarks, bellbirds and tuis trill as we bumped along. Deep fault lines striped cliffs like angry scratches. The landscape was geological layer cake: soil-covered sandstone on gravel over bedrock of lava, pumice and peat. We crossed an open field that rose to crest the promontory where a cluster of brilliant white gannets huddled on a flat round of windblown grass, high above the water. Tourmaline sea thundered below, breaking on black reef, where Maui's Fishhook – a stony crag also known as the Tooth – pierces the water like a towering shark's fin.

Awkward on land, gannets are built to soar, like albatross, and can fly thousands of kilometres. We exited the bus in their midst, the colony indifferent to our presence, their black-tipped wings, super-hero eye masks and metallic gold heads shimmering in the sun. Some had red seaweed – nesting material – trailing from beaks like scraggly ginger beards. Collectively, they craned their necks skyward and I found myself looking up, wondering what they saw. And together they called, an eerie, muted screeching like a lead-up to a Hitchcock murder scene. They struck me as a singular organism, the colony swaying as though in a trance – a congregation on the cusp of endless horizon.

From the shiny black Moleskine, written in pencil:

I chuckled as we drove past the sign "No Engine Brakes in Urban Areas." It's where a tanker truck had veered from the highway, bumped over a ditch and slammed through a house. Maybe the driver was obeying the sign.

No one had been seriously hurt, and I slowed to gawk. A news reporter said, with relief, it was only a milk truck, not beer. Apparently, the truck driver had a candy sucker in his mouth, hands-free, which he choked on, blacked out and drove off the road. The rig carried on through a yard and punched through a home. The house frame remained intact, save for the truck-sized hole clean through the middle. As the truck thudded to a stop, the sucker popped free of the driver's esophagus. He came to and was quite all right, albeit surprised to be idling, partway through a house and adjacent yard. The homeowner had been watching TV when the truck and trailer rammed through his porch, kitchen and living room. Miraculously, the homeowner only suffered a broken ankle, and, I presume, badly soiled shorts.

We'd been methodically working our way around the country – up, down and side to side, across both North and South islands – the occasional short-haul flight, buses, ferries, water taxis and a lot of time in a car. We made an overnight stop in Palmerston North ("Palm North") to break up a long drive. Within a short while, it seemed a rerun of *Frasier* and clipping my toenails would be the highlights of our stay. According to John Cleese, "If you ever do want to kill yourself but lack the courage, a visit to Palm North will do the trick." But late that evening, a few determined sundogs broke through a leaden sky and we enjoyed a walk along a muddy trail beside the slow-moving Manawatu River, leaving us with a not unpleasant feeling toward the little town.

Back on the road, we drove past the place with the longest name in the world, Taumatawhakatangihangakoauauotamateaturipukakapiki-maungahoronukupokaiwhenuakitanatahu. It's Māori for a hill. Not "a hill," that would be silly. But a *specific* hill. The Welsh, however, claim with pride that *they*, in fact, possess the town with the longest place name, Llanfairpwllgwyngyllgogerychwyrndrobwllllantysiliogogogoch, which I believe is pronounced like cartoon swear words: hash marks, at symbols and exclamation points. I suspect the name just keeps growing, the Welsh systematically adding Ls to bulk up the ridiculous name of their town. And don't bother counting letters. I can assure you there'll be more next time you check.

A black-backed gull circled a farm named Whāngaimoana, reminding us we were near the sea. We crested a hill to see Cook Strait meld with Pacific, a mottling of turquoise and inky indigo. Big blocks of lava funnelled crashing surf, breakers smashing onto black sand beach. We parked the car near sunbathing fur seals – outsized, blubbery slugs that smelled of herring – and hiked a dry riverbed of round rock flecked with pyrite and fossilized cockles, making our way to the pinnacles.

Unlike the statuesque, golden rock towers in Western Australia, these pinnacles are walls of dusty grey hoodoos – weather-worn, dark sandstone. Cicadas buzzed – a static-like hum, as we climbed a trail of carved mud and rock steps through windblown foliage under a canopy of tea tree and fern. Magpies hopped by, while a red-headed finch wheeled overhead and a lark sang from a high plateau like a welcome. We reached a viewing platform, and across a broad valley the stone pinnacles loomed like a massive pipe organ, an abandoned fortress facing the sea.

From the same black Moleskine:

I thought of the classic exchange in Tolkien's The Fellowship of the Ring *when Frodo admits to Gandalf that he wishes none of this had happened during his time. To which Gandalf nods agreement, but adds a grey-to-white clarity by stating the only thing we need to determine is what it is we choose to do with the time we're given. Simple. And profound.*

Back in the capital of Wellington: home to Peter Jackson, Flight of the Conchords, the Parliamentary Beehive and other stuff I didn't bother to learn. We'd made our way to the bottom of North Island, this particular foray weaving together volcanic mountain spines with coastal paths and cities, a blend of urban, wilderness and sea, impossible to pack for but expansive in a way that reminds us each day we experience much more than we can ever prepare for.

From a breakwater a man cast for sea trout, what we call steelhead in British Columbia. We stopped to visit with him as we walked the seawall fronting Oriental Bay, then made our way to the Museum of New Zealand (Te Papa Tongarewa), where we joined an energetic crowd of all ages crushed around the "World's Fastest Indian" (an Indian motorcycle). It was particularly fun as we'd just seen the movie.

Deb caught up on correspondence and I explored another Saint Paul's Cathedral, Wellington Museum, park-like Bolton Street Cemetery, the Peace Garden and a city pitch where an excellent cricket match was in progress. I strolled from the Botanic Garden along the City to Sea Walkway and Harbour Walk, where a children's fair was underway, squeals and laughter ringing through a sea of colourful tents.

From the capital we drove toward Paraparaumu and Raumati Beach. I took a wrong turn, as I do, leaving us on the winding high road rather than the smooth, straight low road. It was the one time I regretted taking the high road. There was no one around. No one, that is, except for a lone gunman.

It was the main story in the news, and he was currently hiding out somewhere near where we were, coming out every so often to pick off passing motorists. Authorities explained they were closing in on him, although it was akin to looking for a needle in a haystack. But rather than a haystack, it was the heavily forested mountains of the Lower Hutt Valley, and instead of a needle, it was an arbitrarily murderous rifleman. With grim humour, Hutt Valley had been renamed "Hunt Valley." And I really wished I'd taken the right turn.

Despite the slight but real possibility we might be shot, I cleared my throat awkwardly and pointed out how lovely the sea views were from the remote, mountainous locale. Eventually, the road wound gradually down the cliffs, like a snake toward the water, and the relative safety of a seaside community. And, despite a tense silence in the vehicle, I felt a modicum of solace knowing we were effectively, albeit slowly, serpentining.

Why, you might ask, didn't I simply turn around and go back the way we'd come to link up correctly with the low road? Well, we'd already come a great distance on the high road by the time we realized my error, so the choice was either carry on a little ways farther, take our chances with what in all likelihood were relatively low odds of being shot and killed or add another couple of hours' travel time to an already very long day in the car. Plus, I really wasn't keen on having to top up the gas tank with petrol that was nearly three dollars a litre.

From a small yellow Post-it, on a pad we used
to mark guidebooks and maps:

Rock, paper, scissors. Maybe the best haircut experience ever.

I followed the quiet, curving main road into the village centre and spotted the rotating striped pole of a barbershop. The sign in the window read, "Haircuts $8." I did the conversion from New Zealand dollars to Canadian. About $6.50. At that price the results are irrelevant, combined with the fact I have too little hair to care – it looks the same no matter what (not to brag). I also have a bottle of shampoo that's lasted 11 years. I like to believe it'll last forever.

As hair first vanished from the top of my head and began its determined and aggressive growth from everywhere else, I enjoyed making the joke that I felt whoever cut my hair was less of a barber and more of an ear, nose and throat specialist. It was comic gold on the Rotary lunch circuit. I just had to say it very loudly.

It was early morning and, although the shop had been open awhile,

I was the only one there. The barber was a dead ringer for Ron Perlman from *Sons of Anarchy* – big, badass, grey-haired and wearing a black leather biker vest. There was a solitary barber's chair and the compact shop was filled with *Rolling Stone* magazines and rock concert programs, the walls a kind of shrine to classic rock. It was a great array of memorabilia – and, surprisingly, predominantly Canadian bands – Triumph, BTO, April Wine and Rush. There was also a host of All Blacks artwork and team photos, the players looking especially vicious and mean in each of them. One exceptionally well-done poster was a computer-generated action shot of the All Blacks in a gruelling battle with bloodthirsty lions, as though the team were Christians tossed into the Colosseum for Nero's Sunday Service. The All Blacks, however, were winning.

A few years prior, we met a couple of players from the national team while waiting in LAX for a flight to Christchurch. We were standing together and I noticed their All Blacks gear didn't look like the stuff you'd buy at a souvenir store. I put on my Hercule Poirot hat, but it was fairly obvious. The one guy was about six-foot-nine and had a nose that bent sharply to the left (his *and* mine), while the other guy was about five-foot-nine, both ways, and sported two fresh, dark, black eyes that looked as though he'd been struck in the face with a mallet. I asked them if they were on the team and their bemused looks told me they were probably famous. They said they'd just finished a European tour and were coming home from Italy. I asked them how they did. They gave me those looks again.

"We won," they both said, somewhat flatly.

I realized it was like asking someone who dropped something which way it fell. Of course they won. It's what they do. The All Blacks have the highest win percentage of any team, in any sport, ever. They also hold the record for total number of wins and wins by the largest margin, once defeating Tonga (a decent team) 102 – 0. While we chatted, a couple of boys shyly approached the players for autographs. The oversized men smiled and nodded to me, concluding our visit, fished well-used black Sharpies from their bags and went to work.

Back in the barbershop, Ron Perlman directed me to the chair, which looked as though someone had just emptied a mohair pillow onto it. Either that or his previous customer was a high-altitude sheep (possibly merino) and he'd yet to remove the pile of shearings. I stood facing the chair for an awkward moment, thinking he would sweep the sweater-like lump to the floor to make room for me, but instead he just held the plastic cape open and also waited, somewhat awkwardly, for me to get in the chair. I figured for $8 Kiwi I shouldn't expect too much, exhaled a great puff of air in the direction of the chair as though I were sighing and settled into the nest of matted hair. Once the creep factor dissipated, it was actually remarkably comfy, like a seat cushion you might use on stadium bleachers, or some kind of post-surgery blow-up ring.

We had a superb early morning barber – customer conversation of sorts, exchanging a total of four words, two nods and a grunt. Unbeknownst to him, I'd spend much more for the luxury of such brevity. He buzzed electric trimmers around my head, a delicious experience when done properly and silently, and I enjoyed the view my peripheral gaze allowed. I did some mental math, wondering how a guy makes a living giving an $8 cut in what was otherwise an empty shop. It was then I noticed a rack of hats – ball caps – for sale by the till. They were $40 each. Logic (and cynicism) told me perhaps I shouldn't trust a barber offering haircuts for $8 and caps for $40. The cut, however, ended up being all right – aside from the large bald patch he left on top.

15

SOUTHERN OCEAN

From our trusty companion, the waterlogged, coiled journal in green. The passage I'll share, fittingly, will reveal itself in due course.

I could go on about the soft-covered green journal, but you're probably familiar with it by now. There's no point in belabouring my fondness for this coil-bound stack of lined paper. However, I found this one rather fun, itself a discovery, as we decipher my water-stained, treasure map/journal together.

I'd settled into a soft sofa with a coffee, trying to make sense of the notebook with the clumped pages and scribbles in faded pencil. It had been in my pocket on a long solo hike when I was caught in the hardest rain I'd ever experienced – a fire hose on full. A 20-kilometre loop, the trail undulated over rough rock, through forest and tidal coast track, and my technical clothes simply couldn't stand up. They'd become a pasty second skin.

I had a 20-dollar bill in my pocket and, staggering back into town, I popped into a convenience store to buy a bottle of wine. I sloshed a trail of water through the small store and apologized to the clerk as I did so, giving him the 20, which felt like a washcloth after a long bath. He said no worries, he was used to it as the store was across from the beach, and most of the money he took in was soaking wet.

When I got back to our unit, I realized the cheap green notebook was a bloated wet ball and I feared my record of this bit of viking was lost forever. But I began to methodically peel apart pages, allowing the soggy little pile of tatters to dry. Faint pencil slowly became legible over a few days, like revealing invisible ink. I discovered one entry I particularly liked: *Devastating setback. Urine at best.* I had no idea what it referred to. All I could come up with was perhaps I'd suffered an ailment and then recovered, maybe an improved bladder condition I'd forgotten about. Then again, I could've been describing something unpleasant I'd consumed that tasted like pee. We'll never know for sure.

We left North Island on a ferry from Wellington under morning sun, puffy cumulus and bright blue sky. On the water, severe wind blew through Cook Strait, reminiscent of Perth's Fremantle Doctor. We were on the inter-island ferry going from North to South island, ironically travelling in a northerly direction, as the ends of the two land masses extend a short distance beyond each other.

We were en route to Picton, and the boat rocked sharply in steep swells and intense wind. On deck, I couldn't keep a cap on my head as we squinted against gale-force northwesterlies. We took shelter inside, watching the Marlborough Sounds heave past through Plexiglas portholes streaked with spindrift, and lunched on a cafeteria platter of deep-fried lumps. Everything was hot, smelled mildly fishy and tasted of well-aged oil. A Schweppes ginger beer and plate-sized slab of ginger cake not only anchored me like ballast against the pitching of the boat but the ginger kept it all down as well.

We trained from Picton to Kaikōura, past a sea salt refinery and fields of grazing cows and sheep. The train punched through black lava tunnels on the coast, passing uninterrupted stretches of smooth, sandy beach. The area was the oldest inhabited part of the country, settled a thousand years ago by Polynesians who arrived from the north in double-hulled, long-distance sailing *wakas*, reminiscent of the *Hōkūle'a* from our first *Gone Viking* adventure. Here on the northeast coast of South Island, fog hung directly offshore and rain crept down the windows in jagged smears. Through streaky water and mist, I glimpsed fur seals diving in dark surf, where bull kelp swirled like mermaid hair.

Despite a foul day – cold wind and heaving black breakers – I went to a rocky beach, lugging a monstrous surf-cast rod, weights and tackle. I struggled in the wind, fighting off gulls while baiting hooks, my hands slowly numbing. The only thing I caught was the start of a cold, but despite frustration and futility I was pleased for the experience.

Weather improved and we explored Kaikōura's Fyffe House, a 160-year-old home built on a foundation of sperm whale vertebrae stacked into lumpy pilings. A monarch butterfly fluttered in the garden. The butterflies were self-introduced to the country, leaving us to wonder how far they'd flown. There was also a preserved moa egg on display. The moa was a massive, ostrich-like bird the Māori hunted to extinction. Slow-moving, flightless and tasty, the birds were doomed to a short existence. ("It's an island. We didn't have a lotta protein.")

We strolled around town – a long, thin community strung along the seaside, and lunched on crayfish the size of Atlantic lobster (the 30-dollar half-order will be plenty, thanks). Afterward, we meandered through the serenely beautiful Garden of Memories – a cenotaph park awash in coral, pink and white roses, yellow buttercups and lapis bluebells. Cabbage trees, pohutukawa and sturdy Norfolk pine threw shade and sheltered the little sanctuary from ocean winds. Whale jawbones, resembling ribs, were planted like towering fence posts. The bones arched upward, meeting and slightly overlapping, creating a corridor like walking beneath massive, crossed swords. There was a positive energy, and we found ourselves dawdling until lunch wore off and we were hungry again. We dragged ourselves away, but lingering in the oddly comforting white cage of bones, you couldn't help but feel like Jonah.

Next morning a bedside alarm woke me nauseatingly early. (What we'd later refer to as vomit o'clock.) I left Deb sleeping and walked to town in near blackness. By dim yellow streetlights and a handful of stars, I made my way the couple of kilometres to the train station, walking along the water. Tide was slack, the ocean quiet.

At the station, I went to an inner room to meet with a whale-watching group. It was warm, dimly lit and quiet. A video played on a wall – whales in slow motion, mewling to an instrumental soundtrack like a lullaby, transporting me to Robyn's shockless van and the long, queasy drive to Telegraph Cove. Only this time I fell asleep, immediately, upright in a hard plastic chair. I suspect the other 20 people joining the tour were drowsing as well. My head lolled until a train thundered past, a freighter that didn't stop. I snapped awake, expecting the train to smash through a wall. The floor bounced, vibrating my feet in circles, an erratic soft-shoe shuffle.

A coach arrived (alas, still no sign of Craig T. Nelson). We boarded and weaved our way around the headland under the looming gaze of the Kaikōura Range. As we reached the pier, the weather turned. A sharp easterly gusted in. Moored boats rose and fell on steep waves. We loaded into a heaving boat, where we were greeted by Captain Chevy.

"Oim Kippin' Shivvy. Theessah moy vesso," he said.

As we fell into seats, he explained two things: how to use the life preservers and how to use the sickness bags. And with that we lurched into growing swells.

A short way from shore, deep ocean troughs provide ideal feeding grounds for sperm whales, the most highly sought species in the lucrative whale-oil trade. In the 19th century, European and American whalers arrived, doing their best to eradicate whales and disseminate syphilis, effectively replacing highly intelligent life with quite the opposite.

We trundled out several kilometres, Captain Chevy's high, spring-loaded seat rising and falling nearly a metre with each wave. Clutching at handrails, I weaved my way onto the deck, where the horizon moved like mercury. Petrels bobbed, shearwaters skimmed the breakers like surfers and a massive Gibson's albatross soared past, its four-metre wingspan a banner.

Swells gradually subsided and more people crept to the gunwales. A sperm whale was spotted and we motored toward it. Passengers were huddled on the port side, so I made my way to the starboard railing, where only one woman stood. Then I realized why. She was vomiting with loud wet gags, an impressive quantity, splattering in the surf with an oddly musical vibrato. *Thar' she blows!* I thought, then moved upwind and enjoyed a relatively private viewing spot despite the disturbing ambient soundtrack.

The whale logged, oxygenating its blood, preparing to dive for giant squid two kilometres deep in the canyon-like underwater trench. After a short while it dove – the money shot moment – giant flukes sliding perpendicularly into the water, barely rippling the surface. A tiny circle of water moved like a drain, a watery black shutter, closing to end scene.

From that once-bloated ball of a waterlogged journal, pencil lead continuing to reveal itself like lemon juice in candlelight:

Again I'm reminded of high school English lit and long-dead mentors, having trekked a trail toward (the original) Canterbury – now I get to do it again, in a car, here in the South Pacific.

Spending time in and around Christchurch in New Zealand's Canterbury region, we discovered the best fish and chips in existence at a place called Monger's. Imagine, if you will, the finest piece of fish you've ever eaten. Now imagine it prepared even better. Flawlessly, in fact. The server whisks the perfect fish from the grill (not the fryer) and presents it to you for viewing. All you can do is smile. Now imagine this taking place over a busy take-away counter. Your immaculate meal is then passed to you in a little (compostable) cardboard box, and away you go to enjoy your perfection wherever you choose and somewhat ruining you for fish and chips anywhere else, ever again. Inside the front door, a scrawled note was taped to the wall: "This is *the best* fuckin' fish and chips – rock on!" with a happy face and Jack Black's signature. Apparently, he'd come here every few days during filming of Peter Jackson's *King Kong*, following an after-work joint. I felt Jack's review was spot on.

From Christchurch we made like Chaucer, swapping tales as we ventured through Canterbury, travelling south around Lyttelton Harbour to the Banks Peninsula and the small French village of Akaroa, Māori for Long Harbour. A farmer's dream, this unique pocket of land is situated on a deep harbour with fertile volcanic soil and was settled by English, German and French immigrants. The French, however, thrived, populating the area with a boatload of settlers from the cheese mecca of Rochefort.

To get here, we followed the only road in, a sharply winding highway blasted through a wide, dark volcano. The road was in a constant state of repair, the drive an exercise in stopping, starting and patience. Tourists would simply stop on the road to take pictures of stunning coastal views. Road workers did their best to hurry drivers along where they could and stop them when they had to.

The other impediment to the drive were brash, cheeky keas – alpine parrots – that strutted up and down the centre line like bowlegged little gunslingers from a western, looking for a draw. The squat green birds, about the size of Chucky, were entirely unafraid of traffic, or people, and exceedingly adept thieves, snatching anything valuable, edible or otherwise interesting from open car windows or unattended packs and purses.

French flags fly around Akaroa town centre. Street names are also in French. Shortly after we arrived, a storm rolled through – hard, blinding rain. We took shelter in a cafe, nibbled dense gateau and the strongest espresso I've ever had, actually feeling it wash away tooth enamel and stomach lining. As we stared through a wet window, an enormous truck rumbled past – a road train of sorts. Three long trailers were each packed with three storeys of sheep, noses poking through slatted sides. There must've been a thousand of them, bleating and rattling past on their one-way transit.

Christchurch is a key departure point and scientific centre for Antarctic exploration, and I went for some indoor viking and research at the city's International Antarctic Centre, a joint project of Kiwi, American and Italian interests. I was also keen to make up for the disappointing South Pole display at Auckland's MOTAT.

At the entrance to Christchurch's Antarctic Centre I was greeted by a ragtag bunch of rescued birds in varying states of recovery, including Morgan, a little blue penguin who'd decided he no longer cared for the water. Morgan was a bit of a celebrity and on some level struck me as a well-dressed Buddhist, patiently waiting for his next reincarnation to something more land-based, truer to his calling. It reminded me of a trip Deb and I made to a museum farther south, where a taxidermied king penguin met us as we entered.

"Another herring?" I asked.

"Oh, I couldn't. I'm *stuffed*," it replied, in my mind.

The Antarctic Centre was geared to kids. I fit in. A group of us were ushered into a preparatory room where we were given bulky hooded coats, mitts and fat foamy boots. After a short wait a red light came on, a door slid open and we shuffled into a recreated Antarctic landscape complete with snowy hills, tunnels, an icy slide and a vintage Hägglund Antarctic vehicle.

Once we were inside, the door slid shut, sealing us in. The Hägglund rumbled to life and an Antarctic storm simulation began. Two digital displays glowed on a wall, one showing the temperature, the other the amount of time remaining until we'd be released to thaw. Wind increased and the temperature dropped. We were effectively sealed into a massive industrial freezer with added wind chill, crunching about with nostrils frozen shut, gradually losing feeling in extremities. For this we paid 20 dollars.

At one point I imagined an evil voice would purr through a speaker, demanding we divulge classified M16 information while Jaws (not the fish, but the villain with the metal teeth) would flash his wicked, glinting smile through the glass. And, not unlike my partial drowning in the watery tent on West Cracroft, the Antarctic Experience was uncomfortable, unnerving and, in hindsight, oddly pleasant.

Later a long, winding drive took us to Lake Tekapo, a teal-blue glacial lake nestled in the snow-capped Southern Alps, roughly in the middle of South Island. We could've been in Switzerland or Alberta's Lake Louise. We'd passed fields of dairy cows, farmed deer and countless sheep. (I tried counting but invariably fell asleep.) The air here is reportedly the clearest in the southern hemisphere. No such thing as tanning, simply varying degrees of burns. This chunk of the country, apparently, is also beneath the hole in the ozone. Without heavy SPF sunscreen, I could nearly watch myself toast like grilled cheese under a broiler.

Boggy ground surrounding the lake was thick with lupine, an impressionist's palette of soft colour. The lake turned a polished, abalone blue-green as we walked to the Church of the Good Shepherd, a small square stone building on the lakeshore. Richly layered organ music seeped from the church and I felt we were entering a 1940s radio serial. A tiny, dark-haired woman was tucked neatly in a corner, playing the organ and working the pedals with concentration, while in the pews another solitary woman sat, head bowed, hands clasped in silent prayer.

From another Moleskine, this one in puce (that's right), half-lined, I could clip a tiny pen to the spine, all of it fitting neatly in the pocket of technical pants:

THIS, I felt was the ultimate antipodean, viking sojourn –
DUNEDIN – Scottish capital on the underside of the world!

Founded in 1848 by Thomas Burns (Robbie's nephew), Dunedin is the southern hemisphere's Edinburgh. Burns settled the town under the Free Church of Scotland. Back home, the rest of the Presbyterians in the traditional Church of Scotland had begun asking for donations. No one's certain if the donation request was the reason Thomas et al. fled the country, but you have to assume it's quite likely. Trust a Scot to travel halfway round the world in search of a new home, bypassing countless warm South Pacific islands and instead choosing to settle in rugged southern New Zealand, its climate cold and harsh for much

of the year. I could imagine that first conversation as they sailed into
Otago Harbour:

"Och, buggerr me, Misterrr Burrns, bu' tha's fookin' coldt!"

"Eye, McTavish, she's brracing, bu' bonny, nay?"

"Eye, bonny asa' lass."

"Och, eye."

"So, is tha' i' then?"

"Eye, tha'll do."

The Scots settled here and built a thriving town at the bottom of the
world, turning it into a wealthy, powerful city following the discovery
of gold in 1861. Having travelled around the country, we too made it
home for a while, a base to explore the Otago and Southland regions.

I walked trails around Dunedin's Botanic Garden and through the
University of Otago grounds, recognizing a creek running through
campus featured in Michael Palin's *Full Circle*. Beyond the city we
explored Port Chalmers, Portobello, the surf beaches of St Clair and
St Kilda, and visited Taiaroa Head, home to a colony of enormous
royal albatross.

We were in the southern Scottish city for Robbie Burns Day, a
downtown party featuring the old country sounds of the Red Hot Chili
Pipers. Across town, fireworks popped for a Chinese New Year's celebration, creating a unique fusion vibe. In true Highland fashion, the
day turned dreich. And I did my part to recognize my Scottish heritage, popping into a pub, having a Laphroaig and not tipping.

Grabbing a rental car for a day, we headed up the coast to wander
amidst the Moeraki Boulders – massive, spherical stones spat slowly
from the earth that sit in shoreline sand like giant rock marbles.
Eventually, the stones wear down and break apart to reveal a geologic-
ally unique honeycomb centre.

While in Moeraki, we stopped at Fleur's Place – a small, nondescript
building at the end of an unmarked road that houses a rustic little restaurant where it's nearly impossible to get a seating. Fleur Sullivan is
a low-key, nearly unsung celebrity chef, if such a thing's possible. Her

fan base is enormous, but there was no TV show, no products, just a few of her books for sale at the till and a steady stream of patrons filling her tables. A dedicated fishing boat supplied her restaurant. Rick Stein, England's seafood guru, was apparently commissioned by the *London Times* for a single story. He could name the place, anywhere in the world he wanted to go for a meal – the paper would pick up the tab – he just had to write a story. And he said he didn't even have to think about it. He had to go to Fleur's.

It was well before noon and the restaurant had just opened. Our guidebook said to not even bother trying without a reservation well in advance. However, we poked our heads in the front door, where a woman stood at a small reception counter.

"Any chance we could have lunch?" we asked, figuring we knew the answer.

She turned pages in a big, leather-bound book. *Flip. Flip. Flip.*

"Sure," she said. "But we'll need the table in under an hour."

Feeling fortunate, we were shown to a tiny upstairs table. Nearby windows looked over a pier and boats in a compact bay. A stained glass window of a whale's tail cast a strip of blue-green light onto downstairs tables. We ordered soup and blue cod in creamy bacon sauce. Our soup bowls arrived – the size of helmets, filled to the brim and exquisite. Unable to *not* finish, we mopped it all up with bread and were stuffed. But then creamy, bacon-flavoured cod was set before us, artfully served with vegetables nestled around a polished abalone shell and finished with an edible orange daisy. Once more I made those noises I made while eating Haimin's squid-ink pasta in Taupō, submerging my face in my food, not resurfacing until the plate was empty. I had, however, paused briefly for a pre-meal photo, which was fortunate. All that remained afterward was my impeccably clean plate, a slightly distended belly and a Cheshire Cat grin.

From the back of a sealed #10 envelope, a piece of unaddressed junk mail left at our rental unit, which I repurposed as foolscap:

Presbyterian spires dotted low skyline as we strolled through Dunedin under imposing architecture of late nineteenth century affluence – heavy sandstone, local bluestone and dull brick – stodgy as the Calvinists who built it.

Everything resembled a refined old bank, and a disproportionate number of buildings had been just that. The one exception was Dunedin's train station, standing back from the city centre like an ostracized child at the edge of the playground. It was as if every bit of playful creativity and whimsy excluded from the rest of the city's conservative buildings went into the station's design. It looked like something by Hans Christian Andersen – a fairy-tale castle made of gingerbread, gumdrops and white frosting. The interior felt as though the city had reached a stage where it had simply run out of ways to spend money, doing its best to drain the coffers on this single structure. Royal Doulton custom made the tiny, ornate floor tiles. A stained glass locomotive loomed overhead, seemingly about to run you down, and threw muted blue light throughout the interior. The colour and tiles cooled the room, adding a sense of sterility more in keeping with an infirmary than a train station. When we arrived, a farmers' market was set up outside, adding life to the place and warming it into a proper community.

We made our way to the central town square, which is actually an octagon, beneath (its) Saint Paul's Cathedral and an oversized bronze statue of (Uncle) Robbie Burns, working on something on a roll of parchment. There's writing on the "paper," but you need to jump and scramble a bit to glimpse it. Conveniently, Robbie chose to write this particular piece upside-down, allowing passersby to read it. All I could make out was something about Mary, which confused me as I thought the Farrelly brothers wrote that for Hollywood, but apparently it was Burns, in the mid-18th century.

A short while later a small bus picked us up near Dunedin's Octagon. (Which I didn't capitalize earlier because it didn't make sense then, but now it does.) We dodged through town, joined the highway and made our way west and south to the edge of Otago Region and the rugged Catlins coast.

Following serpentine highway, we crossed the Clutha River and stopped at Invercargill. When the Rolling Stones arrived here in the 1970s, in what we can only assume was a booking error, one of the band emerged like a springtime groundhog, looked around and asked how they'd wound up in the middle of the arsehole of the earth. I've read that quote credited both to Mick and to Keith. Whoever said it, it just won't go away, and locals refer to it with a mixture of resentment and pride.

We loaded a few people from the earth's arsehole into the van, bringing our little group's tally to seven, including our driver–guide Mike. He drove us to Waipapa Point Lighthouse, where we beachcombed a windswept shore of straggly kelp and iridescent seashells. We'd been on the bus a long time and it was barely midday. The vehicle wound along a bumpy narrow isthmus separating Porpoise Bay from open sea at New Zealand's southern tip. A compact general store was our only food option for a lot of hours. We had a choice of frosty ice cream or very old candy. There was also an ossified meat pie under a heat lamp, perhaps as a curio, and I wondered if that was how this minuscule town – Curio Bay – got its name. A sign read "Population: 11." And this hamlet was home to a pod of Hector's dolphins, the smallest of its species in the world.

We scrambled to shore down a bank of low dunes – windswept sand and sea grass, and scanned the water. Sun filtered through gossamer cloud – the same flat, bright light that illuminated the start of this viking excursion, and the bay was the colour of aluminum foil, crimped in rippling breeze.

Amongst the smallest of all cetaceans, Hector's dolphins are only found here. The species is comfortable around humans, but the water's icy, wetsuit cold. I couldn't imagine getting in the water, but there was an outsized photo of people cavorting with a pod. I suspect the shot was taken moments before the smiling swimmers succumbed to hypothermia.

From the relative warmth of dry land, we stood on the beach, scanning the cold grey water. And before long we spotted a small pod porpoising out in the bay – pale grey backs on chunky, torpedo bodies. Aside from their size, the most distinctive feature of Hector's dolphins is a rounded dorsal fin, reminiscent of a sea turtle flipper. We were treated to a simple, rewarding show – flashes of small, curving bodies rolling briskly through a swath of metallic sea.

Back in our coach we motored on, stopping to traipse through a petrified forest on the shore and hike a wooded trail beneath fuchsia trees to McLean Falls, a veil of water that drops 30 metres to crash onto mossy boulders. Our tour carried on to Kaka Point and Cannibal Bay, where we learned disappointingly ungrisly history and crept past a blubbery sea lion nestled in sand at the base of grassy dunes.

Back in the van, Mike connected his phone to the sound system and asked for requests.

"Cold Play's 'Paradise,'" someone called from the back.

"Yeah, 'Paradise,'" the rest of us chimed in. We'd already heard it twice – it was still getting a lot of airplay but seemed an ideal fit to an exceptional day and good scenery.

"Jesus!" Mike said with a smile. "Always 'Paradise.' I've got over 2,000 songs and every trip, every group, 'Paradise'! Any other requests?"

"'Paradise'!" we said again.

Mike sighed, indulged us and we belted out the lyrics one more time.

Following a long day, we eventually arrived at our final destination, Nugget Point, one of New Zealand's most iconic views. We walked a narrow footpath along plummeting cliffs through waving yellow grass to a lighthouse on the headland. Wind whipped over tumultuous water far below and the sky was cloudless, brilliant blue. We carried on to the end of the trail, end of the coast and end of the country, with nothing between us and Antarctica but a couple of uninhabited islands and the stormy Southern Ocean.

We made a short detour on foot to a viewing hide, where we spotted a yellow-eyed penguin making its way from the water. On the long drive back to Dunedin, conversation lagged and heads bobbed. I rode up front and socialized with Mike. Passing a field, we watched a sheep run full speed, headlong into a mesh fence, bounce back, fall over and leap back up, as though that was exactly what it meant to do.

"Jesus, those things are stupid," Mike chuckled.

The sheep looked down as we passed, as though embarrassed. I'd say it looked sheepish, but that would be redundant.

Scribbled on a regular-size napkin (self-serve), from Dunedin International Airport's food court:

The Otago Peninsula glowed, the harbour reflecting muted light in the sky. Then morphed to a Hallmark sympathy card as sun broke through a cloud bank, fanning sundogs across Dunedin.

A huge manuka framed my view with gentle hills south of the city. A blackbird hopped across the grass. There was a pitch-perfect, single note call of a thrush and the soft bleating of sheep across the bay. Sun dipped below the cloud, igniting it like a torch, and sunset sky bled red into tangerine and mauve, gently fading to black.

Late that night, a party blared from our bathroom while we sat in the living room, uninvited. The party wasn't *actually* there, mind you. It was echoing up the hill and pounding through our little unit, reverberating as though the live band was in our bathtub. It was midnight, our flight was leaving early in the morning and things weren't fun anymore.

The band started playing "Sweet Child o' Mine" and I was teleported back to bleak New Year's Eve in Napier. I called the landlord (who lived on the property) and he said there was nothing he could do. We packed our bags, simply needing to be elsewhere, and drove toward Dunedin airport.

I envisioned a night of aimless driving and gas station coffee, but we decided to try our luck at the airport. It was a long drive with few signs, winding through unlit farmland. After some time we spotted tail lights up ahead – a taxi. *It must be going to the airport*, I thought, and followed it. After a few kilometres, the taxi driver slammed on the brakes, leapt from his cab and ran at us like a bull elephant charging a Jeep.

"Why are you following me? *Why are you following me?!*" the man howled.

The poor guy was terrified. My pursuit on the long dark road had him worked into near hysteria. I did my best to calm him down.

"We're just going to the airport," I said in the most soothing version of my voice, the one I use with rabid dogs and the insanely irrational. I gently repeated it and he calmed to about an eight on a scale of ten.

He went back to his vehicle, glancing over a shoulder, and drove away. We waited for his tail lights to disappear and then carried on toward the airport. It was the only possible destination on that road at that time of night. Given his reaction, I felt he'd made a poor career choice.

Eventually, we rolled up to the airport, where an underlit sign of an albatross greeted us as we veered in. It was just past 1 a.m. and the sign was the only light on at Dunedin International Airport. Our flight was seven hours away and everything was locked and dark. We pulled to the curb, cracked a window to avoid asphyxiation, pulled up jackets like blankets and pretended to sleep.

"Ah, the glamour of travel," we said in unison and laughed.

There was a tap on the window, which, surprisingly, didn't startle us in the black. After the charge of the raging-bull taxi driver, I suppose nothing could've rattled us. I looked out and there was a giant peering into our car. *Objects are closer than they appear*, I thought, and rolled down the window.

"You can't park here," he said, his voice a deep, gentle rumble.

I sighed, prepared for the "move along" speech the sheriff gave Sylvester Stallone in *Rambo* to get him out of Hope, which, for those of you who don't know, is just outside of Vancouver.

"Okay," I said, steeling myself for the drive back to town and an inevitable night of gas station coffee. But I was wrong. He asked what we were up to and I told him.

"Pull over to the other side," he told me, which confused me, but I did what he asked and then got out of the car.

He walked over to where we were and said, "I'm John Buchanan. You'll be all right parked here for the night. Follow me. We'll see if we can't set you up inside."

Deb and I looked at each other, shrugged and followed John Buchanan. It turned out he was airport security – the *entire* airport security. He unlocked the Dunedin International Airport, showed us to a small room of long bench seats, ideal for snoozing and conveniently located next to some vending machines and a loo.

"I'm afraid I can't put the lights on for you. They're on a central timer and won't come on 'til morning. Take this," he said and passed us his flashlight, which was the size of an arm. "I'll check back on you, but I'll be quiet. Good night."

John Buchanan, the gentle giant, turned an otherwise brutal night into a rather pleasant experience, and we got a bit of sleep we assuredly would not have gotten in the car or our rental unit.

A few hours later, we woke to birdsong. Sunrise was a vast sky of lavender. Sparrows were already busy in leafy trees lining the airport drive. Windows were thick with frost and I shivered, imagining what it would've been like in the vehicle. We moved the car to rental returns, got our gear, shuffled through the terminal and tracked down John Buchanan to thank him and return his giant flashlight – this being one of those magical travel moments, experiencing the kindness of strangers.

I wrote this on an ad for Subaru (pronounced locally "su-BAR-oo") from Kia Ora, Air New Zealand's inflight magazine:

*The howling scream from the back of our airborne
plane told us something was horribly wrong.*

It keened to a high-pitched wail and I realized with a modicum of relief it wasn't human. The captain came on the PA to tell us it was nothing alarming, just the door at the rear of the plane was open.

"Just a little," he said, after an endless second or two, before adding, "We're gonna take 'er back down and see if we can't get that thing closed. Please remain seated with your seatbelts securely fastened."

As if we needed to be told. All I saw in my mind were those blurry photos of that Hawaiian flight when the door popped off and a passenger or two were sucked out to plummet toward the Pacific. I clutched Deb's hand a tad firmly, feeling something crack. Then again, it may've been the hand of the fellow on the other side of me.

A flight attendant came down the aisle, stiff-legged and white knuckling the chair backs. She was doing her best to explain that things were, in fact, quite all right, really, reminding me of the faux banks in Grand Cayman after the hurricane. Her expression was unconvincing.

She leaned into our row. "Would you like anything?" she yelled over the trumpeting rush of air.

"Do you have a clean pair of underwear?" I hollered.

Her expression told me (I suspect) that she thought I was questioning her hygiene. Of course, I was leading up to a doody-free joke, but it was clear she was done with me. She clutched at seats and went down the aisle where she addressed a Japanese tour group, none of whom spoke English. They all looked terrified as the screaming plane wheeled sharply over snow-capped mountains. The look of fear needs no translation.

The flight attendant leaned in stiffly, trying to instill confidence, her strained smile a frightening clown grimace. Having successfully scared the tour group even more, she slowly made her way, Frankenstein-like, back to her seat for landing.

Despite jarring turbulence, the pilot eased the jet neatly into the tight gap between rugged mountains and a deep indigo river. We bumped to a stop on the runway.

A couple of maintenance guys in coveralls – characters from *Fletch* – sauntered over to the plane. They banged on the rear door with heavy tools and then slammed it shut like an old Buick.

The captain came back on the PA: "That oughta do it. Buckle up folks. Let's try that again." And we taxied back the way we'd come and took off. We'd barely begun our ascent when the piercing howl screamed from the rear again, only much louder than before.

"Well, folks," the captain said. "I guess that's as good as we're gonna get. Sorry for the inconvenience."

And we carried on. Then I looked around the cabin. There were fewer passengers than the first time. I'm sure of it. How they left the plane, I never knew.

I'd been watching *Pilot Guides*, the Lonely Planet TV show, usually hosted by engaging travellers, my favourites being Ian Wright, Justine Shapiro and Bradley Cooper (yes, *that* Bradley Cooper), inspiring me to write this across a map of Cook Strait:

*A surreal travel moment – sitting by a train, waiting for
a bus to take us to a ferry – from there, we'd walk.*

We left Wellington once more, island hopping toward a multiday hike on the north end of South Island. On the destination side, we passed a nondescript aquarium and a short but spectacular shoreline walk past a tidy row of towering Phoenix palms. We were in the commuter town of Picton, a hub for ferries from Wellington and trains from Christchurch. The town seemed nothing more than a throughway, a means to elsewhere, but there was charm to be found the moment you looked.

A series of trails wound through the Victoria Domain with water views, where we watched stingrays swim in iridescent blue water. I went to the Edwin Fox Ship and Visitor Centre and crawled around one of the world's oldest ships. The *Edwin Fox* transported convicts to Australia and was one of the first vessels equipped with a refrigeration system, used to ship frozen lamb to Britain, igniting New Zealand's economy-sustaining export trade.

Making the most of the area's perennially pleasant weather, we took a rest day and joined a tour of Marlborough wineries where we met George, a lumbering, affable man who reminded me of Brian Dennehy. A former ambulance driver and retired cop, George was our tour guide. Immediately likeable, the big man told jokes and pointed out things of interest as he drove our little bus through vineyards around Blenheim, one of New Zealand's well-established wine regions.

By the sixth and final winery of the afternoon, I'd become remarkably witty and doubtless an exquisite dancer. George pulled the bus directly up to the front step of the winery, two strides from the front door, where a smiling host awaited us with a tray of sparkling wine in fluted glasses. Displaying my rapier wit, slurring only slightly, I complained to George it was unthinkable that we should have to carry ourselves the entire distance (two metres) to the winery entrance, and was that really the best he could do?

"Right!" he replied smartly. And, plucking me from my seat, he slung me over his shoulder like a sack of fermented grain and carried me, giggling, from the bus to the tray of champagne, neatly combining three of my favourite things: being airborne, being tipsy and being the centre of attention.

From a pad of unlined paper:

I imagined myself somewhere in the lyrics of the Tragically Hip song "Looking For a Place to Happen," when adventurers had just one job. To explore.

A lugubrious day, grey pall over water and steep volcanic hillsides. Leaning on a gunwale, we watched our wake curl away in a dancing white *V*. The water taxi was hauling us to the Queen Charlotte Track (QCT) trailhead at Ship Cove on New Zealand's South Island. Last time through these waters, we'd scattered a raft of little blue penguins as we passed. This time, a different boat on a different day, we were watching for seabirds when Deb spotted something in the water, breaking the surface. We couldn't make it out. Then the water exploded – 30 bottlenose dolphins diving around our boat, chasing our hull and piercing our wake. It carried on for some time, our skipper slowing to make it last, until gradually the pod moved on and it was over too soon.

Bands of cirrus smeared over charcoal sky – a painter's monochrome brush strokes – and my mind drifted with the cloud. We rounded an isthmus where Captain Cook had landed, a white memorial just visible in the distance. I thought of the places he'd been and how many we'd visited, over 200 years later, viking our way through the ages. During Cook's epic second journey commanding HMS *Resolution*, he wrote in his journal, "The truth is, I was willing to prolong the passage in searching for what I was not sure to find." I felt the same way. (This particular journal of his, by the way, was a 750-page, leather-bound tome, the captain's handwriting fine and meticulous, full lines crossed out as he searched for more accurate words.)

On Vancouver Island, a brass hook hangs off a rock bluff in Victoria where Cook anchored his ships. Captain Vancouver used the same moorage years later. I mentally cross-referenced our respective viking routes. Like Cook, we'd travelled up and down the west coast of North America and around the Pacific – Australia, New Zealand and the Hawaiian Islands. We'd even been to where Cook was killed as part of our first *Gone Viking* endeavour.

The event that ended Cook's life was sadly trivial, another example of an assuredly avoidable catastrophe. Kamehameha was supposedly there, in the melee where Cook was mobbed and brained. I couldn't help but wonder if the captain was an unwitting victim of a cruel and unfortunate misunderstanding, some local having asked Cook if he'd like a club sandwich, the way you might offer a Hurts donut, a knuckle sandwich or, in this case, a Hawaiian punch.

Our boats slowed as we pressed deeper into the Marlborough Sounds. We passed Resolution Bay and Endeavour Inlet, both named after Cook's ships. I'd crawled around an H M S *Endeavour* replica in Sydney's Australian National Maritime Museum, built to exact specifications. The replica housed an excellent display of historical items and I was forced to stoop as I walked through the captain's low-ceilinged quarters. Cook had shared the room with six-foot-four Joseph Banks, making me shudder at the idea of living and working asea for years in such cramped conditions.

On the flip side of the Dunedin food court napkin:

Although an ocean or two from the earliest Viking routes
around northern Europe, we remained,
I felt, on the heels of the more modern variety,
over the past three or four centuries.

Now we'd left cars, buses and boats behind. For the next several days we'd be on our own, getting from A to B (and then C, D and E) on foot, packs on backs, a trail map, guidebook and the occasional directional sign hammered into the earth by New Zealand's Department of Conservation, known locally as the DOC. Our accommodation would be a series of small lodges where we could get a cooked meal and have a modicum of overnight comfort as we trekked our way around the north end of South Island from Cook Strait, through the Marlborough Sounds, and around Tasman Bay.

The water taxi (our last motorized transport for a week) approached a pier fronting the trailhead to Queen Charlotte Track. It was a stopping point for some of the world's most famous voyagers, reflected in place names, the Sounds melding Cook Strait with Tasman Bay.

Abel Tasman was one of the first Europeans to sail to New Zealand. The Dutchman arrived in the 17th century seeking new trade opportunities and, I presume, teaching islanders to pay for their own meals. Jean François Marie de Surville of France followed a century later. A settlement was established on New Zealand's southeast coast and the French thrived, farming and introducing locals to smoking and infidelity. Again, I presume. Arriving the same year as the French, Cook sailed under the Union Jack, claiming land for the British Crown and passing on long-standing traditions of overcooking food and abandoning oral hygiene. By the time missionaries arrived, some years later, it seemed the only thing left for them to impart was the notion of mono-positional intercourse.

As I channelled the Continental racism of my Via Rail breakfast companion (in the words of Dave Chappelle, "You racist, hilarious bastard!"), my mental meanderings came to a shuddering stop as we banged against the pier at Ship Cove. We jumped to the dock and hoisted packs that somehow kept getting heavier. I wished I'd chosen the lite peanut butter, and regretted packing extra bags of apples and oranges. I hoisted the awkward lump onto my back, twisting and spinning, fighting to stay upright as we went ashore. A weka waddled past, sizing us up, as though it too knew we'd eaten one or two of its distant relatives. We avoided eye contact and carried on.

Just beyond the present-day prehistoric bird, the trail rose like a wall. And, as the water taxi burbled away out of sight, we were left with only one way to go. I thought of Bill Bryson's friend Katz from *A Walk in the Woods*, hiking the Appalachian Trail, growing tired of the weight of his pack and simply throwing stuff away amongst the trees – clothing, food, pots and pans. Just chucking shit. *That would feel fantastic*, I thought.

I was sweating buckets and already feeling chafing from the heavy pack. I made the mistake of checking my watch and calculating distance. We were about one kilometre into our 71-kilometre trek, which would end up being over 80, as I would eventually (and inevitably) make a wrong turn. But we were buoyed by optimism and surrounded by beauty. A green-blue sea peeked through pockets of dense ferns, tall pines and fat, furry palms. Sun shone warm and the sky was a palette of blues. Fantails rustled through underbrush and wood pigeons swooped through high branches, their heavy wingbeats thudding like helicopter rotors. Ahead on the trail, Deb saw a wild piglet scurry through the ferns, grunting and snuffling, and we hoped we weren't close to its parents.

Following our initial ascent over a slippery blanket of pine needles and around spotted orange mushrooms like something from *Alice in Wonderland*, we gradually descended from the ridgeline to water level, down a treed corridor to our lodging for the night. We were greeted by a friendly, black, Chesapeake retriever. We learned his name was Stokes, and I immediately wanted a sidekick named Stokes. Or to be a sidekick named Stokes. Either way. We'd work the streets, dancing the thin blue line, doling out our own brand of vigilante justice from a souped-up Charger, or possibly a Camaro, and needless to say there'd be a Mike Post theme song. (Younger readers: Post was the Pharrell of his day.)

A Jacques Cousteau (or SpongeBob) voice-over:

Zee sea...she eez com. Bud...beneez zee sur-FASS...
we 'unt...zee eeloo-SEEF...cod bleu.

The little aluminum boat swayed as I leapt in from a tilting pier. The lodge's handyman held the boat for me, rocking beside the wharf. I cranked the throttle and gave a mighty tug to start the rusty old outboard. It caught with startling enthusiasm, tearing the boat away from the pier, bow thrust at the sky. I didn't want to look back, certain I'd see the handyman's hand gripping the gunwale, his severed arm trailing in the water. But when I snuck a peek he was on the pier, laughing and waving, his arm still solidly attached.

We'd eased into our multiday tramp with a rest day at our first lodging, and I took advantage of the gorgeous cold water to try my luck at hand fishing. (Which, by the way, is fishing *by* hand, not *for* them.) I throttled down and bumped my way into the fjord. Heavily wooded hills rose on both sides of the long channel. A gull called from somewhere and a high sun sparkled in the water. I took inventory in the little fishing skiff: a spool of thick monofilament line, a rusty nut for weight, two hooks on leaders forking from the single line, a disintegrating bucket that was more air than plastic, a block of frozen squid bait and a wicked filleting knife – more rust than steel, like something Cousteau would recover from a sunken Phoenician galley. *That's not a knife!* I thought. But, I decided, if forced to defend myself, I could certainly give an opponent a nasty case of lockjaw.

I tied to a buoy, hacked off some softening squid, baited the hooks and lowered the line, hand over hand, into the water, watching a trail of bubbles descend into deepening shades of green. Sun beat down and the boat rocked gently, lulling me with the lap of the water. My head bobbed until I felt the line go gently taught and slack, taught and slack – something nibbling far below. A bead of water rolled down the line, vibrating nearly imperceptibly, and I set the hook with a sharp upwards tug. The line ran and slowly I began to draw it in, the same hand-over-hand motion, this time in reverse, the way anglers have done for thousands of years.

I saw the fish swimming in inky green water far below, felt it in the touch of the line, exhilarating and primal. It was a good-sized blue cod – an ugly, thrashing, wet cylinder that would make a fine lunch. Hauling it in, I double-checked its size against daubs of paint on the gunwale, fumbled for the prehistoric knife in the shattered bucket and gave it a lethal dose of tetanus.

I kept moving through the bay, tying at different buoys and slowly working through the lump of squid. I ended up spending a great deal of time simply feeding the fish, offering up morsels for them to snatch deftly from the deadly little hook buffet. But I did pull up a mottled red, tang-like fish with big, puckered lips that reminded me of Linda in Seattle. After releasing it, I looked it up in my fish guide. It was a moki, with the exceptional English moniker "bastard trumpeter fish." I felt that would make a superb name for a brass band – Herb Alpert and the Tijuana Bastard Trumpeters.

I found myself humming Alpert's "A Taste of Honey" as I put the last of the bait on the hooks. Within a short while, I felt the now familiar sensation of exploratory nibbling. When I set the hook, the line ran hard and I felt like Hemingway's Santiago, back off the coast of Cuba, before the sharks arrived. But, hauling the line toward the boat, I realized I had fish on *both* hooks; *two* fat cod on the end of one line. *Forget Santiago*, I thought. *This was downright biblical.* All I needed was a loaf of bread and I was ready to feed the masses. Keeping the larger fish, I released the other, which swam away with a near-audible, fat-lipped "Phew!" to relay its whopper of a tale in school.

The lodge kitchen was closed, but we'd befriended the amiable chef, who prepared us late lunch, grilling the fresh cod and plating it with fries and salad. He sat with us and shared stories of fishing and diving for abalone, a regulated skin-diving sport that ensures conservation. Anglers can't use oxygen tanks and the water can be 18 metres deep. It was demanding. Abalones have to be prised from the rock, where they cling determinedly with surprising strength. A simple screwdriver is the preferred lever amongst divers.

While we visited, savouring our cod, Stokes came by, smiling and wagging his thick black tail. We sipped dark beer and watched other hikers come in off the trail until sun set, which happened quickly behind steep hills, the land around us changing from green to blue to black.

From a journal I had a long time before using it: thick, almost square, in navy blue. No elasticized band on the cover. I would've liked an elasticized band on the cover. On the fly-leaf I wrote:

Yogi Berra said, "When you come to a fork in the road, take it."

On the trail, I did just that, took the fork, inadvertently leading us the wrong way down an embankment with thick brush and high, tripping roots. Eventually, we found a home tucked between ferns, asked directions and, a mere half-hour later, were where we wanted to be.

Another rest day followed, and I fished, again, this time from a red plastic boat in a private bay under radiant, high-UV sun, pulling up another moki and blue cod. Next day, with a belly full of fish and eggs, I wandered to the water, enjoying the space before we had to move on. An octopus crept past like living liquid, clever and slithery, just beyond reach in clear shallows.

Reloading our packs, we climbed a calf-burning slope to the faintly marked trail we'd missed trying to get here. Two hard hours of climbing followed. We were forced to use one or both hands as we scrambled up sheer slopes, hauling on tree roots, narrow trunks and low-hanging branches on a blanket of slippery leaves. The gruelling climb got us back to the QCT, and from there we began another five-hour trek.

Later we stood on a pier jutting into a crystal blue-green inlet – a remote dent in New Zealand called Portage. Another couple stood nearby, doing the same thing, admiring the water. We began to visit and learned she was from South Africa. It turned out her best friend from childhood was the spouse of my former co-worker who hailed from Winnipeg, long odds that shrank the world and made us laugh. It's the only other place I've been to called Portage. In Manitoba, it's where canoes were hauled between the Red and Assiniboine rivers. Here on New Zealand's South Island, it's where Māori lugged *wakas* through a narrow pass 100 metres high to eliminate the snaggletooth chunk of land that sprawls in every direction, creating the myriad Sounds. From a muddy-brown river in the centre of Canada that marked the start of this viking journey, to an impossibly blue fjord at the base of the world, once more we're connected by people, one slender degree of separation. As we stared at the water, it became a snow globe – translucent parachutes of jellyfish pulsing past, a delicate, undulating dance.

Following an overnight nap (windows that didn't close, doors an inch from the floor, neighbours' conversations as clear as if we were roommates), we climbed once more to the trail and spent half a day on the march. Nearing the end of our 80-kilometre hike, we met another couple at QCT kilometre one. We'd hiked the trail in reverse, and were taking pictures to commemorate completion of the tramp. The two we met had done the same. We exchanged cameras, posed for photos and wished each other well, but wound up at the same little cafe in tiny Anakiwa, having coffee. They were waiting for a water taxi. We were waiting for a room.

They were Leslie and Veit, from Germany, travelling around New Zealand before Veit started a new job. He worked with the consulate, moving around and taking postings, as he put it, in cities with good opera. It reminded me of a teacher I had who'd only take jobs at universities in proximity to ironman triathlons, his competitive pastime.

I asked Veit where he'd worked.

"Vienna was a plum posting," he said. "And we're about to start a three-year stint in Sydney."

We socialized awhile and compared travel plans, as we too were peregrinating somewhat arbitrarily. Their water taxi arrived, we said goodbye and checked into our nearby accommodation. Our room was furnished with a 250-year-old mahogany canopy bed, which, we were told, had belonged to an Indian raja. I asked about ghosts and the subject was deftly changed. Made entirely of wood, the bed could be neatly disassembled. During hot Indian summers it would be taken apart and hauled to a higher, cooler locale by elephant, where it was reassembled for the season. After dinner, ensconced in the antique bed with windows open, we fell asleep to the haunting hoot of a morepork owl.

The next week, in Kaikōura, we ran into Leslie and Veit at a grocery store. They'd taken our accommodation recommendation and we were at the same motel. Timing was a coincidence, as our itineraries were still solidifying. We met for drinks and swapped stories, respective travel routes evolving as we spoke.

Roughly a month later, we were walking in a crush of commuters and tourists around Sydney's Circular Quay and remarkably ran into each other again. They were going to the Opera House for a performance and came to our place for drinks, as we were close by.

A short time later, also defying long odds, we ran into Vancouver acquaintances in the Rocks. We cooked them dinner and a few nights later met up for a restaurant meal in Darling Harbour.

Seated at a table next to us, a fellow was having dinner with his elderly parents. They'd travelled to Australia from France, he explained, to see him. He was a pastry chef and it turned out he made the restaurant's desserts. He mumbled something to a server and, as we finished our meal, a platter of pastries and baked goods was set down, covering our table. Our friends, both lactose intolerant, swallowed some pills, rolled up their sleeves and led us into the obscenely large mountain of sweets.

From the back of a DOC leaflet:

Awaroa Inlet can only be crossed within an hour and a half before, and two hours after, low tide. Along the track, the scenery alternates between sandy beaches and rocky headlands of regenerating kanuka. (Like manuka, kanuka is a tea tree known for its honey blossoms, the result a fragrant medicinal honey the colour and flavour of caramel.)

We returned to the north of South Island for another of the country's Great Walks, a short distance west of the QCT, another multiday tramp over gold sand beaches and jungly volcanic hills, this one being the Abel Tasman Coast Track. Let's jump into the trek, to Awaroa Lodge, shortly after arriving at this blend of mountain and sea.

pluviophile – (noun) a lover of rain; someone who finds joy and peace of mind during rainy days.

I'm not a pluviophile. As rain poured down windows like a car wash, we shivered in our cold, damp room, scratching mosquito bites. I found the hole in the screen that was to blame or, more accurately, I found some screen surrounding a hole disguised as a window. Outside it was miserable. Almost, but not quite, on the scale of my journal-drenching hike in the biblical deluge.

The lodge we were nestled into for a couple of nights backed onto an estuary, which at the moment was nothing but fog. A bird sang from somewhere – a ridiculously complex, freestyle trill that lasted over two minutes without a break. The forest that surrounded us was beautiful in the light, *and* in the dark for that matter, but in the in-between sludgy grey, it was bleak and oppressive. I brewed another strong cup of black Ceylon tea and wondered if we should start calling it Sri Lankan tea. No one had asked my opinion, so I let it go.

The room was tired. I wondered if it had changed since we'd last been here, or if we had. Probably both. Previously, we'd set the bar high, arriving by helicopter – a slick new EC 130, with a front row of three bucket seats to accommodate Deb, me and Andrew, the pilot. Skimming steep volcanic hills, we'd soared over deer farms and paddocks of sheep, banking over the Tasman Sea to follow the coastline – a winding band of sandy gold. Seals drifted on a reef and stingrays glided in the shallows – dark oblongs and diamonds in cobalt water. We swept over the yawning mouth of the Awaroa River and inlet, descending over waving palms and pines to land, touching down next to a chef's vegetable and herb garden. We'd travelled non-stop for 30 hours, yet still felt energized, excitement trumping fatigue. Shouldering packs, we thanked Andrew and made our way down a narrow dirt trail under a canopy of beech and ferns to the lodge.

Weather cleared and we dined outside. It was just the two of us on the patio, nestled amongst ferns, palms and pines, a short stroll from the sea. I ordered an all-Kiwi coastal meal: abalone starter, eel entree and kumara (sweet potato) cheesecake for dessert. Another person strolled onto the big, wooden deck, a bottle of wine under his arm. He smiled, exchanged pleasantries and we encouraged him to join us. His name was John. He insisted we share his hearty Californian red, and the three of us watched sun set over forest into the Tasman.

John was 50, with thick, salt-and-pepper hair and an open face. He wore shorts, flip-flops and a crisp golf shirt. He topped up our wine and after a while shared his story. He explained he'd broken up with his partner; she just didn't know it yet. I thought he was sharing a tasteless old joke, but he wasn't at all, simply articulating a revelation he was having in real time.

He lived in California and was travelling on his own, touring New Zealand and thinking about relocating, possibly finding new work – the ultimate vocation vacation. He was spending a lot of time hiking, enjoying the land and figuring out what he wanted to do next.

"I feel as though I'm ready for a change," he continued, thoughtful. "I just don't know what."

We nodded. The buzz of cicadas picked up.

"I was a millionaire at 32," he said. "And broke at 34. You realize how important relationships are. And values. My ex? She'd never put a pack on her back and tramp around New Zealand like this. It was all Prada and LV. Bullshit stuff. She'd put $50K on the card in a day – a day!" He smiled, thinly, somewhere in the past. "My dad and my sister passed away. It's just Mom and me now. It makes you appreciate family; those connections."

The light dimmed, softening the ambiance. John poured the last of the wine. His brow furrowed, just for a moment, then he grinned. "I'm looking for my next adventure now," he said. "I hope I'll know it when I see it."

Sometime later I thought of this when I met Willie, my seatmate from New Zealand to Canada. He worked on his family farm on South Island. They farmed deer, selling most of it to Germany for a range of venison products. Willie was friendly but shy, his hair a smootheddown clump of dirty blond, his shirt plaid flannel. Soft-spoken and thoughtful, he chose words carefully, making what he said worthwhile. He explained that his dad was ready to retire and it was up to Willie and his brother to take over the business and run things now. He didn't seem keen, the responsibility a heavy obligation. I asked him what was taking him halfway across the world.

"A girl," he said, grinning sheepishly.

"What's her name?" I asked, smiling back at his infectious grin.

"Kelly," he replied. "K-E-L-L-Y."

Woody's song from *Cheers* immediately played in my head and I had to cut it short midway through the chorus.

"Ye-ah. She was in New Zealand, studying and working on a farm, finishing her degree in agriculture from the University of..." he paused, then said, "Sa...Sa...Saskatchewan," like it was a sneeze.

"Now she's back on her family farm," he carried on. "Outside

Saskatoon, working with her parents. I'm going to surprise her for Christmas," he smiled. "She doesn't know I'm coming." Then he paused, his smile fading. "I'm going to ask her to marry me," he added.

"Way to go!" I said with enthusiasm, unsure how to read his expression, which struck me as tentative, as though he was unsure what her answer would be, or what it meant going forward.

"I wouldn't mind if my brother ran the farm back home," he said, adding some clarity.

I nodded, and he did the same, pensive. It felt as though I was in the back of the bus with Dustin Hoffman and Katharine Ross at the end of *The Graduate*, decision made, limitless future, terrifyingly directionless.

"Good luck," I said.

"Ye-ah, thanks," Willie replied. And his smile returned, partway.

From the plain pad of paper:

Once more I felt I was living out lyrics, this time from Colin Hay's "Beautiful World," recurring lines echoing the title.

Like the Queen Charlotte Track, we completed the Abel Tasman Coast Track a couple of times. Following the somewhat high-end arrival by chopper the first time around, the subsequent trip we came by water taxi – a steel-hulled tank with partial cabin, not unlike the boat that hauled me along with Robyn and Herta into the rainforest. The skipper, however, could not have been more different. This one was a friendly Kiwi named Darren.

We were the only passengers, and Darren went out of his way to show us some wildlife and burble slowly around picturesque Split Apple Rock – a massive sphere of cracked basalt over 100 million years old. The rock's twice the age of the country's current land mass, and was sitting pretty much as is when New Zealand was still attached to Australia, Africa and India. It sits high in the water, a short distance from shore. It's naturally split neatly in two and lays partially open like a huge, prehistoric stone butterfly. We got some pictures from different angles, morning sun providing lighting for our little shoot, glinting off clear blue water in blinding pockets of gold.

Darren took us north, the Tonga Islands visible in the distance. We motored through Torrent Bay and Bark Bay, all of it washing into the Tasman to the east. He deftly manoeuvred the boat into sandy shallows where we splashed into the surf to find the trail and start our trek.

The trail meanders through Abel Tasman National Park, following the shoreline around wide river mouths with sand flies and stingrays, then passing through heavily wooded forests of beech and fern trees with fantails and silvereyes, along high sandstone cliffs and long expanses of bright sandy beach, all of it requiring careful timing for tides and shoreline crossings.

We'd started in Motueka, a dusty town built over a century ago that felt like the Wild West. I strolled past an old theatre that showed silent movies – when they were new. A tumbleweed actually blew across my path, making me wish I was bowlegged, wearing chaps. I walked around the garden of Motueka's St Thomas church, a parched little patch of yellow grass centred by a massive monkey tree, easily 100 years old, that towered and spread out like the world's largest prickly patio umbrella.

With a series of water taxis, we completed the trail (that particular time) in a few large chunks, pieced together like a trekking jigsaw, and finished by marching out after a long day to the tiny seaside village of Marahau. Dirty, tired and thirsty, we dropped enormous packs in a small motel room and made our way to a pub situated near the water. The quaint little establishment was called Hooked on Marahau and we felt much the same. We drank Mac's Black beer and ate fish and chips while a softly mauve moon rose over the water, adding an ivory glow to rocky islands in the bay. Fighting to keep our eyes open, we stumbled back to the motel and threw ourselves onto a thin lumpy mattress that felt like heaven.

Two days earlier, as we were closing in on the end of the trek, the Tasman Sea was gold leaf, late afternoon sun rippling on low chop. A stingray glided by in the shallows and a cozy bay of sand, ferns and podocarps yawned before us like open arms. We'd hiked through hot hills and dense foliage all day, packs heavy on our backs, chafing shoulders and hips. Our lodge was somewhere ahead, hidden in trees, but the water beckoned. High hills surrounding the bay created the illusion of water rising to the horizon – a tilting infinity pool. My boots were laced over a shoulder. I tossed them above the breaking tide and plodded through soft, sucking sand, easing my pack from raw shoulders and hoisting it in the direction of my boots. Peeling off my shirt, I packed it like a snowball, threw it at the beach, then traipsed toward the horizon and dove.

The sea was like a cooler after a long hot picnic, when ice has melted and clear, frigid water is all that remains. But the chill soon vanished and I hooted at the majesty of it all. We were on our own – just the hills, trees, the sea and who knew what, swimming with the stingray and me. And I laughed and splashed, doing watery somersaults, immersed in absolute freedom. In the words of English writer Henry Green, "That blessed state when you forever cease to give a damn."

Following the exquisite sleep on the shabby mattress, we caught a bus that made a leisurely route from Marahau, stopping at small dairies (general stores) to deliver newspapers and bread and pick up the occasional passenger.

René, the driver, learned we were Canadian and recounted fond memories of travelling through Canada during the Montreal Olympics in 1976. As he spoke, it became obvious he'd fallen in love while in Canada and carried that with him – a distant memory of a young woman and the country where they met. Filled with nostalgia, he barely kept us on the winding road, hanging the bus over tight, switchback turns atop plummeting seaside cliffs. He turned to face us as he shared his stories, his back to the road as we snaked along craggy cliffs, making me clutch the seat and involuntarily point at the road ahead.

From the half-lined puce Moleskine, now
with a coffee cup spill ring:

We shared a laugh with the couple at the next table,
having ordered the same items for the same courses.

Before long, we'd pulled our tables together in the small dining room. Her name was Serene and his was Shane. After dinner we moved into the lounge together. Shane bought a bottle of port and poured. Serene had long, dark hair and almond eyes – a South Asian melting pot. She'd worked as a writer in Sydney, London and New Zealand. Shane looked like Jason Statham (trimmers on setting #1, in a gym each day) and worked for the secret service in Wellington, protecting the New Zealand prime minister. Deb asked if he talked into his collar. He laughed and said it was all in the wrist now.

Married five years, the couple had a 12-year-old daughter and their conversation focused on her. Serene struck me as a tentative tightrope walker – balancing free spirit with responsible parent. The restaurant emptied and we were the last ones in the lounge. The conversation got meatier, like our transition from wine to port. I referred to the "Live Laugh Love" ornament in our home, and asked what these things meant to them.

Shane shifted in his seat. "I'm more a math and science type," he said. He drummed his fingers, thinking, then soldiered on. "But the meaning of life...I like to think there's *something* more."

Serene's brow furrowed. "Now that I have a daughter, I find I'm more concerned," she said. "More afraid for the future. I wonder about God and if there's an afterlife; if there's anything else."

The love for their daughter was clear; she seemed to be their anchor. Funnily enough, when not talking about her, they spoke almost exclusively of their differences.

"I love to laugh," Shane said, aptly with a laugh. "I like when someone's takin' the piss, and I love *The Simpsons*."

"I need to laugh more," Serene said with a frown. "I guess I'm more literal. But opposites attract, I suppose."

We talked about experiencing the world and new connections. Whether seeking or escaping, travel, like ecdysis, demands, rewards and enlightens. Growth invariably tags along; these viking journeys I like to believe are ongoing.

Our new friends were good company, offering sentiments we all share. We touched on big things, common around the globe, but the cozy room in a faraway land encapsulated it in an intimacy analogous to a shrinking world.

Paul Theroux:

"One of the greatest thrills in travel is to know the satisfaction of arrival, and to find oneself among friends."

We returned to Vancouver (the flight on which I met Willie, making his way to Saskatchewan and possibly a new life). I was spending more time in the car than I was used to, covering ground with events and readings.

I had a book signing at a suburban retailer, where I tried not to get lost in sprawling square footage. I was set up at a table at the front of the store, wedged between a promotional booth and a Starbucks. There were glossy signs promoting the event, my name, remarkably, spelled correctly. Things looked promising. Buyers were even queued before my arrival, friendly people keen to visit, requesting signed copies of my recent book. We clicked selfies in Viking helmets. It was all quite fun.

As the afternoon wore on, I admit, my enthusiasm waned, along with my breath mints. Then something wondrous occurred. One of those Frank Capra moments when the instrumental score surges dramatically, ensuring that you know, even if you weren't paying attention, that something special is happening.

I'd decided a break was in order – a coffee to muddy my air-freshener breath. So I bumbled into a sort-of lineup. There was no discernible queue. Those of us there looked at each other, shrugged and did our best to form a schoolyard line, which wasn't easy around the displays. A lone woman in our clump smiled, nodding in my direction. I returned the salutation. Then a server made eye contact with me. I indicated the smiling woman should be served next. The server complied. But smiley was certain I was next in line. So she ordered her coffee and insisted on buying whatever I was having, one of those pay-it-forward moments we love and first witnessed in that movie with the child actor with three names. What I felt in that moment was optimism in humanity.

My inclination was to decline, with thanks. An obligatory, "I couldn't *possibly*..." But something I remembered from years earlier – the teachings of Bodhisattvas and possibly Ann Landers – went *ping*. When offered a gift from a stranger, a stranger with good intent, always accept with a simple thank you. My dad never read Landers (he may've touched on Buddhism in our Time Warner encyclopedias), but, being Scottish, he knew when to simply say thanks to free coffee. And so I did, knowing in my heart Siddhartha, Ann and Dad would approve.

Back at the table of books, sipping my gifted java, I had more genuine visits, kind people with stories to share. And then another remarkable encounter ensued. A middle-aged guy with the energy of a sugared-up tween came at me with an onslaught of enthusiasm and smiles. He knew everyone. Anyone he didn't know intimately, he'd worked with. He told me of his time travelling and fighting fires. He told me of his manuscript, literary praise and his pride in the craft. It was simply a matter of time before our Venn diagrams intersected. Which they did. His editorial consultant and mentor was the same guy who made up half the judging panel who scrutinized my very work stacked on the table – the award that earned a sticker on the cover and got me a year's worth of speaking gigs. Small world? Maybe. But I suspect given enough time this affable guy would find the thing or things he had in common with anyone, and everyone.

"Wait here!" he said, like a kid on Christmas morning. "I got a book for you!" And he was off, race walking at an Olympic pace.

I figured I'd be getting a copy of his book, and maybe we'd do the author swap thing. But, no, there was simply a title he wanted me to read. So, as well as buying one of my books, he found the other title on the shelves, went back to the till, paid for everything, then brought me this additional book as a gift. He wrote a fun inscription, listing the people we both knew, along with his nickname, so I'd remember who he was. Which of course I will. Once more, the kindness of strangers.

Maybe that, more than anything, is why we say yes. Yes to leaving the house, meeting new people, leaping from comfort zones. Yes to the unknown. And yes to the goodness of people. Oh, the book he bought me? Well, it was Matt Gutman's *The Boys in the Cave: Deep Inside the Impossible Rescue in Thailand*. The man who bought me the book knew one of the guys involved. I think. Degrees of separation were unclear.

If you don't know the story, 12 Thai boys – part of a U15 soccer team, and their coach – went for an after-practice hike into the underground caves near their town. It was a popular hike – you can clamber and creep a mile and a half into the earth, the caverns the result of monsoon erosion.

The team (ages 11–14) finished practice and, along with their coach, made their way to the popular local hike. It wasn't yet monsoon season. They weren't irresponsible. They weren't misbehaving. Just a group of boys with a well-intentioned coach doing something more than simply practising. But they got caught in the caves amidst an atypical early flood that made exiting impossible.

To ensure their safety, they were forced to move farther inside the underground maze as water accumulated, cutting off their only possible exit. The downpour filled the series of low-snaking caves behind them with a torrent of water – an instantaneous, raging river, leaving the 13 cut off with no means of escape. They managed to find a small, tilting shelf of sandy rock, and there they waited for water to slacken, or for rescue. The water was due to recede, perhaps, in three or four months. Snacks got eaten. Their pocket of stale air turned slowly to carbon dioxide with each exhale. The book follows the ensuing story from a reporter's perspective – government, navy and civilians doing their best to rescue the boys from a dismally inaccessible, submerged labyrinth.

The only possibility of survival for the team, albeit remote, was rescue – a rescue unlike any other. Cave diving is a unique and highly skilled endeavour. A handful of people on the planet are capable of a dive like that – in pitch black, through narrow, snaking caverns with stalactites and sharp rocky floor with no clearance, not to mention dragging a dozen non-swimmers a mile and a half underwater, buried in cellphone- and GPS-impenetrable rock. In other words, it was never intended to be a rescue, only recovery. The first diver discovered the boys and their coach ten days after they were stranded. Ten days. And *then* the rescue planning began.

Spoiler alert: if you want to read the book and be surprised, skip this paragraph! The ending to the tale is happy. Predominantly. The team and their coach were rescued, against unfathomably long odds. A Thai Navy SEAL died early in the rescue attempt, likely from a tainted oxygen tank and subsequent drowning. He became the face of the rescue – the hero who didn't make it. The surviving heroes were many. The story's a good one. For many reasons.

When I first wrote this excerpt for *New Reader Magazine*, the world was in another wave of pandemic lockdown, each of us doing our part to flatten curves, wondering what the vaccine would mean going forward. Until then, more optimism and uncertainty. Most would survive. Many would not. And to believe things would return to pre-pandemic normal was a myth. Our lives, like the boys in the cave and all involved, have changed forever.

I hadn't undertaken this series of viking voyages with the express intention of picking, poking and prodding at what exactly life means. Even articulating that struck me as arrogant. Besides, we all have a pretty good idea of what's important – truly important. Mind you, lobbing that kind of an enquiry into conversation can (usually) make for exceptional dialogue between strangers and friends over coffee or wine. Chances are, we've thought about it in one way or another. Maybe not in quite the same manner as Greek philosophers, and probably not with the intention of *actually* figuring it out, but still, a curiosity about some of the bigger questions – life, death, the universe. The stuff that creeps into peripheral vision unannounced, leaving us to wonder what came before and perhaps what's next. In other words, where our next viking excursion will lead us.

Fast forward a bit. I was on our tiny deck, just before northern hemisphere winter. It was cold – Vancouver cold, right around freezing – and I was ignoring the elements, grilling meat (flank steak, marinated in horseradish and soy). As I cooked, I was nibbling potato chips (all right, I don't *nibble* chips, I jam them into my gob by the fistful, but for the purposes of this, let's just say I was nibbling). The grill was coming to temperature, making the space around it wavy with contrasting heat in the cold, the look of hot desert highway. Through the squiggly barbecue air, mountains to the north with their blanketing forest were dusted in snow, a white quilt that crept toward town.

Virus vaccines were being produced and distributed, and the world looked promising once more. Or still. The extent to which we'd freely travel again was uncertain. But one thing remained, unwavering, and that's whenever (and wherever) we long for a taste of adventure, for exploration, we can invariably discover something new, be it through a window, a book or the pages of handwritten journals.

I read somewhere that Nelson Mandela stated every journey's important. And no journey is impossible. While he spoke of the difficulty of *all* human journeys, he emphasized there's clarity and nobility in simply being a journeyer. Which I liked. And wondered if he knew that "viking" was a verb. Once more I thought of the bigger perspective, travel so frequently used as a metaphor for life. Movement being (for most of us) a relatively natural thing. Doing so with some clothes, a book and a journal in a bag struck me as no different than breathing – revitalized wonder, connections and fresh views. Like so many of us, I relish the new along with the paradox of never wanting that to change. The pull to go viking remains, a yearning to explore. Imperative, perhaps, to our survival: a fire-starting kit. We carry the tinder. Our spark is internal. A suitable environment and oxygen are all that's required for combustion, igniting the next adventure.

CONCLUSION

As well as a gathering of people, places, perspectives and journals, this saga became an amalgam of transport modes, more often than not over water. Which got me, suitably enough, drifting down a tributary of recollective thought, paddling a canoe. (What many Oceanians call a kayak; what I consider a canoe, they call a Canadian canoe.)

Canoeing was integral to my childhood. And as an adult, for that matter. The last boat I bought was Kevlar – lightweight and strong, and, of course, bulletproof. I believe. Never actually had it tested. Just felt safe from snipers. It was red, by the way. And that lovely red boat became an array of things: a place of solitude, communing with the outdoors, a slender floating home and a receptacle for hand-caught kokanee and trout.

It also felt like a nod to my dad, as he and I paddled together when I was young, which itself felt like homage to our country – from portaging fur traders to Pierre Trudeau (Justin's dad). In fact, a slice of that wood-grained Canadiana (a piece of Pierre's paddle) found its way into Jowy Taylor's Voyageur guitar and eventually my hands on a stage. All this from a canoe, a thread of history as long and varied as the bodies of water we've traversed in our travels together.

It struck me as a kind of ekphrastic experience – inspiration derived from other forms of creativity. The expression's morphed somewhat since Greeks first coined the term, describing art based on other art – the addition of layers to enrich the overall experience. Like bacon. Adding it simply makes things better.

Everything, I suspect, has a facet of ekphrasis to it. Reading a book is more than a visual undertaking. Opening a print publication entails multisensory stimulation – the tactile feel and aroma, be it heady new ink or the scent of old paper and glue, a dusty hardback from a second-hand bin or well-thumbed paperback left on a train. Every book has a mixed-media personality, stories to share beyond the representation of words.

This came to mind again on the water, aboard an 80-year-old, round-hulled wooden boat – an ark, more or less – when I saw a sea eagle, the second I'd seen in my life. And while neither endangered nor rare, they're far from common. The sighting felt as though I'd been admitted to some sort of exclusive club, an avian order. Seeing that eagle soar across Arctic sky was as mesmerizing as cloud gazing – intoxicating and freeing, leaving an intense connection not only to the bird but everything around it.

It took me back to a falconry display at a Scottish castle, blending adrenaline surges with primordial fear – witnessing a hunter hunting. It was in part for food, clothing and survival, but still very much a blood sport. A thing of terrible beauty.

With that I'd like to share a piece I wrote shortly after those encounters, the sea eagle sighting in particular, my mind overflowing with Norse exploration and mythology. This has appeared a few places, including *Pandora's Collective*, *Plum Tree Tavern* and *Forever Cast in Endless Time*, and it's called "Yggdrasil."

Yggdrasil, the world tree, mother ash
stands astride a Nordic knoll
beyond Uppsala's temples
where every god – the real ones
take meat and mead amongst the Norns
Wyrd, Verðandi, Skuld

atop the tree the eagle with no name resides
witness to our lives and spindle whorls of fate
an eyrie shared with a hawk called Veðrfölnir
witherer of wind

when I saw the eagle I was drifting on a wooden ark
in looming crags of crystal leaded ice
"Nattoralik," whispered the Greenlander
aurora eyes squinting into cloudless Arctic sky
following the nameless one in flight

and together we watched the giant sail
across a canvas of calcium blue
the hawk invisible to us
its presence though we felt
in the eagle's sweeping gaze
removing every trace of wind
breath sucked silent from our lungs
a contour feather *whoosh*, the only sound

Following the release of *Gone Viking: A Travel Saga* and publication of
"Yggdrasil," the League of Canadian Poets asked me (for World Poetry
Day) to write about a world of poetry. *A world of poetry?* I thought.
This, I understand. And, in doing so, recapped two decades of viking,
discovery through the eyes of a traveller, specifically one with a poetic
bent. Once more with the aid of journals, mementos and photos, I re-
lived and recounted the voyage.

I remembered being witness to stomped-verse haka in Waitangi,
the lyrical thrum of outback didgeridoo, breathy sax in a wet
London underpass, red-slashed characters on a mud wall in Hebei,
tanka blurred through joss smoke in Kyoto, the guttural slur of a
Greenlandic hymn and a master's spoken word reverberating on old
timber, sibilant sea hissing through cracked glass. Musicality of lyrics,
prose and rhyme. All of it a poem. Of course, we have this everywhere, from familiar land masses and sea, bound in part through
flags and food and song.

A particular visual stayed with me – a midwinter night in the bleak-beauty grit of an urban neighbourhood *not* in transition. Boarded shopfronts. Needles underfoot. The oddly comforting cacophony of one-sided conversation, solitary souls broadcasting to the world. I took refuge in a pine-walled bookstore, poetry stacks beyond retail rationality. Authenticity accumulating dust.

I was one of the misfits keeping a poetry reading series on life support. Resuscitation by mouth-to-mouth. We'd done a decent job, packing the compact space, a standing-room-only affair. But it was the makeup of the room that warmed me – a community snapshot, an LGBTQ2S+–Indigenous–Eurasian rainbow framed in maple leaf red and white. Poets shared their work – spoken word and storytelling – humour, horror and healing.

I'd read with some of the artists at a Talking Stick festival – communal meals of bannock and salmon with moiety heritage bound in verse, part of my cross-country viking travels I'd undertaken by rail, road and air. From west coast islands, tent towns and high-rise glass, through foothills and lowlands, Great Lake vistas, *la belle province* and Atlantic, with swathes of taiga and tundra. I envisioned pins thrust in a topographical map, linking this globe with poetically spun yarn, memories scribbled in well-weathered journals and on mismatched scraps of paper:

The stammering of a young poet, first time before a mic, reading work she'd never dared to share until that moment, seeing dimmed light begin to brighten.

At the bear-footed base of a squat cedar totem, witnessing raw anger dissolve through cadence of rap; half-lisped, half-screamed.

Embraces at a grief-filled reading, mourning children none of us had known, tears binding strangers.

The dissolution of a stuffy conference as 100 suits exploded in diaphragm laughter, ennui of P&L statements replaced with rhymed couplets and play.

The jarring joy of off-tempo clapping to accompany layered song – a round – young and old rising from seats, swaying and singing, an improvised druidic dance.

Rail wheels on steel – pine tar ties the unending lines of open-end verse.

A community centre, the essential untuned piano, mismatched chairs in a lopsided oval. Typewritten pages (typewritten!) read in the warble of vulnerability. An RN's hand-painted A4 accompanied work-based ekphrasis – her experience – sonnets of death and syringe.

Low-ceilinged library, upstairs and echoey, where a scowling stone bust spends life on a sill, disapproving of everything.

Watercolour shades that can only be learned through a life of repression, removed.

And the rubbery hum of whitewalls on asphalt – mile after potholed mile – biblical wheat-belt storms, antenna scratch of AM radio on watery roads and harbour towns where every chanty's sung alongside psalms.

At the opposite end from where I began, that first cross-continent trip, I ate lobster, ripped into buttery chunks in a roll and listened to an O'Brien sing his craft – meter of four-four, concrete-mixer baritone of early Sunday, the gravelled pitch of artists on the road. Somewhere in that onshore breeze, a whiff of salinated Heaney. From a dark-lacquered, high-top table I glimpsed a great big sea, home of the same-named band. It would be seven months and 7000 kilometres in the other direction before I'd meet the man named Alan who hailed from that compact bend of coastline, shifting his words from lyrics to prose, transnational poetry set to bodhrán.

That journey wound down in a tiny room in a tiny town. I drank weak coffee and listened to a grab bag of wide-eyed youth, odds stacked against them in more ways than any of us could conceive, each of them writing with unabashed adolescence. Later, in a university, I heard a doctor write in the voice of the dead, scant weeks before he learned of his pending demise. And in a pocket of lakes I read the stilted verse of a young mom, optimism of new life in a world we too easily discount.

Hope remains in our midst, the cling of rudimentary organisms, determined and eternal. It's too simple to write of doom, Orwellian views and endless sweep of searchlights. We know better. Sure, our shores recede as seas encroach and livability wanes in its inconceivably juxtaposed connection to GNP, while Janus looks the other way. But like a new, incessant weed, a blade of grass appears, breaks through broken concrete, certain that this world is good. In life we persevere, explore, the best way we know how. Through written, spoken words we share in rhyme and verse and song. A world of poetry, of music and of viking. This, I understand.

EPILOGUE

From the journal that started this voyage, shaped like a wedge, with a map of the world and a photo of me and my dad:

I made my way to the water through heavy, midsummer air, flip-flops thwacking a slow and shuffling beat.

A dusty haze covered the coast, a billowing translucence that blurred views and softened morning light. Low tide, briny and recycled, melded with late blossoms, jasmine and lilac, colours and smells that sharpened the senses like coarse salt, strong and invigorating. Onshore thermals picked up, passing ten knots, shifting northerlies to the west and the first whitecaps began to break, pulling a smile across my face.

From an open boatshed I carried a six-metre mast like a wobbly caber, avoiding high-ceiling lights and water pipes, dragged a heavy Escape catboat onto a wheeled dolly, tossed a rudder and tiller into the boat and lugged it all down to the sandy shore. A pair of cormorants flew past like sleek black darts and a gull alighted on an old wooden pier, punctuating it with an echoing call.

I pulled on a wetsuit and life vest, rigged the mainsail, attached rudder and tiller, and slid the yellow-hulled boat into the bay. I dropped and locked the centreboard, and with a shift of weight and a tug on the mainsail sheet, the little boat took off. And I was sailing, like the man in the half-silent film in St Mawes, an eye to the horizon, my grin smeared ear to ear, the city shrinking behind me.

ABOUT THE AUTHOR

Bill Arnott is the award-winning author of *Gone Viking: A Travel Saga*, *Gone Viking II: Beyond Boundaries*, *The Gamble Novellas*, *Forever Cast in Endless Time* and the #1 bestseller *Bill Arnott's Beat: Road Stories & Writers' Tips*. For his travel expeditions, Bill's been granted a fellowship at London's Royal Geographical Society. When not trekking the globe with a small pack, journal and laughably outdated camera phone, Bill can be found on Canada's west coast, making music and friends. @billarnott_aps